Urban-Regional
Economic Growth and Policy

A volume in the series entitled
Man, His Community and Natural Resources
Donald R. Field, Series Editor

Urban-Regional
Economic Growth and Policy

James R. Prescott. Professor of Economics,
Iowa State University, Ames, Iowa.

W. Cris Lewis. Associate Professor of Economics,
Utah State University, Logan, Utah.

ann arbor science PUBLISHERS INC.
POST OFFICE BOX 1425 • ANN ARBOR, MICHIGAN 48106

PREFACE

Subnational diversity is an apparent characteristic of nations the size of the United States. The spatial impacts of economic growth and technical change may be quite uneven, resulting in an array of special development problems at various regional levels. This diversity has as yet precluded a comprehensive policy in the United States toward regional economic growth, though some significant beginnings have been made and will undoubtedly continue to be developed.

This book deals with numerous problems along the size continuum of subnational regions and issues of policy at the local, state and national levels. Our principal objective is to analyze some of the major difficulties encountered at each spatial level and to suggest how various methods may be used to estimate empirically their impacts. The regional units include rural communities, labor markets, river basins and metropolitan areas. State taxation, locational economic incentives and urban resettlement are topics included in the policy chapters. The methods used in analyzing these problems include econometric multiequation models, linear programming, multivariate statistics, regression analysis and input-output techniques. Within the chapters we have tried to integrate the discussion of the substantive issues and methodological problems encountered at each regional level.

This volume is intended for readers who share a concern for the various issues of regional development and an appreciation of modeling techniques by which these problems can best be analyzed. Though the topics covered are not exhaustive we hope the discussion reflects the diversity of issues that typifies the field of urban-regional analysis.

James R. Prescott
Ames, Iowa

W. Cris Lewis
Logan, Utah

v

ACKNOWLEDGMENTS

Our principal debt of gratitude is to those individuals who as graduate students at Iowa State University or co-authors of articles have contributed substantively to the analyses in this book. These include Professor Gary Carruthers (University of New Mexico), Professor Gene Gruver (University of Pittsburgh), Mr. David Holmes (Washington, D. C.) and Professor Walter Mullendore (University of Texas at Arlington).

The editors of the following journals have kindly permitted us to revise previously published articles appearing in the indicated chapters: Annals of Regional Science (Chapters 1 and 5), Papers of the Western Agricultural Economics Association (Chapter 2), Proceedings of the American Real Estate and Urban Economics Association (Chapter 5), Land Economics (Chapters 6 and 7), National Tax Journal (Chapter 6), Journal of Regional Science (Chapter 3) and Water Resources Research (Chapter 7). At Utah State University, Professor B. Delworth Gardner, Dean Robert P. Collier and Dean Doyle J. Matthews are thanked for the financial support that allowed this book to be undertaken. The National Science Foundation and Agricultural Experiment Station at Iowa State University also supported the research reported in this volume.

CONTENTS

1

Introduction: Development Concepts and Spatial Delineation

For the past two decades, a good deal of professional effort within the social sciences has been devoted to problems of urban-regional development and resettlement. The substantial growth in indicators of national wealth and real income have been realized only within the context of considerable variation among regions within the United States. The post-World War II focus on the growth and cyclical effects of national economic policy has been complemented more recently by the realization that the spatial distribution of economic activity is a similarly legitimate concern of policymakers at the local, state, and federal governmental levels. Though at a rudimentary stage, the broad contours of a national urbanization policy are beginning to be developed.

It is apparent that such a policy must be based on the principal socio-economic problems encountered at each level in the size continuum of urban-regional places. Historically the effects of agricultural productivity on the out-migration of rural families has been as important to the economies of metropolitan regions as the suburbanization of their residents. The limits that congestion may impose on the size of our largest urbanized regions will probably be reflected in growth problems encountered by the smaller cities. The effects of resource development may also be spread throughout the full scale of settlement sizes within the applicable region, and governmental policies in the transportation field may differentially influence the accessibility of firms and households in cities of alternative sizes to markets and productive resources. These interdependencies have important implications for the spatial distribution of economic activity and are not easily dealt with by traditional governmental units within the public sector.

The purpose of this book is to identify some of the major economic interdependencies and development problems within and among settlements along this size spectrum. Chapter 1 describes the principal economic concepts underlying regional analyses and their relation to the areal delineation of the spatial units considered in this book; the last section provides a detailed organizational description of the studies. Chapters 2 through 5 proceed from the smallest to the largest regional unit, including the rural service center, low density labor markets, water resource regions and high density metropolitan centers. Chapters 6 and 7 describe policy problems at the local, state, and federal levels that are related to the various regional entities discussed in previous chapters. Throughout these chapters we draw on some on-going and previously published studies of urban-regional structure to illustrate the principal characteristics of the various spatial units; our interest includes the structure of models we have found useful in analyzing economic problems of subnational development. Though arranged in a sequence from the smallest to largest spatial unit, each chapter constitutes a self-contained discussion on the particular region considered; the principal results are summarized in the concluding chapter.

LAND USE AND THE RURAL-URBAN CONTINUUM

The gradual increase in employment and residential densities is the most visible characteristic of the rural-urban continuum. The agricultural, manufacturing, and services sectors are typified by successively smaller land/labor ratios reflecting (among other factors) a declining locational dependence on primary resources. The capital and labor components of value-added tend to increase through successive productive stages to final consumption, and contiguity to urban markets becomes an increasingly important locational consideration. Sectoral production functions that allow a substitution of capital and labor for land tend to typify enterprises with the highest employment densities. Technological innovations among sectors that favor the substitution of these factors have been an important determinant of the changing patterns in land uses within urban areas. From the viewpoint of costs, the relative expense of input procurement and product distribution is an important element in the firm's locational decision along the low to high density scale.

Households have an analogous set of spatial expenses, the relative importance of which varies between the rural and urban resident. (1) Goods and services procurement entails shopping expenses at nearby towns or shopping centers. Since retail establishments usually are spatially distributed in proportion to population densities, the time cost of shopping per trip tends to decline along the rural-urban continuum. Though the rural resident is disadvantaged in the purchases of retail goods, his self-sufficiency in the production of low-order goods is an option not open to the urban dweller; it is at least possible for the rural family to incur zero shopping expense. (2) Labor, the product of the household, is distributed from the residence to the place-of-work. Since the home and place-of-work are contiguous for the farm family, journey-to-work expenses are nearly zero. Conversely, urban areas are typified by an extreme spatial specialization between the residence and employment site, so the urban resident must be sensitive to the relationship between housing location and commuting costs; many of the congestion problems in high density urban communities are attributable to this spatial variation in land uses.

In addition to input procurement and product distribution costs, both firms and households purchase or rent land for productive and residential purposes. Traditionally, urban theory has given less emphasis to the costs of input procurement, and both firms and households consider the trade-off between the costs of site rental and product distribution to market. Firms purchase inputs at the same competitive prices at each site but incur lower transportation costs nearer the marketing center; hence, bid-rents per unit of land increase near the central distributional point. Households may incur higher commuting costs to central workplace locations at sites further away from the city center, but are compensated by the lower rentals on land for residential purposes. Both firms and households bid freely for sites along this distance continuum, with this competition resulting in the locational patterns of land uses within the urbanized region.

Figure 1 illustrates these relationships. The bar chart shows increasing widths of the lots offered for sale from the marketing center (0) to increasing distances from that center; the height of each bar is the rent per acre offered by firms or households. Services firms are successful bidders for lots 1, 3, and 5, and manufac-

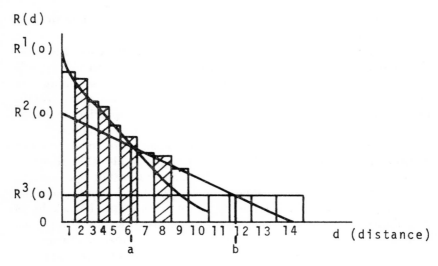

Figure 1: Bid-rent functions for three productive activities.

turing firms occupy lots 7 and 9. Agriculture is conducted on all parcels exceeding (and including) number 10. Its residential component is assumed to be included within land parcels used for production. Lots 2, 4, 6, and 8 are hatched to indicate their use for housing residents who must commute daily to the marketing center. For all activities excepting agriculture, the rent per acre of land rises toward the central city; the interspersed activities are due in part to the indivisibility of parcels offered for sale at various distances from the marketing center.

The bid rent functions for the production activities shown in Figure 1 are attained by connecting the midpoints of their respective bars. Services firms (along with the highest density dwelling units) are located within the approximate range of *Oa* miles, and **manufacturing firms** (along with lower density suburban housing) are found in the approximate range of *ab*; farmers market products at transportation nodes other than the city's distributional center, and each site has equal access to these processing centers. Though these functions overestimate the locational radii of services and manufacturing (*e.g.*, agriculture actually begins at lot 10), the three types of bid-rent relations shown have particular significance. These may be represented as:

$$R^1 \ (d) \ = \ R^1 \ (o) \ . \ e^{-\alpha_1 d}$$
$$(\text{services}) \qquad (1)$$

$$R^2 \ (d) \ = \ R^2 \ (o) \ -\alpha_2 d$$
$$(\text{manufacturing}) \qquad (2)$$

$$R^3 \ (d) \ = \ R^3 \ (o) \ = \ \text{const}$$
$$(\text{agriculture}) \qquad (3)$$

Assuming competition within and among industries, the bid-rent of a firm for land is the residual of gross revenues over nonland input costs and transportation expenses. Since the latter varies with distance only for services and manufacturing and the other cost and revenue components do not depend on distance, Equation 3 does not vary with distance. Equation 2 assumes that the ton mile cost of transportation is constant and that declining distances to the center are reflected in proportionate increases in rent available for bidding on an acre of land. The services equation makes an additional assumption that capital (which is fixed in price) may be substituted for land (whose price increases near the marketing center), so the additional savings are reflected in the rent-offer for land. Hence, the capital/land ratio must fall in the range Oa; it is constant within the ranges ab and exceeding b miles from 0. Considering the land intensive nature of agriculture, it also falls between these ranges as distance increases.

Residentiary densities tend to decline as distance from the central city increases since land prices fall. Apartment dwellers near the central city accept residentiary congestion and capital intensive housing structures in order to be near the central workplace, while suburbanites substitute cheaper priced land for the increased costs of commutation. Assuming a minimum scale of serviced population necessary for the retail firm, marketing radii for these firms increase with distance from the central city as do the costs per shopping trip. At the central distributional node the resident population per store is likely to be less than this minimum scale since the density of home-to-work destinations is high. (The highly mobile urban population will consider nonresidential origins in deciding on the spatial distribution of its retail purchases.) Increasing returns to scale in retailing may or may not increase the shopping costs of residents as distance from the distributional center rises; shopping centers offer a vastly expanded range of goods and services whose search costs can be consolidated in a single trip, but such savings also depend on the preferences of households.

Figure 2 summarizes some of the principal relationships expected along the rural-urban continuum from the discussion above. Households and firms within the distance Ob incur commuting and transportation charges that vary proportionately with distance from the marketing center. Land prices per acre fall exponentially to Oa, at a

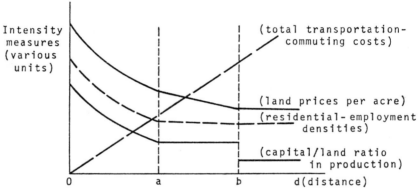

Intensity measures (various units)

(total transportation-commuting costs)

(land prices per acre)
(residential- employment densities)

(capital/land ratio in production)

0   a   b   d(distance)

Figure 2: Summary of intensity measures along the rural-urban continuum.

constant rate from Oa to Ob, and are constant for parcels in the agricultural hinterland. Residential and employment densities (per unit of land employed for these respective purposes) fall from the marketing center to b and are constant for farms in the agricultural sector. The capital/land ratio also declines nonlinearly for industries capable of substituting these factors and should decline similarly between the manufacturing and agricultural sectors. Although the units vary among these characteristics and exceptions to the regularity of the relations shown in Figure 2 invariably appear, the graph suggests a continuum of attributes that must distinguish the boundaries of the urban and rural resident. As discussed later in this chapter (p. 17) several delineating criteria have been suggested, each having advantages in relation to its particular use.

THE ECONOMIC BASE

A second theoretical construction distinguishes between the export and services component of employment within a region.

Known as the export-base model, employment in the export and services sectors is recursively related to population growth within the region; the primary source of regional growth is attributable to export demand. The model may be summarized as:

$$E_b = E_b^o \qquad (4)$$

where E_b = employment directly attributable to exports of goods and services

E_b^o = exogeneously determined levels of export employment

$$E_n = a_1 + b_1 E_b \qquad (5)$$

where $b_1 > 0$, and

E_n = employment directly or indirectly servicing the export sector

$$E_t = a_1 + (1 + b_1) E_b \qquad (6)$$

where $E_t = E_b + E_n$

$$P = a_2 + b_2 E_t \qquad (7)$$

where P = total population

$$P = a_2 + b_2 a_1 + b_2 (1 + b_1) E_b \qquad (8)$$

This recursive sequence takes exogenous levels of export employment and determines nonbasic or service employment in Equation 5. Total employment is exhaustively distributed between its export and service components and determined by export employment in Equation 6; population levels are expressed as a function of total employment demand in Equation 7. Substituting Equation 6 into Equation 7, population levels may be directly expressed in terms of basic employment as in Equation 8.

Though our interest is primarily in the delineating implications of the model, several criticisms of the export base model should be noted. (1) Economic growth within the ultimately largest region cannot be explained by the equational sequence summarized above. Increased factor input supplies, technological progress, and the elimination of resource misallocations are among the sources of growth within the totally self-contained spatial economy. (2)

Prices of exports and resident factor inputs do not influence the equational sequence shown in 4 through 8. Assuming a fixed output/labor ratio for both E_b and E_n, neither the prices of exports or prevailing wage rates influence employment levels. (3) Levels of E_n are linearly and positively related to E_b, so the relative price of export and service labor does not influence the allocation of employment between sectors. If $a_1 = 0$ in Equation 5 and a common output/labor ratio prevails for both labor sectors, the implied production function has an expansion path with a slope $= b_1$. Other productive factors such as capital and land are similarly excluded from explicit consideration.

Though many of these criticisms could be incorporated within the export base model, its essential feature is the assumption of an autonomous increase in one component of product demand. Since all recursive systems must make at least one such assumption, the model's inherent weakness is shared with many other sectoral economic models that are used extensively. Neither is the spatial source of the demand increase particularly crucial to the equations of the export base model. If ''export'' products can be domestically marketed, an autonomous shift in local demand curves for such products will result in essentially similar results at least so far as Equations 4 through 8 are concerned. The important assumption relates not so much to the spatial location of the shift in commodity demand curves but to their unexplained nature.

As household residentiary services are an important component of E_n, we expect employment densities in this sector to be positively correlated with population densities. Most of the housewife's work falls within this category, and the per acre intensity of this activity is higher in multifamily residential areas than in single-family suburban tracts. Convenience retail outlets are similarly more concentrated where higher density residences are located, and shopping centers tend to have a substantially larger marketing radii. Wholesale outlets for residentiary services must consider the land intensive nature of this activity in addition to the distribution of retail stores that they service. Bulky, low-valued commodities such as food are usually received at rail terminal sites while more compact, high-valued items (*e.g.*, tobacco products) may be centrally warehoused. The inherent variety of goods for final consumption suggests the corresponding locational variance for wholesaling activities.

Business services are an additional component of E_n; their locational characteristics vary with the type and frequency of the service offered. Business services that regularly provide routine maintenance and repair work for office buildings tend to be centrally located within the city, while independent marketing research firms may be substantially more "footloose." Professional services are often complementary in location; lawyers locate near governmental offices and municipal courts since the latter provide needed inputs and are a source of employment for members of the legal profession. It is also expected that since larger firms are able to internalize needed services their export and services components of employment will tend to be more locationally congruent than are those of smaller enterprises.

Among cities of alternative sizes, the marginally hierarchical service will usually have a central location. Since the obstacle to the service's existence in smaller cities is market scale, only a single firm will generally provide the service in the city size class where it initially appears. A central location is thus expected in the first size class, and the activity may or may not be substantially dispersed in size classes exceeding the minimum scale. Exceptions occur particularly where the activity has a high land/output ratio or population alone is not the inhibiting market determinant. Professional sports stadiums are more likely to locate in peripheral sites within large cities, and services demanded by only the very highest income families may have specialized, noncentral locations.

The E_b component of employment naturally remains stable as long as its marketing destination falls outside the delineated regional boundary; where destinations are along a continuum of distances the ratio of (E_b/E_n) falls as the regionally delineated radius increases. Figure 3 shows some alternative distributions of market destinations for a nodal exporting activity at A. The following characteristics should be noted:

    1. If A's services are provided to a uniformly dense population within the city then its employment ratio (E_b/E_n for the CBD regionalization) is approximated by the proportion of the land areas in the outer and inner rings.

    2. Unstable export components are shown for the single destination B and the circular set of destinations immediately surrounding A. All employment at A is export activity for regional radii less than the origin-destination shipment distance,

but service employment for regional radii just marginally exceeding this distance. Estimating errors may be quite substantial for activities with singular shipment distances.

3.   If A provides services radially emanating from the origin then (E_b/E_n) falls continuously as the regional radius increases. If the depicted service is contained within the municipal boundary, $E_b = 0$ and $E_n = E_t$ if the city is the appropriate regional unit for that activity alone.

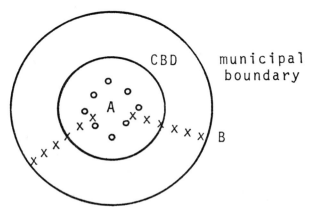

Figure 3: Delineating effects of alternative regional boundaries on E_b and (E_b/E_n).

The above discussion suggests that the ratio of (E_b/E_n) should fall as regional size increases; at the limiting case of a single region E_b is zero and all employment is within the services category. There are clear exceptions to this case, however, depending on the characteristics of the nodal center; for example, the ratio of E_b/E_n is much lower for monasteries than for manufacturing firms or households. However, the rule is consistent with gravitational principles since export shipments must decline as the attractional force of the destinations is successively internalized within the region. Subject to these qualifications, it should be noted from Equation 5 that for $a_1 > 0$, the ratio (E_b/E_n) rises for regions of increasing size or is at best constant if $a_1 = 0$.

The degree of spatial specialization would also seem to influence significantly the sensitivity of alternative regionalizations to the appropriate classification of residentiary and nonresidentiary activity. Spatially self-contained units may be subject to considerable variation in the allocation of employment between these two categories; homogeneous activities with unique and distant shipment destinations will be delineated more accurately under an array of alternative regionalization principles. From Figure 1 it is generally expected that for regions of increasing radius (from 0 along the distance axis), more stability will be achieved because the central city encompasses a rich array of land uses; the more uniform land uses in the agricultural sector add land increments to the regional unit, which normally have more stable ratios of E_b to E_n.

Figure 1 also shows that increases in the export demand for agricultural products limit the growth of activities shipping to the central city. If agricultural output increases on the extensive margin, the degree of this limitation depends on the price and output adjustments in this sector and the shape of the bid-rent curve at the edge of the urbanized area. Adjustments in land use at this margin will be minor if competing gradients are steep and land is highly productive in urban-related uses; the opposite occurs if the manufacturing bid-rent function is flat and land in either use is a ready substitute. Also, among cities of alternative sizes (with similarly shaped bid-rent gradients at the competing margin), a given upward shift in the agricultural bid-rent function retires proportionately more land from urban use in small than in large cities. This is compatible with an assumption that the rent-gradients of smaller cities may be approximated by shifting the origin (0 in Figure 1) successively further out along the distance axis. Though this is consistent with generally declining central rentals per acre in smaller cities and the comments above about the central location of marginally hierarchical urban activities, cities of given sizes may also be quite specialized within a broader regional community.

Finally it is likely that the criticisms of the export base model are successively more valid as regional size increases. Demand curves for exports become more inelastic as the number of included firms approaches the total for the industry; a corresponding effect is expected on the demand curve for factor inputs. Similarly the supply curve of labor becomes increasingly inelastic as the number of firms within industries are aggregated within the larger region. Though the importance of E_b tends to decline with increasing regional size, the necessity of including the various price effects on outputs sold and inputs hired depends on size of region and not solely on the employment categories distinguished by the export base model. These comments apply to perfectly competitive markets for products and inputs; where firms or unions can exercise significant market power the critical regional size at which these considerations become important may be significantly smaller.

URBAN SYSTEMS

A third major consideration is the interrelated nature of nodal units within a broader regional community. Central place theory provides an economic rationale for the inverse relation between the number of cities by size class and the size of city; spatial indivisibilities caused by minimal market scales for different goods and services limit urban size and the variety of activities found in successively smaller size classes. Hierarchies of goods and services are, therefore, found along the size spectra, and the various combinations of city sizes within the delineated region will influence the mix of economic activity found within the region.

One formulation of the relation between city sizes in the spectra can proceed directly from Equations 4 through 8. Assuming all family members are employed, E_b' and E_n' are the populations of the rural market area and the smallest sized service center in the spectra. Hence,

$$E_n' = k(E_b' + E_n') = k(E_t') \qquad (9)$$
$$0 < k < 1$$

denotes the productivity of the service center k in providing goods to itself and families in the exporting sector E_b'. From Equation 9, terms can be rearranged so that,

$$E_n' = (k\ E_b')/(1\text{-}k) \qquad (10)$$

and

$$E_t' = (E_b')/(1\text{-}k) \qquad (11)$$

If we further assume that the total regional population of the next highest order includes s satellite populations of the lower order plus a central city of its own order, then the second order region is

$$E_t^2 = E_n^2 + s\ E_t' = k\ E_t^2 + s\ E_t' \qquad (12)$$
$$s > 0$$

and solving for E_t^2 we have

$$E_t^2 = (s/1\text{-}k)\ E_t' \qquad (13)$$

Since Equation 13 shows the relation between successive size classes, $[s/(1\text{-}k)]$ to the appropriate power (say, n-l) will indicate the relation between the nth-sized region and the lowest order regional population ($n = 1$). Also, substituting Equation 11 for E_t' in 13, we have

$$E_t{}^n = [E_b' \, s^{n-1}/ \, (1\text{-}k)^n] \qquad (14)$$

Several characteristics of this formulation should be noted. (1) Equation 14 is the hierarchical spatial analog to the simple export base model. Knowing basic employment (*i.e.*, rural population) of the lowest order region, the model directly predicts the urbanized and total populations of the largest metropolitan regions. From Equation 6, if $a_1 = 0$, $b_1 = [(1/1\text{-}k)\text{-}1]$ in Equation 11. (2) The predictive capability of the model depends on the regularity of the constants k and s among successive orders in the urban hierarchy. If these are relatively stable, Equation 14 generates city size distributions that closely follow the rank size rule.

The stability of k among regional size classes depends on the productivity of hierarchical activities added at each level and possible scale economies attained as regional size increases in goods provided at all levels; preference patterns of residents may also influence the composition of economic activity. If low money incomes in smaller regions preclude labor intensive personal services (chauffeurs, domestics, etc.), then k is likely to rise as regional size increases. For services less sensitive to income, the productivity of the activity added at larger regional levels may be greater or less than the average k for the immediately smaller regional center; if the market indivisibility is substantial, k will probably fall in the first size class in which it is found and may rise thereafter. (One professional sports activity requiring a franchise in a city of at least 1 million persons provides a monopolized service for cities marginally under 2 million, but larger than 1 million, in population.) Where smaller communities have sharply divergent preference patterns for particular services, discontinuities in the hierarchical provision of the service among city classes may appear, and k will probably fall as city size rises due to differences in per capita consumption of the service.

A stable system of hierarchical goods and services also suggests the imperfect substitutability of economic activities along the city size spectra. Complements to the marginally hierarchical service extend the market for firms providing lower order goods and probably increase the proportion of economic activity in the nonbasic sector. Though it is likely that services activities in larger cities may operate closer to the margin with this additional competition, their survival suggests that the elasticity of demand for lower order goods and services is not appreciably influenced by the size of city in which the activity is located. Though high school cultural and sports activities may be recreational substitutes for the residents of smaller towns, these events are also found in the largest metropolitan centers.

Though the productivity coefficient is assumed to be constant in the equational system above, it should be noted that the ratio of urbanized to rural population rises as regional size increases. Comparing the rural to urban population levels at orders 1 and 2, it can be seen that the principal difference in regional population must be attributable to the additional city at level 2. The lowest level ratio is (E_b'/E_n') and the second level's ratio is $(sE_b'/[E_n^2 + sE_n'])$, which implies that

$$\frac{E_b'}{sE_n'} > \frac{E_b'}{E_n^2 + sE_n'} \qquad (15)$$

Therefore rural population declines relatively as total regional size increases. The central city of level 2 may now be a significant importer of agricultural products and an exporter of services to both lower order central cities and farms in the basic sector; as with the economic base (p. 6), the ratio of nonbasic to basic activity rises with regional size as basic employment becomes internalized within the region. Increases in k will cause this ratio to rise at an even faster rate with increasing regional size.

The number of satellites, s, may vary with regional size if a substantial amount of city specialization occurs at any particular level in the hierarchy. Regular market areas, such as hexagons, seem more likely where commodity preferences are quite homogenous, as between service centers and their surrounding rural populations. Where a particular population has distinct tastes, services otherwise provided at a higher level may be found at a lower one and other consumers in nearby satellites of a similar order may break the regularity of their particular market areas. Such specialization would tend to reduce the central city's population since at least a part of employment normally accruing to the marginally hierarchical service is now provided noncentrally. This is a potentially important characteristic of cities capable of growing through the strict regularity of satellite sizes suggested by central place theory.

Though cities tend to vary over time in their relative position in the urban size spectra, it is less clear whether this specialization is systematically related to city size. Small communities within the labor markets often serve as retirement centers providing specialized medical services to other urban places of approximately equal size; much of the growth of larger cities in the southwestern states is attributable to increasing demands for particular services such as recreation. Also, it is likely that much of the urban specialization that does occur is unrelated to regional variations in consumer preferences. Governmental installations (universities, defense-related activities, etc.) often account for much of the observed variation in employment mixes among cities of given sizes and these services frequently have market radii far exceeding those for other cities within the same size class.

Assuming a constant k and s in Equations 9 through 14, the distribution of cities closely follows the rank size rule; this distribution is illustrated in Figure 4. Two characteristics (the population of the largest city, *max* E_t, and the number of cities, p) completely describe this distribution where the product of population and rank is constant for all cities in the system. This constancy implies that the areas, (*max* E_t) and $[(E_t/p).p]$, are equal in Figure 4 and each

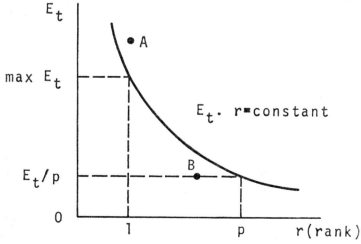

Figure 4: Rank-size distribution for a constant product of population and rank.

city's population is attained by dividing the largest city's population by the rank of the city of interest. Variants from the strict constancy of the product of rank and population may be obtained by statistically estimating the equation illustrated in Figure 4 where the data imply an equational form other than a rectangular hyperbola. Deviations from either strict constancy of the population-rank product rule or its variants suggest irregularities of k and/or s within the equational system described above; two types of deviant behavior are of principal interest in delineating urbanized regions.

The population of the central city exceeds that predicted from the average product of population and rank for all other cities in the system; this situation is shown as A in Figure 4. Dominance of the central city suggests that k rises or s falls between successive levels in the hierarchy. The largest city may be providing highly labor intensive services due, perhaps, to a central concentration of high income households or the location of governmental activities. A specialized service, previously provided in one of the lower order centers, may be relocated in the central city causing a regional redistribution of service employment. Whatever the cause, central dominance may indicate that the appropriate spatial radii of the region included by all cities within the distribution is underestimated.

At the lower end of the population spectra, rural communities may be smaller than would normally be predicted by the rank size calculation; in combination with A, point B in Figure 4 results in a distribution of cities whose population-rank product falls as city size declines. As suggested above, the central city may become competitive with a smaller satellite community in the provision of a specialized service. The economic base of the smaller towns may be considerably more sensitive to declining incomes and employment opportunities in the agricultural sector; k falls though the number of satellite towns may be uninfluenced. Since the marginally hierarchical service will normally have the spatially broadest marketing radii, it is expected that the marketing area of the smaller city (B in Figure 4) is somewhat smaller than would be predicted from the rank-size rule.

A combination of both of these influences increases the variance in observed populations within a given city size distribution over time. Since (for a given number of cities) the variance in r is constant, deviations from the rank size rule are caused solely by changes in the variance of the population among cities; both an increase and decrease in the population variance may suggest spatial inconsistencies among hierarchical levels in the urban system. In the former case, the market radii of the central place may significantly transcend the radii expected of lower-order satellites; households shopping in the central city may be purchasing lower-order commodities in satellites not included within the system. The opposite may occur if the population variance decreases; households located in the smaller towns may be purchasing higher-order goods in a central place located outside of the regional boundary encompassing all cities in the distribution. These spatial changes in market areas among cities complicate the interpretation of statistics summarizing distributional changes over time for a given regional system.

For purposes of spatial delineation, central place concepts emphasize the congruity of market boundaries for a wide variety of economic goods and services. At the spatial margin separating two urban systems are marketing boundaries for all commodities provided within the two regions, a characteristic not true of locations nearer to the regional centers. As the number of hierarchical levels rises, the significance of delineating errors along the regional boundaries also tends to increase; the smallest chance of making a delineating mistake is for households and economic activities that are located in the center of the largest city if the spatial radii of all services do not vary substantially within the region. Though we expect these radii to vary among regions, the spatial inclusion of a substantial number of activities is a characteristic of regionalizations closely based on central place principles.

SPATIAL DELINEATION

The appropriate spatial delineation of regions is one of the more important problems of urban-regional analysis. It is not difficult to conceive of an alternative distribution of states, counties, and urbanized areas that might substantively change our view of the types of socio-economic problems that have important spatial dimensions. Where a fixed number of spatial units are aggregated into regions of various sizes, an attribute (per capita income, unemployment, etc.) may vary in value from the over-all mean with zero variance to the range value (absolute difference) between the extremes indicated in the smallest set of units. The extreme variances that are usually possible under delineations of intermediate-sized units will substantially influence perceptions of both the importance of a particular problem and the appropriate policy instrument for its resolution.

Two somewhat related assumptions underlay most empirical delineations of regions. (1) The sets of regional units are spatially exclusive so that their boundaries are closed and unique to a particular self-contained unit. These are characteristics of most political subdivisions and may impose restrictive constraints on the analyst. Closure suggests that no elements shall remain undelineated, though usually few principles of classification provide sharp distinctions for all cases. Every U.S. resident is physically located in one of the political subdivisions, for example, and he enters and exits that political jurisdiction by crossing its boundary. Though space may be readily demarcated along politically convenient dimensions, the appropriate boundaries for socio-economic characteristics may be substantially less clear. In addition, the unique character of each region precludes spatially separate (noncontiguous) combinations of subunits; this restriction is undoubtedly more confining, though administratively and analytically convenient. (2) The set of regional units spatially exhausts a predetermined space. This is an additional restriction that may encourage inappropriate delineating criteria since there is no *a priori* reason to believe that socio-economic attributes are necessarily congruent with a particular spatial domain. Variations in the spatial dimensions of the delineated units introduce similarly disparate measures of density because land area is the basis for most variables measuring socio-economic contiguity. It should also be noted that such density estimates may be very inaccurate measures and that the importance of physical space is probably overrated within the context of these assumptions. Three delineating criteria are important to the regional units considered in this book.

Homogeneous and Heterogeneous Regions

Given a predetermined number of spatial subunits, regions might be selected that minimize the variance of a particular characteristic within units and maximize the among-region variation. The success of the delineation depends on the spatial distribution of the attribute and presumes some regional variation in the characteristic. (The test is dependent on the relative variances within and among spatial units and, hence, cannot distinguish separate groupings if the overall variance of the characteristic is zero. Some heterogeneity must be present in the criteria to delineate homogeneous regions except in the redundant case of a single spatial unit.) Statistical tests utilizing analysis of variance techniques may be used in empirically delineating the appropriate set of regions for a single characteristic; covariance and factor analytic tests are appropriate for a set of attributes.

Homogeneous economic regions tend to be both specialized and dependent; hence, external trade and export-related domestic activities are important characteristics of these spatial units. Agricultural supply and resource regionalizations are perhaps the most internally consistent examples of economic homogeneity. The corn and cotton-belt counties of the Midwest and South are highly specialized in a single crop and share a common dependence on demand conditions in external markets; natural resources such as forests and mineral deposits tend to be even more spatially specialized than agricultural activity. The concentration of homogeneous production units minimizes the extent of intra-regional trade and results in exports of primary products to markets and manufacturing centers. These exports constitute a major source of earnings to regional residents and are expended on needed imports of goods and services. Since the productive complementarities of primary products are not extensive, trade among regions delineated on the basis of agricultural supply characteristics tends to be minor.

The number and size of homogeneous economic regions often depends on (1) variations in preference patterns in consumption, and (2) the ability of producing units to substitute unique local resources for other factor inputs. Indeed, where all demand and supply functions for goods and services are virtually identical in space, there is little basis for regional differentiation. As final consumption is an inherently nonspecialized activity of households, market radii for goods and services tend to be spatially restricted, and heterogeneity among regional units is easily discerned on the basis of general delineating characteristics. Supply areas are often spatially extensive in accordance with the specialized nature of production and, therefore, more readily distinguished among regions. Where utility and/or production functions allow for considerable substitution of commodities or factor inputs, the potential number of regions increases; consumption complementarities and the even spatial diffusion of production technologies will usually restrict the number of spatial subunits.

From the viewpoint of factor returns and the variety of potentially consumable goods and services, intra-regional trade increases the homogeneity of producing regions and the heterogeneity of marketing areas. Supply regions specialize in commodities utilizing abundant factors of production so their among-region returns tend to be equalized and the incentive for the producing agent to migrate is reduced. (Factor returns are equalized, though commodity and resident factor specialization is increased.) The possible variation in consumption patterns among market regions is increased, and competition will tend to reduce prices in locally concentrated producing industries. Regional trade may, therefore, substitute for labor or capital migration, which might otherwise produce similar pressures toward factor price equalization among spatial units. Though we may expect earnings differentials by industry or occupational class to narrow, per capita average income differentials among regions may remain due to variations in skills, managerial abilities and consumption preferences; regional variations in per capita real income are not *a priori* evidences of economic inefficiencies despite the prevalence of this assertion in the regional literature.

The opposite criterion to that suggested above chooses regions on the basis of homogeneity among and heterogeneity within subunits. These regions are usually characterized by high ratios of nonbasic to basic employment and a substantial degree of functional independence. Standard Metropolitan Statistical Areas (SMSAs) are population concentrations delineated by the U.S. Bureau of the Census on the basis of (1) size of central city, (2) degree of nonagricultural employment, and (3) extent of daily commutation into the region. These three characteristics usually insure that the SMSA includes a relatively complete array of goods and services necessary to support the residentiary needs of households and businesses. Functional Economic Areas (FEAs) are even broader regions encompassing all employees commuting daily to a central place within the region. As the FEA is not subject to restrictions (1) and (2) above, the number of regions and their total population are more inclusive of urbanized regions in the United States compared to SMSAs; their boundaries internalize the spatial area within which residents conduct almost all of their daily employment and residential activity. The variety of economic activities within units and the common functional independence among units is the salient delineating characteristic of both the SMSA and the **FEA.**

Two characteristics of the homogeneity/heterogeneity criterion noted above may be summarized as follows. (1) The homogeneity-within variant of the criterion typically fails to spatially internalize the extreme dependence of the regional unit. As the external influences substantially affect the unit's economy, the determination of the spatial origins of these influences may be quite difficult. The advantage of the criterion is that regionally differentiating characteristics are usually emphasized. (2) The homogeneity-among variant has the opposite set of characteristics. Economic independence typifies the SMSA and FEA so that the necessity of tracing external influences is lessened, but the variation among units tends to be confined to differences expected solely due to the characteristics of various sized central places; the attributes that sharply distinguish regional units are less apparent.

Finally empirically delineated units often have important characteristics exemplified under both variants of the criterion. Small rural communities typically service their surrounding farm populations, but also may specialize in a particular activity for a broader regional population. The functional independence of labor markets that vary in population from 250,000 to 16 million may be substantially less important than the different mix of services and the types of economic problems among regions of this size. Excessive emphasis on either variant of the criterion may subvert characteristics of importance to the analysis of a particular problem.

Nodal Regions

From the viewpoint of empirical delineations, nodality is a special case of the heterogeneity-within variant of the criterion discussed above; two characteristics are usually used in defining nodal regions. (1) Density variations within regions are the primary characteristic, and the delineating attributes may or may not vary among subunits. Central place concepts and employment or residential land use densities are frequently utilized as the basis for delineation. (2) A single center usually constitutes the base for calculating density variations within regions, and boundaries are determined by estimating the spatial domain of an activity at the center. Multinodal regions are usually excluded and the spatial boundaries do not depend on the among-region variance in the characteristic.

These restrictions facilitate considerably the determination of the number of regional units, and delineating errors arise principally from variations in the characteristic among nodal centers. Ideally, the number of units should be the result of maximizing differences in the within- and among-region variances under the two variants of the homogeneity criteria, but this is often impractical in empirical work. Choosing centers that are just large enough to supply the same marginally hierarchical good is a much simpler procedure and, if accurately done, should result in centers of approximately equal size; in a well-defined central place hierarchy, this method should also exhaust the spatial area of an urban system. If the centers provide different goods at the hierarchical margin, market radii overlap and some of the regional boundaries will be underestimated where all spatial elements belong to a unique regional unit.

As suggested in the sections on land use (p. 2) and urban systems (p. 12), centrality may be due to efficiency in the locational patterns of productive and residentiary activity and spatial indivisibilities in transporting goods and services. Marketing centers within cities attract firms selling products incurring substantial costs of distribution; households locate near to employment centers to save on commuting expenses. The fixed cost and bulk efficiency of commodity transportation result in distributional centers of various sizes that are quite evenly diffused throughout the regional hinterland; the number of these centers depends in part on the ability of transportation technology to overcome the costs of providing goods and services in space. Centrality is, therefore, a characteristic that can be defined at numerous levels in the spatial economic system and provides an extremely general concept for the delineation of regional units.

SMSAs and FEAs exemplify regions based on nodal principles, though a substantial variation in the size of centers is allowed. SMSAs must have at least 50,000 persons residing within their central cities, and at least 75% of employment within the central county must be in nonagricultural occupations; a substantial variation in nodal size among regions is possible even with the minimum population restriction. Labor market regions (or FEAs) are delineated solely on the basis of commuting behavior, so their central city populations may be substantially smaller and the among-region variance higher than for SMSAs. Since both regions approximate the labor market area for a well-defined central place, the marketing radii for the marginally hierarchical good may be less than the one-way commuting distance for small regions and substantially in excess of this trip radii in large regions. As wage and salary payments constitute the largest expenses for productive factors, the FEA and SMSA provide approximations to a spatially internalized "household expenditure" region; in most cases, the region generating receipts to firms will be substantially larger.

Residents on the boundaries separating nodal regions are least advantaged with respect to purchases of central goods and may experience some instability in the spatial distribution of their expenditures. Depending on the nature of the central good offered at the node, noncentral residents will usually consolidate shopping and business trips and (with the exception of commuting) travel less frequently to the nodal center. Since, for these households, the purchases of low- and high-order goods in the nodal center may be complementary, nodal firms providing low-order goods have an interest in the competitive capabilities of businesses producing the marginally hierarchical commodity or service. Among nodal centers, competition may cause households on the periphery to vary their shopping destinations, particularly in the absence of complementary trip purposes at a particular center; rural farm families probably best exemplify this situation. Nodal firms providing goods at the hierarchical margin may be more concerned about peripheral customer "good-will" than with the purchasing habits of households nearer the center and, hence, less likely to shop at other market centers.

Though nodality implies declining population densities from the center to the periphery, the aggregate market effects of peripheral households should not be underestimated as lower-order centers are successively aggregated within the region. The often observed exponential decline in population density from urban centers to the periphery is offset by the geometric rise in land area implied by increases in the radius of a circle; the cumulative distribution relating land area to population may or may not reflect "equity" (*i.e.*, equal cumulative percentages at all increments to distance from the center to the periphery in these two variables). If city size was inversely correlated with distance from the nodal city and the constant population-rank product rule held, land area and population would in all likelihood be equally distributed within city systems. (This assumes that distances among cities in each size class are not specified.) The spatial nesting of smaller cities precludes this phenomenon, of course, and the locational regularity of lower-order systems suggests considerable instability in this cumulative distribution for successively small increments to the regional radius. This same regularity, however, insures that the number of included cities should rise at an average rate exceeding proportionality to distance increments from the center to the periphery. Though we may, therefore, expect the degree of nodality to vary among regions (as evidenced by the shape of the population-land area Lorenz curve), peripheral firms and households constitute an important market for businesses in the nodal center.

Policy Regions

A third spatial unit of interest is the governmental body responsible for the administration of economic policies influencing urban-regional development; the federal, state, county, and municipal governments are traditional units having substantial policy impacts on their respective economies. None of these geographical units are solely delineated for the purposes of effectively administering the tax and expenditure programs at their disposal and, with the possible exception of municipalities, boundary changes are rarely indicative of the spatial dynamics of economic development. Primarily as a result of this stability, numerous special districts and administrative regions of the federal government have been created to reflect more effectively the locational economic changes that have occurred historically.

Though strongly influenced by the legal separation of powers, the tax and expenditure programs of these units are not totally unrelated to an appropriate economic jurisdictional division. Stabilization policy is unlikely to be effective when left to the uncoordinated actions of the numerous state and local governments; the restrictions imposed on the debt and money-creating functions of these units further impair their role in dealing with cyclical fluctuations in employment and output. The progressivity of the federal personal income tax and the traditional role of this unit in the welfare and Social Security programs provides the federal government with substantial leverage over income redistribution. The role of local governments in providing fire and police protection is at least partially justified through the financing of these services by the property tax. Numerous economists feel that the function of urban governments should be confined solely to the provision of public goods within the allocative objectives of policy, financed to the greatest possible extent through user charges.

Several additional considerations relate to the optimal size of governmental units providing a particular service. (1) Possible scale economies attained through the consolidation of service districts may be offset by the disadvantages of internalizing highly variant preference patterns of households within subunits. Public utilities (water, gas, sewerage) are most likely to be subject to spatial scale economies with minor variations in local preference patterns for these services. (2) Merit goods, such as education, should be provided on a spatial scale sufficient to insure an equitable distribution of the service. Small school districts may result in tax enclaves and an inequitable distribution of financial resources necessary to ensure that this objective is achieved. (3) The unit's size may or may not internalize benefits sufficiently to ensure a socially optimal level of resources budgeted for the service. Out-migration of high school graduates may, therefore, result in suboptimal budgets for small school districts though it is likely that the public interest evidenced in local schools may outweigh this effect. Control districts for air and water pollutants must be sufficiently large to spatially internalize these external dis-economies and the realities of modern warfare preclude adequate defensive measures taken at anything less than a multinational level.

In substantial contrast to the more general delineation principles discussed above, relationships among policy units may influence the optimal distribution of function and effective size of unit. Proposals to substitute general block grants for special purpose programs in urban communities imply a substantively reduced commitment to the income redistributive objective of the federal government. State grants-in-aid have been the major instrument in attaining school district consolidation at the local level in an effort to reduce inter-district inequities in educational opportunity. Taxing powers of state and local governments have similarly been extended beyond their immediate resident jurisdictions. Earnings taxes on suburban residents extend the ability of central cities to shift the cost of daytime services to an important class of users; suburban retaliation will probably be increasingly effective as employment decentralization continues within the larger metropolitan regions. State use taxes on out-of-state sales by residents protect the sales tax jurisdictions of state governments from the tax-avoiding responses of boundary residents. Grants-in-aid by federal agencies have also stimulated local governmental cooperation through the formation of multicounty planning organizations, particularly in the field of transportation. In these numerous ways, intergovernmental relationships may compensate for the traditional rigidity of the geographical boundaries of these policy units.

Special districts are another way in which the public service preferences of residents may be locally differentiated without changing the traditional jurisdictions of political units. The costs of local improvements, such as the provision of sidewalks and gutters, can be internalized to the principal beneficiaries of the service in newly developed sections of the community. Rapid transit districts empowered to levy a tax on resident property provide a special service transcending the boundaries of existing urban and county governmental units. Utilities and fire and police protection are frequently provided on a spatial basis that is not congruent with the existing political boundaries of incorporated cities or townships. These types of districts have generally been more flexibly created and changed compared to the political units and probably better reflect the changing spatial distribution of public service preferences and economic activity.

The diversity of public functions described above suggests that the requirements of contiguity and spatial exhaustiveness of the policy subunits may be relaxed. Spatial units should be chosen so as to encompass and contain all legally-defined constituents to be influenced directly by the particular public policy, but this may only include a highly selective subset of the population. Grants for urban renewal, public housing, and local airport construction are usually administered directly within the pertinent local governmental unit, and many states do not allow their municipalities to participate directly in federally-sponsored grant-in-aid programs. Counties and townships usually exhaust the geographical area of a state but municipalities do not. The specialized programs of the U.S. Office of Economic Opportunity have been administered within small and highly specialized districts of the largest metropolitan regions. Due to the different eligibility requirements inherent in various public programs, there is little reason for their administrative subunits to be spatially contiguous.

The relevant variant of the homogeneity criterion applicable to a specific policy regionalization depends on the nature of the public service considered. Efficiency in operation is probably best attained by isolating heterogeneous spatial subunits so that some degree of administrative specialization is attained; the field offices responsible for subsidies provided by the U.S.D.A. undoubtedly reflect a substantial degree of such specialization. These possible efficiencies may be attained at the expense of "unequal treatment of equals" where the spatial heterogeneity attained is considerably less than perfect. Legally required uniformity in the administration of the federal personal income tax laws and the more even spatial distribution of incomes effectively preclude a substantial amount of specialization among districts of the Internal Revenue Service. As suggested above, the variety of policy functions of the various governmental levels makes it difficult to apply regionalization principles of a general nature.

Another problem associated with the delineation of policy units is the tendency for the largest and most stable political regions to be chosen as official statistical units. The detail and probable accuracy of data available for analyzing regional growth problems is inversely related to the size of the political unit despite the likelihood that smaller units (particularly municipalities) are best able to adapt their boundaries to the realities of spatial economic growth. From the viewpoint of political decision-making, these priorities are undoubtedly justified, but problems arise in making behavioral inferences from these data to regionalizations more appropriately reflecting the spatial socio-economic community; the latter are the relevant statistical unit, not time series or cross section data based on rather arbitrary spatial regions. Because of the lack of information on smaller spatial regions, problems of data disaggregation are of particular interest to urban-regional economists.

An example will illustrate the types of inference problems arising from the use of official statistics on political units. Suppose that workers commute daily from state A to state B and report income on a residence basis. Assume further that A's workers shop in state B so at least a part of consumption expenditure is reported in B's statistics. Under such circumstances, one of the household's characteristics (consumption expenditure) is split between two political jurisdictions and the other (income) is not. In utilizing state cross section data to estimate the relationship between consumption and income, the variance in consumption expenditure is overstated relative to the variance in income and the marginal propensity to consume is biased upward. A problem of this type may become more serious over time as labor markets transcend state boundaries if the locational specialization of residence and employment between states A and B increases.

A final problem to be noted is the impact of disparate policies among contiguous jurisdictions on economic development. When the effective regional community overlaps the political jurisdiction, boundary economies may become spatially specialized, imposing limitations on the freedom of a political unit to pursue an independent course of action. If state A alone tries to restrict the marketing of a particular commodity, firms from state B will move to A's border, and unless stringent policing of the restriction is accomplished, the policy fails. When policing is not enforced, the policy restriction tends to be differentially applied to the border and interior residents in state A, and land use patterns at border crossings are inefficiently distorted. The ultimate extent of the distortion at the boundary depends on the number and unique nature of the restrictions imposed by states A and B. If the legislatures of A and B restrict different goods, all the "bad" commodities are offered on the opposite sides of the border; alternatively, if both states restrict the same goods, the border offers no differential locational advantage for firms producing these commodities. If the different restrictions of A and B are extensive, the states may even trade households consuming "bad" goods through migration and the specialization at the border would cease. Though this is an extreme case, it illustrates the practical limitations on policy diversification among political units and distorting effects of policy on locational patterns of economic activity.

The discussion above has emphasized the compensations and distortions stemming from the inflexibility of traditional political units to adapt to the changing spatial organization of economic activity. There are good reasons for this inflexibility, mostly related to the stability of expectations regarding governmentally provided services affecting land uses and property values. However, it is worth noting the substantial costs of this stability. Virtually all of the commonly discussed environmental and fiscal problems of urban development stem from externalities generated by existing patterns of land use and the inability to spatially adapt to locational change. The traditional means of urban governments in promoting efficiency in land use have not always included safeguards against these external effects; the so-called crises of municipal development and finance are, in large part, crises of spatial change.

ORGANIZATIONAL INTRODUCTION

Both the regional development theories and delineation principles discussed above provide a background for the studies in subsequent chapters. The first four chapters include regional units varying in size from the very smallest rural towns to the larger metropolitan communities; these units represent the extremes in economic dependence. Labor markets are an important example of regions delineated on the basis of nodality and river basins combine several of the principles described in this chapter. Policy units include the local, state and federal governments; instruments of policy unique to each governmental level are used to illustrate their various effects on urban-regional development. The following topics, by chapter, are discussed:

(Chapter 2). The smallest rural towns exemplify dependence on a contracting employment base in agriculture and inadequate access to residential services and amenities. These towns may specialize in particular services and/or compete with larger cities in providing low-order goods to rural residents. Recent policy approaches to their development problems are discussed.

(Chapter 3). Labor markets provide one focus for the application of the "growth centers" development strategy. Nodality is a key feature of this approach; governmental programs are centralized within the largest city of the labor market. Several models that examine the structure of cities within the smaller labor markets of the United States are discussed.

(Chapter 4). Water resource regionalizations integrate a population base with the distribution of a particular natural resource. Waterways provide connecting linkages between supplying and demanding regions within a country, and the commercial traffic along these waterways depends on the shifting comparative advantages of regional production and population growth. Because of the importance of planning inland waterway improvements on a spatially comprehensive basis this chapter provides a detailed discussion of the problem of estimating interregional commodity flows. Methodological issues are stressed in this chapter to emphasize the numerous difficulties of reconciling regional diversity within the simplistic structure of maximizing models.

(Chapter 5). Metropolitan planning models incorporate a variety of demographic and economic variables designed to facilitate comprehensive sectoral planning; the interdependence of policies designed to influence land-uses and their spatial distribution are an important element of models on which such planning is based. Among urban areas, disparities in factor returns may influence population migration and city sizes; a model analyzing the locational aspects of interurban earnings differentials is discussed.

(Chapter 6). State policies influence regional growth and may equitably (or inequitably) redistribute fiscal resources within the state. A discriminant model of interstate competition analyzes locational incentives attempting to foster industrial growth. The allocative effects of tax exemptions are also discussed.

(Chapter 7). National policy approaches toward urban-regional development may focus on population redistribution. The development of large metropolitan communities (experimental cities) and new towns are a part of this development strategy. The problems of integrating the development of existing urban regions with these new communities and the specification of planning criteria are stressed in this chapter.

A final chapter summarizes our discussion and suggests some methodological and policy issues that are based on the analysis in previous sections.

GENERAL REFERENCES

Alonso, W. *Location and Land Use* (Cambridge, Mass.: Harvard University Press, 1964).

Andrews, R. B. "Mechanics of the Urban Economic Base," *Land Economics*, **29-31**, 1953-1956.

Beckmann, M. "City Hierarchies and the Distribution of City Size," *Econ. Develop. Cultur. Change*, **6**:243–248, 1968.

Berry, B. J. L. "Cities as Systems Within Systems of Cities," *Papers Reg. Sci. Assoc.* **13**: 147–163, 1964.

Berry, B. J. L., and A. Pred. *Central Place Studies: A Bibliography of Theory and Applications*, Bibliography Series No. 1 (Philadelphia: Regional Science Research Institute, 1965).

Berry, B. J. L., et. al. *Metropolitan Area Definition: A Re-Evaluation of Concept and Statistical Practice*, U.S. Department of Commerce, Working Paper 28 (Washington, D. C.: Government Printing Office, 1968).

Blumenfeld, H. "The Economic Base of the Metropolis," *J. Amer. Inst. Planners*, **21**, 1955.

Borts, G. W. and J. L. Stein. *Economic Growth in a Free Market* (New York: Columbia University Press, 1964).

Boudeville, J. R. *Problems of Regional Economic Planning* (Edinburgh: Edinburgh University Press, 1966).

Christaller, W. W. *Central Places in Southern Germany,* 1933 translated by C. W. Baskin (Englewood Cliffs, New Jersey: Prentice-Hall, Inc., 1966).

Duncan, O. D., et. al. *Metropolis and Region* (Baltimore: Johns Hopkins Press, 1960).

Hoover, E. M. "Transport Costs and the Spacing of Central Places," *Papers Reg. Sci. Assoc.* **24**:255–294, 1970.

Hoover, E. M. and R. Vernon. *Anatomy of a Metropolis* (Cambridge, Mass.: Harvard University Press, 1959).

Lewis, W. C. "A Critical Examination of the Export-Base Theory of Urban-Regional Growth," *Annals Reg. Sci.,* December, 1972.

Losch, A. *The Economics of Location* (New Haven: Yale University Press, 1954).

Mills, E. S. *Urban Economics* (New York: Scott, Foresman and Company, 1972).

Perloff, H. S., et. al. *Regions, Resources and Economic Growth* (Baltimore: Johns Hopkins Press, 1960).

Romans, J. T. *Capital Exports and Growth Among U.S. Regions* (Middletown, Conn.: Wesleyan University Press, 1965).

Siebert, H. *Regional Economic Growth: Theory and Policy* (Scranton, Pa.: International Textbook Co., 1969).

Tiebout, C. M. "Exports and Regional Economic Growth," *J. Pol. Econ.* **64**:160–164, 1956.

Tiebout, C. M. *The Community Economic Base Study,* Supplementary Paper No. 16 (New York: Committee for Economic Development, December 1962).

2

Rural Community Development

The smallest rural communities of the nation comprise the lowest-order settlements in the urban hierarchy and are the most dependent economic units considered in this book. Agriculturally-related business and residentiary services are an important element in the community's economic base and the increasing mobility of residents within the surrounding market area intensifies competition with the more densely populated centers in the region. Relatively low incomes and limited access to high-order private and public services combine to restrict the range of work and leisure-related alternatives available to the small town resident. The sectoral changes affecting per capita income usually occur outside the town's political jurisdiction, and the agriculturally-related emphasis of public investments have at best indirect effects on these smaller rural communities.

From the discussion in Chapter 1, these communities may be characterized as follows. The rural town exports services to hinterland families in the agricultural sector and possesses primitive centrality in land uses; both the central business district (CBD) and the residences surrounding it are low-density land-using activities. These communities tend to be homogeneous with respect to their residentiary and business services base among towns within their own size class; particular communities may occasionally specialize in the provision of services for a broader regional community. The town is a focus of social activity, residentiary purchases of low-order goods and often a transhipment point for agricultural exports. Excluding these activities, however, nodality is not an important characteristic of these cities. As the smallest order centers, there are no high-density satellites within the market radii of the city.

The development problems of rural communities must, therefore, be analyzed within a broader regional framework. The condition of the town's CBD does not fully reflect its accessibility to commercial and residential services; the automobile, highway-related investments and the growth of contiguous cities have continually broadened the economic community of which the small-town resident is a part. Labor markets are a useful approximation to this broader regional community. The commuting radius to the region's largest city internalizes the home-to-work trips of most regional residents and spatially contains most of the retail and services expenditures of its households. Accessibility to employment opportunities and higher-order residentiary services will usually decline from the central city to the peripheral boundaries of the region, so the decentralizing trends expected from regional growth may substantially benefit the residents of the smallest towns.

These small communities may benefit from decentralized growth in at least two ways. (1) Market thresholds are reached so that the decentralization of higher-order services is possible. The smaller cities are able to compete with larger communities in providing goods and services to rural residents. (2) Specialized economic bases may be possible for particular towns in the hinterland. These communities provide services for numerous cities within the region in addition to low-order goods for households within their immediate market areas. In both cases, the city's position within the rank-order distribution of central places is strengthened at the expense of centralized growth. Policy strategies that complement decentralization of economic activity may also be structured along the specialized/nonspecialized focus of spatial growth.

The purpose of this chapter is to analyze employment changes within labor markets that may be expected to influence the competitive abilities of the smallest rural communities. The first two sections cover economic changes in the basic and nonbasic employment sectors and the spatial distribution of these activities within labor markets. To illustrate these developments, we draw on a large sample of multicounty rural labor markets for the period 1958–63 and contrasting trends in two Iowa labor markets for the period 1960–70; the latter includes a three-county urban region centered on Scott County and a declining seven-county rural labor market centered on Union County. Policy approaches are then discussed and some planning efforts designed to complement decentralized growth are analyzed. Some evidence relating to the stability of city-size distributions in one of Iowa's more spatially homogeneous labor markets (a six-county region centered on Ft. Dodge) is then presented.

EMPLOYMENT AND POPULATION GROWTH

Economic growth should enhance the development prospects for small towns by diversification of the rural employment base and improvement in incomes earned in secondary sectors that substitute for agricultural activity; these changes should substantially affect the locational patterns of employment and residences within the labor market region. From 1960–70, the substitution of manufacturing for agricultural employment was discernible among and within these regions, resulting in some narrowing of income differentials. The spatial distribution of these changes was not uniform, however, either within given states or among states of the nation. Furthermore, growth rates in manufacturing have not been sufficiently high to fully absorb employment declines in the agricultural sector. These trends are encouraging, however, in that the instability of excessive spatial specialization may be reduced.

Manufacturing Employment

From 1962–69, about 20% of the 3 million net job additions in manufacturing occurred within predominantly rural labor markets (Haren). This growth has been particularly strong in the South, the Great Lakes industrial belt and the states of Minnesota, Iowa and Missouri. This decentralized growth has been accompanied by diversification in the mix of manufacturing activity within these regions to include industrial machinery, leisure-related products, and various types of metal-working industries. Much of this growth was evenly sustained over this period and is due to improved marketing technologies, the desire for less congested living environments, and improved access to these regions because of the interstate highway system.

There is also some evidence of manufacturing employment decentralization within labor markets during an earlier part of the decade. From a national sample of 86 low-density labor market regions for the period 1958–63, total manufacturing employment grew by 11.9%; the growth within central cities of these regions (all with less than 100,000 residents in 1960) was only 7.1%. In towns outside the central city, manufacturing employment grew at about twice the rate of the central city (14.4%) and secondary job opportunities per resident increased. Agricultural employment declined an average of 5.3% annually, and indicators of sectoral change within agriculture are highly correlated with manufacturing activity in the smaller peripheral towns of these regions. Manufacturing establishments in the regional periphery seem to be particularly sensitive to declining job opportunities in the farm sector. (See Table I for sectoral employment growth rates.)

These secondary employment increases may have different impacts among city-size classes and may be categorized as to their business and residentiary components. (1) It seems doubtful that the services purchases of firms will be strongly internalized either within the smaller cities or the region generally. Plants located in small towns probably purchase limited amounts of noncommodity inputs from the central cities, and locational changes are often contingent on the previous existence of needed services. From the viewpoint of these smaller regions, many services are in fact basic industries; activities such as recreational products, private colleges, commercial laboratories, and business consulting firms are examples of decentralizing enterprises dependent on external markets. Locational inducements (as discussed in Chapter 6) may deplete fiscal resources in the short run and a substantial proportion of new manufacturing employment may accrue to new regional residents. Also, the plants of large corporations usually retain centralized purchasing connections for services and intermediate inputs further restricting the internalization of the secondary effects of manufacturing employment growth. (2) Residentiary purchases by manufacturing employees may have a more substantial impact on public and private services offered within the region. The addition of managerial personnel and the substantially increased average incomes of production workers should be reflected in the demand for income-elastic, higher-order retail and services purchases. Nonagricultural employees are also less able to substitute at their place of residence for the absence of recreational facilities provided locally or supplement real incomes by home produced goods and services.

This labor market sample also suggests that the decentralization of manufacturing employment is consistent with existing differences in labor costs and productivity between the center city and peripheral towns; differentials in the scale of plant indicate, how-

TABLE I

Employment-Population Growth and Decentralization within Rural Labor Markets, 1958–63

	Labor Market	Central City	City Class (5-10,000)	(2.5-5,000)	(less than 2,500)	Outside Central City
Employment:						
Retail	4.0%	0.7% (161.1, 175.8)	1.9% (153.3, 152.0)	7.8% (163.9, 160.0)	10.8% (52.4, 54.3)	---
Wholesale	11.9%	8.6% (184.1, 175.8)	10.2% (132.5, 144.0)	10.9% (59.9, 57.5)	---	---
Selected Services	11.5%	6.8% (190.1, 181.9)	5.6% (138.3, 138.4)	12.2% (127.8, 124.0)	19.2% (48.5, 47.0)	---
Manufacturing	11.9%	7.1% (159.1, 146.1)	---	---	---	14.4% (79.8, 82.3)
Agriculture	26.7%	1.1%	---	---	---	25.7%
Population	6.3%	12.9%	12.6%	8.8%	0.1%	---

Source: Lewis, William C., *An Econometric Model of Urban-Rural Structure and Development*, unpublished Ph.D. dissertation, Iowa State University, Ames, Iowa, 1969. See p. 32 f. of this reference for a detailed discussion of these employment characteristics. Growth rates appear in the top row of each column above. The indices in the second row are defined as $(E_i/P_i) \times 100$ where E_i is the percentage of regional activity accounted for by the ith class and P_i is the percentage of regional population accounted for by the ith class. These indices provide some adjustment for the base on which the growth rates are calculated; the 1958 and 1963 indices appear in order below the growth figure.

ever, that there may be a substantial amount of spatial selectivity between communities within labor markets. Value-added per employee rose from $10,296 (all towns outside the central city) to $10,683 (central cities) in 1963, while the all-manufacturing average annual wage was $374 higher in the central city. Differences in the average size of plant were more substantial. Value-added per establishment was $635.2 thousand (central cities) compared to $455.1 thousand (peripheral towns), a differential of about 40%.

The changing mix of basic employment within regions may also influence daily transportation patterns in several ways. (1) The substitution of manufacturing for agricultural employment increases site alternatives for new firms. The diversity of locational determinants for firms producing fabricated products and the resultant diffusion of new plant locations should result in some decentralization of the origins and destinations of commercial deliveries. (2) In freeing the residential site from the place of work, average journey-to-work distances should increase. Smaller towns may find it easier to specialize as bedroom communities for manufacturing employees, and the daily shopping radii of families may increase to the extent that retail purchases are made during the journey-to-work. Both of these factors may increase the demands for transportation improvements within labor markets and the decentralization of trip patterns may be quite costly from the viewpoint of highway investments. The extent to which transit patterns diffuse to smaller towns within the labor market depends in part on the residential site decisions of regional residents.

Population and Migration

The national sample of labor markets suggests that relatively higher population densities were to be expected within central cities of these regions. The dominant urban centers grew by 12.9% over the period 1958–63 while the rural towns increased by only 0.1%; the overall regional population growth rate was 6.3% or about half the rate experienced in the largest cities of these regions. (See Table I for the population growth data.) Although the central counties of labor markets tend to increase faster (or suffer slower rates of decline) than peripheral counties, a wide variation is undoubtedly present in the national sample. Within the state of Iowa, for example, Union County (the central county of a rural labor market in the southwestern part of the state) declined by 1.1% over the period 1960–70; this was about 10 times slower than the seven-county labor market average decline in population. Scott County (the center of a rapidly growing three-county labor market in eastern Iowa) increased by 19.8% compared to a 13.8% increase for the entire region over the same decade.

The components of net natural increase may substantively influence average money incomes, the demands for public services, and the specialization of small towns within labor markets. Stable or slightly declining death rates and earlier farm retirements increase the needs for specialized medical care and encourage the development of retirement centers within regions. Declining birth rates will restrict primary school enrollments in bedroom towns close to the central city, and it is likely that the populations of these suburban areas may stabilize as the fixed costs per pupil of recently constructed school systems increase. Though substantial specialization by city-size class will be expected only in regions subject to population and income increases, these demographic characteristics may increase the variance in crude birth rates among communities within labor markets.

Migratory flows also favor population retention in the central counties of labor markets and may influence the educational-skill content of the resident labor force. Net migrant rates for the Union and Scott counties labor markets in Iowa are −2.8% and 5.5% for central counties compared to −10.4% and 1.6% for their respective regional averages; the declining rural region centered on Union County had attained a zero net natural rate of population growth from 1960–70. In declining regions, the out-migrants probably include quasi-marginal farm families and younger adults who are part-time labor force participants. Average per capita and family incomes for the region may rise, and it is likely that the loss of numerous high school graduates reduces the average educational attainment of the region's residents. For industrializing labor markets, the income increase is probably due to the substantially higher average incomes earned by manufacturing employees and in-migrants are likely to be better educated than the average adult resident in the region.

The locational characteristics of demographic change are not particularly conducive to the objective of "balanced urban-rural development" within labor markets. Policies seeking such balance must encourage urbanization where it is least likely to be successful or at least let present developments take their course in regions subject to declining population and employment opportunities; the opposite must occur in growing labor markets. The Union County region, for example, increased its urban population from 15% (1960) to 22% (1970) despite substantial losses in its total population. Given present trends for this region, locational balance will be obtained under conditions of negative rates for both the net-migration and natural increase components of gross population change. Conversely, the Scott County labor market was 80% urbanized in 1970 and must reverse present locational trends if the objective of population balance is to be attained. Low income regions with declining populations are thus converging on the balance objective and high income regions with increasing populations are diverging from it. Whatever the merits of this objective, its attainment should be sought on a broader regional basis than the labor market.

RESIDENTIARY SERVICES

The changing mix and location of new employment opportunities will substantially influence the availability of residentiary services to the small town resident; two sectors are of particular significance. (1) Housing costs and quality will affect intraregional residential locations since commuting is possible within the labor market. *Caeteris paribus,* rising vacancy rates and falling housing costs will encourage centralized growth while the opposite will encourage residential locations in the smaller peripheral towns. (2) Scale and productivity differentials within regions may preclude the decentralized growth of new retail and wholesale establishments. Alternatively, some decentralization may occur if smaller towns specialize in the provision of these services.

Housing

Among and within labor markets in the United States, it appears that important changes in housing indicators have occurred over the period 1960–70. In 1970, there were about 6.5 million housing units in excess of urban families and unrelated individuals, and over this decade net additions to the stock were rising by 21% while net household formation rose by only 11%. Within Iowa's labor markets, percentage increases in housing units generally exceeded rates of population increase over the 1960–70 period; the Union County labor market was one exception as total housing units fell by 11% compared to a population decline of 10.4%. (The Scott County region experienced a growth rate in housing units that exceeded population percentage changes by +4%.) These changes in housing markets appear to have substantially increased vacancy rates within regions.

These changes were accompanied by a notable improvement in the available indicators of housing quality, and the distribution of these changes appears to be similar as between predominantly rural and urban labor markets. In the Union County region, the percentage of housing units lacking adequate plumbing fell by 56% over the period 1960–70 and the crowding index (percentage of units with 1.01+ persons per room) declined by 34%; the comparable figures for the Scott County region are –43% and –23%, respectively. In other labor markets within Iowa comparable large percentage declines are typically found, but no systematic differences appear between the seven SMSAs and the nine remaining labor market regions. Insofar as retirements from the stock increase its average quality, it seems possible that farm consolidation in rural regions and freeway construction in urban labor markets are approximately equal in their aggregate impact.

Within labor markets, substantive differences in vacancy rate changes were apparent between the urbanized and rural regions in Iowa, particularly within their central counties. In urban regions, out-migration from small towns in the periphery has not resulted in tighter housing conditions in central counties whereas vacancy changes have been much less pronounced in the central counties of rural labor markets. Scott County, for example, experienced the highest rate of vacancy increase for all sixteen labor markets in the state from 1960–70, and the lowest rate for central counties of SMSA labor markets was not exceeded by any of the rural regions. These indicators suggest that the continued suburbanization of the central cities of urban labor markets may exert a dampening influence on housing costs.

Several implications of these types of housing market changes should be noted:

1. Relatively declining housing costs in central cities may encourage residential relocations from peripheral communities. Programs that subsidize new housing construction in rural towns may face competition in regions where rates of population increase are less than rates of net additions to the stock of dwelling units and vacancy rates are rising; it seems unlikely that such programs will be successful in retaining rural families in the smaller communities of these regions.

2. Unless offset by the growth of new secondary and tertiary establishments, the demand for new construction may fall as a result of rising vacancy rates in the residential housing sector. Since this tends to be an important secondary employment opportunity for farm families, this may encourage further rural out-migration.

3. The orientation of housing policy in the smaller rural towns might be more usefully directed toward the efficient utilization of the existing stock of dwelling units. The conversion of larger single family structures in small towns for use by retired couples provides one example of a policy that would probably be more efficient than the construction of entirely new high-density dwelling units.

Retail Services and Wholesale Employment

The small town resident on the periphery of the labor market benefits both from the growth of higher order services in central cities and the continued existence of smaller retailing establishments in nearby convenience centers. Small town retailers suffer from their restricted marketing radii and the possible decentralization of large scale enterprises to specialized retailing centers in peripheral counties of these regions. The increased accessibility of these services to rural residents may be attained only at the expense of the commercial health (and, consequently, restricted range of public services) of the very smallest rural towns.

The national sample of labor markets provides some evidence of employment decentralization in these sectors and the probable existence of strongly hierarchical spending patterns among city-size classes within these regions. From Table I, it is apparent that the highest growth rates in retailing and selected services employment were found in the very smallest city-size class; the largest growth rate in wholesaling occurred in cities ranging in population from 2,500 to 5,000. The central cities of labor markets became somewhat less concentrated (relative to population) in wholesaling and services and slightly more concentrated in the retailing sector. Regression estimates (discussed in more detail in Chapter 3) generally confirmed the unimportance of shopping trips made by central city residents to peripheral towns and the substantial leakage of expenditure in the opposite direction. These calculations suggest that about 27% and 31% of additional expenditure on retail goods and services, respectively, accrue to central city establishments from customers in peripheral communities. Though some employment decentralization occurred over this period, it seems likely that central city commercial enterprises will maintain a substantial share of the retail and services expenditures of small town residents.

From the viewpoint of labor costs and productivity, the smaller towns appear to be quite competitive with central cities of these regions. The 1963 ranges in annual average earnings (central city minus towns of less than 2,500 in population) are $258 and $93 in the retailing and selected services sectors, respectively; the wholesaling differential was estimated from the smallest city class of 2,500 to 5,000 in population as $258. The average retail employee in the smaller rural towns accounted for $3,806 more in gross sales (1963) than the corresponding worker in the central city, and similar relationships were found in the wholesaling and services sector. As in the manufacturing sector, scale differentials as measured by sales per establishment substantially favor the central cities of labor markets. Central city establishments are 218%, 152%, and 211% larger in the retail, wholesale, and services sectors, respectively, compared to smaller cities in the labor market sample. These data seem compatible with the decentralization of larger shopping centers to specialized peripheral towns that has been observed in Midwestern labor markets over the past several years.

These developments suggest that though services employment may be substantially unresponsive to changes in other intraregional variables, the spatial composition of changes in the retail sector may adversely affect the smaller rural communities. Services employment (inclusive of these three sectors plus government and construction employees) actually rose in the Union County labor market from 1960–70 despite an overall population decline, and it increased at a faster rate than population in the Scott County region. In the declining rural region, the less-productive service sector performs an important role in absorbing the excess supply of agricultural labor, particularly since manufacturing employment increases are still insufficient to account fully for employment changes in the farm sector. Conversely, the changing mix of basic employment in peripheral counties may reduce small town retailing sales since the higher-income manufacturing employees seem more inclined to shop in the central city of the region. Also, the effect of higher rates of population growth in central cities on the range of residentiary services available there will probably induce further expenditure leakages from households in the rural convenience centers. Even if shopping centers decentralize to peripheral counties, it is likely that they would locate in the largest cities; the competition for retail sales would increase in the very smallest towns.

POLICY APPROACHES

The strength of private market forces influencing the spatial composition of basic and service activity will affect the success of policies designed for the development of the smallest communities. These proposals implicitly assume that governmental activity may encourage the general decentralization of economic growth and/or the ability of smaller towns to develop specialized economic bases servicing the broader regional community; the city-size distribution within regions (as discussed in Chapter 1) can be systematically influenced. Several recent developments suggest the general thrust of policy discussions regarding the smaller rural towns.

Congress has recently demonstrated a substantial interest in the nonagricultural sectors of the rural community. In February, 1972, the U.S. House of Representatives passed a bill increasing the grant and lending programs of the Farmers Home Administration to support projects in housing, water, and sewerage system development in rural areas; $580 million was authorized under this bill. The Senate affirmed the increased commitment to this administrative agency with an additional provision of $500 million in revenue sharing for rural development. Although this bill was ultimately defeated, it included a provision for a new credit system providing for loans to small businesses and public agencies in small towns; new research efforts in rural community development and direct aid in improving public services in smaller communities were also encouraged. These proposals are aimed at providing direct investments in the public and private sectors within small communities; as suggested below, however, this is only one of several policy approaches toward rural community development.

Regional growth should encourage both a decentralization of economic activity and some specialization of function by smaller towns in the periphery of labor market regions. This suggests that four policy approaches might be designed to complement development patterns expected in the private sector. Centralized or decentralized growth might be generally encouraged in combination with policies that promote specialization or nonspecialization of function. The following examples illustrate the four combinations of these approaches toward labor market development.

Growth Centers Development

The growth centers policy is an example of a centralizing, non-specializing approach to regional development. Its proponents would encourage population growth in the central cities of labor markets (communities of between 25,000 and 100,000 in population) by discouraging the diffusion of public investments in the smaller cities of the region. It is a nonspecializing strategy in that all government programs at the federal and state levels would be encouraged to locate in the central city. Additional regional benefits are to be attained by having one city of maximum population size within each of these regions.

Several interpretations may be placed on the development benefits attributable to population size alone. (1) Agglomeration economics accrue to firms in large cities due to their contiguity to other business services; this may result in a limited range of increasing returns to goods and services production. It is unlikely, however, that significant production economies of this nature are found in the smaller central cities of these regions. (2) Population and income growth overcome threshhold barriers to the provision of higher-order central goods in the absence of competition from very large metropolitan communities. The city moves upward in the hierarchy of central places providing a wider range of private goods and services to both its own residents and those in nearby communities. The impacts of existing shopping patterns from peripheral to central cities are detrimental to smaller town establishments already suffering from generally low agricultural incomes.

The impact of (2) above depends on the latent demand in the region for the marginally hierarchical good and additional sales of lower-order goods that occur in the central city. If peripheral customers are already purchasing these goods outside of the region, then the growth of the central city internalizes this expenditure. Also, as long as commodity substitutes and complements are closely grouped in the hierarchical order, the expenditure effects of central city growth will probably be confined to the growth center itself. Since higher-order goods tend to be products of greater durability, higher value, and lower turnover, the effects of lower-order purchases in the same shopping trip will also tend to be negligible in the smaller communities.

The centralization of all governmental services would probably constitute a net encouragement of further rural out-migration and could increase the costs of services provided to rural and small town residents. As a governmental services center, the growth node would add a relatively high income, stable component of employment to its local economy constituting an additional attraction to rural residents. The costs of delivering services to the peripheral communities might increase and biases in favor of confining services to the growth center might result. The centralization of housing and educational programs could provide a further stimulus to population in-migration from the peripheral communities.

Educational Center

The provision of vocational/educational services in the central city may be characterized as a centralizing-specialization strategy; it is specialized in the sense that a specific activity is singled out as a major component of the central city's employment base. Several different interpretations of the role of the educational center are possible. (1) The purpose of the vocational college is to ease (and possibly encourage) rural out-migration by providing urban skills to the agriculturally unemployed. The curriculum is designed primarily with the occupational needs of the larger urban areas in mind in hopes of easing the transitional problems of the out-migrant. The schools are designed to reduce the spatial spillover costs in regions experiencing high in-migration by increasing the skill content of the migration flow; the problem of manpower allocation for regional residents is of secondary concern. (2) The school's curriculum is designed to reduce short-run and frictional unemployment rates within the region. The vocational program attempts to follow projected occupational needs of the region and encourage enrollments by students whose skills are in excess supply. An implied objective is the reduction of net out-migration, which is typically highest in the outlying rural counties of the labor market.

In these ways, the vocational college may supplement the role of the labor market's largest city as a training center for its residents. Its ability to successfully perform this role depends primarily on the range of job experiences and occupational choices it can offer. This, in turn, depends primarily on size though occasionally very small cities are found with occupational profiles closely approximating those of the larger urbanized areas. If the skill requirements of a successful out-migrant move preclude back-migration for employment reasons or unduly long adjustments at the destination, then it seems likely that labor markets should have at least one city in the range of 75,000 to 100,000 persons. It is also likely that back-migration has been reduced in the university-age cohorts by providing two-year transitional programs between high school and the larger collegiate institutions outside of the region.

The vocational and community college program also has implications for the provision of services to regional residents. A higher income component of the employment base is added to the city with this institution, and culturally related services are provided. The institution itself provides regularly scheduled events that may be successfully extended to residents in the smaller rural towns and, in many labor markets, is the only activity capable of bridging the gap between the very smallest and largest urban communities of the nation. More narrowly, it extends for two years the part-time employment base for workers in the younger age cohorts within these regions.

Agricultural Services Center

If scale barriers to the provision of high-order services constitute a major impediment to maintaining the rural population, then the consolidation of these investments may be necessary. Some planners have suggested that several dispersed centers designed to accommodate all the services demands of farm families might satisfy this scale requirement. This development strategy may, therefore, be characterized as decentralized and specialized in that selected services are to be dispersed within peripheral counties of the labor market. The centers would be designed to be complementary with the seasonal demands of agriculture and the services needs of all family members.

Agricultural extension activities would form an important component of the base for the center. Demonstrations of new farm machinery and agricultural techniques would be provided for the male household head, and homemaking displays would be the principal occupational attraction for females. This component of the services center might be initially financed by the state government providing several focii for extension activities in each labor market. Presumably, private agri-business firms would be induced to locate in these centers to the extent that it succeeded in attracting numerous farm families within the region.

If the services base were sufficiently extensive, families might be attracted for stays of several days or weeks. Visits of this length would probably be concentrated in the winter months during the agricultural off-season. Moviehouses, restaurants, and similar residentiary services would be designed at a scale exceeding existent competition within the region. Special activities (touring plays, carnivals, etc.) could be valuable supplements to the center's income if well-advertised within the region. For visits of several days, the centers should also probably be located in areas with access to water-based recreational activities providing an additional impetus to summer visitations. Though a development of this scale might preclude one (or several) centers for each labor market, it could increase the opportunities for one-day and weekend recreational trips within the state by providing numerous complementary attractions at a single location.

Due to the problem of generating sufficient seasonal peak loads, an important on-going component of the center's base is the provision of services competing with those in the smaller rural towns. If there is at least one center per region, the variety and scale of activity might attract over half of the region's weekend (and possibly, weekday) night-time social activity in addition to a large share of the daily shopping within the labor market. This competition would probably have a substantially adverse impact on retail and services expenditures in other communities of the region; the labor market's residents must trade off the benefits of increased service accessibility with a spatial reallocation of commercial activity.

Though many of these services are already provided to rural residents in a more dispersed fashion, proponents of this development plan emphasize the conscious role of legislative policy-makers in spatially allocating state-financed programs. By consolidating offices of particular state services, agglomerating forces in the private sector may produce a type and size of hinterland city that can extend the range and quality of services provided to rural families. It seems likely that the potential effects of such a policy have not been adequately explored in most states; there are few analogies in the governmental sector to the business impact study. Political considerations aside, legislatures have more leverage over these locational choices and the consolidation costs would appear to be minor.

Small Town Subsidization

A final policy approach would be to simply establish city-size priorities for programs at all governmental levels; the efforts of the federal government described above come under this heading. These programs would presumably emphasize (1) the growth of new employment opportunities and (2) the development of residentiary services. Programs of housing, renewal, and education could be combined with state legislation enabling cities to extend subsidies to new business firms locating in these towns. This would constitute a decentralized-general strategy for development in that peripheral towns would be given priority choices in all governmental programs.

Employment goals might include keeping rates of increase in new job opportunities close to declining rates in the agricultural sector. As noted above, the somewhat higher growth rates in peripheral manufacturing employment during the 1960's suggest that this not be an infeasible goal. Property tax forgiveness and subsidized leasing programs are among the many types of locally provided locational incentives found in the various states. These programs require state-enabling legislation and may be supplemented by statewide development corporations providing low-interest loans for new firms and plants. Legislation that selectively discriminated between cities of different sizes might present political problems and it is likely that these programs would be most attractive to communities slightly smaller than the central cities of most labor markets. These incentives could also be extended to retail and services establishments in the smaller rural towns of the region. As suggested in Chapter 6, however, it appears that the effects of these programs have not been particularly strong.

A problem associated with the general decentralization of residentiary services is the very thin diffusion of social overhead capital among the many small communities. Rural housing construction, for example, may be dissipated unwisely in the absence of knowledge regarding the possible specialization of towns as bedroom communities near to the larger employment centers. Also, as previously suggested, it would appear that housing policy may be more effectively focused on the efficient use of existing housing units. A second problem is that existing programs providing residentiary-related services may be inadequately designed for adaptation in the smaller communities of the region. The general uniformity with which the public housing and urban renewal programs have been administered among cities of different sizes suggests the need for more specialized attention to the problems found in the smaller towns.

This discussion provides only a few examples of development policies oriented along the twin spectra of centralizing/decentralizing and specializing/nonspecializing influences on regional growth. It suggests that some additional effort might be devoted to a closer examination of the rural impacts of existing institutions and methods by which they might be locationally constituted to provide a more favorable living environment in rural communities. The choice of strategy should be complementary with the stronger private market forces affecting differential economic growth between the smaller and larger communities within the region.

CITY SIZE DISTRIBUTIONS

The policy strategies described above may have various effects on the size distribution of cities within labor markets. The statement that "growth centers should be encouraged and small towns should be left to die" implies that city-size distribution can be altered despite their presumed stability. Though several distributions are possible, it will be useful to discuss these issues within the context of the rank-size rule. From Figure 4, a stable system implies that the rank-population product is constant or the double-log regression of population on rank yields a statistically significant coefficient of determination and a slope coefficient of minus unity. Several interpretations of instability at the lower end of the population spectra seem possible:

(1) The minimum scale of a viable city rises over time so only the constant term in the regression changes. The variance in population size increases and a break occurs within the distribution below which city size falls; excluding the smallest towns preserves essential features of the rank-size distribution. Though it may seem likely that the smallest towns are essentially divorced from the broader system of urban places, there appears to be no convincing definition of economic death. Within the state of Iowa, only four towns lost incorporated status from 1960–70, and it is questionable whether new suburban incorporations should be treated as independent entities. If legal criteria are excluded, small rural

towns should be treated much the same as neighborhoods in our largest high-density cities and the distribution of population change is likely to be bi-modal (with a higher variance) in the latter compared to rural labor markets.

(2) Agricultural, transportation, and marketing technologies may be systematically biased against the growth of small towns and their sunk investments preclude fluid consolidation and/or de-incorporation; alternatively, equilibrium must be defined in a broader sense than current central place concepts provide. The estimated slope coefficient is substantially less than unity and the double-log plot is nonlinear. For given city-size classes, the ranks of the smaller towns are somewhat lower than would be predicted from the rank-size rule.

The constancy of the number of satellites in each tier of a central place hierarchy provides further evidence of stability. Most of the central places of Iowa's 16 labor markets probably have 6 to 7 subregional capitals; these are typically county-seat towns and act as low-order service centers for the county's residents. Minimum convenience centers are the smallest cities in the three-tiered hierarchy and their numbers should range from 36 to 49; hence, there should be about 688 to 912 incorporated places, or an average of about 800. In 1970, there were 954 incorporated towns and cities within Iowa, suggesting some excess capacity in the state's system of urban places. If we allow the central place of each region to have its own nest of lower-order places, then the estimated number of towns should range from 800 to 1,040, or an average of 920; this number is substantially more compatible with the observed distribution of cities.

Some evidence suggests the instability of city-size distributions within labor markets. In the national sample of regions discussed above, the overall average percentages of urban places increasing and decreasing in population from 1950–60 were 81.1 and 18.9, respectively; the percentages for cities of less than 2,500 persons were 77.7 and 22.3. Within the spatially homogeneous six-county Iowa labor market centered on Ft. Dodge, the standard deviation of the rank-population product rose from 3,218.8 (1960) to 3,532.8 (1970). For the 43 cities in this three-tiered hierarchy, 17 of the 18 smallest towns had negative deviations in 1970 from the overall average predicted by the rank-size rule. The Spearman rank correlation coefficient between the 1960 population (highest to lowest) and percentage change in population (1960–70, highest to lowest) is 0.323, confirming the somewhat larger population variance in the last year of the decade.

Table II summarizes additional calculations for the six-satellite hierarchy constructed for Ft. Dodge, providing further confirmation of the slight instability noted above. The rank-size regressions

TABLE II

Summary of City-Size Distributional Statistics,
Ft. Dodge Labor Market, 1960–70

(1960)	Log R = 8.5753 - 0.8593 (log P) (0.1560) (0.0230)	$R^2 = 0.970$
(1970)	Log R = 8.4113 - 0.8372 (log P) (0.1474) (0.0218)	$R^2 = 0.972$

County	r	k	$\hat{P}_2$	$\hat{P}_3$
Humboldt	1,678.83	0.198	15,661	117,309
Pocahontas	1,369.66	0.373	20,906	200,103
Calhoun	1,395.66	0.423	25,155	261,551
Wright	1,415.50	0.509	35,226	430,388
Hamilton	2,475.66	0.192	22,751	168,423
Webster	7,476.16	0.073	52,202	337,905
Range	(6,106.05)	(0.436)	(36,541)	(313,079)

where $r = P_1 - p_1$ r: average rural population serviced by smallest city

p_1: average population of smallest city

$$k = (p_1/P_1)$$

$$\hat{P}_2 = \frac{6\,r}{(1-k)^2}$$ $\hat{P}_2$: predicted population of subregional capital and hinterland

$$\hat{P}_3 = \frac{36\,r}{(1-k)^3}$$ $\hat{P}_3$: predicted population of labor market

for 1960 and 1970 indicate slightly improved equational tests of significance; the standard errors of the estimated parameters decline and R² rises over the period. Both the constant term and slope coefficient decline, confirming the somewhat increased variance in city sizes within the region. Below these regressions are the predicted sizes of the subregions and the overall labor market based on average rural populations and urban multipliers for each county. (The rural population in each county is apportioned equally among six convenience centers for the six subregional capitals and probably overestimates the true hinterland for the lowest order towns.) As shown in Table II, the variance in the predicted populations of the subregions and the labor market is quite large even for this very homogeneous region. The ranges of the predicted populations are also substantial, suggesting the heterogeneity of the relation between rural and urban populations in each of the counties.

There is also some evidence of primacy within the Ft. Dodge region, a characteristic often associated with city-size distributions in the less developed counties. In both 1960 and 1970, Ft. Dodge's deviation of its population from the average rank-population product was positive and about four times the next largest positive difference. This evidence is at least consistent with the centralized population growth for U.S. labor markets earlier in the decade (1960–70) and the more urbanized regions within the state of Iowa. This centrality may impede policy strategies that encourage decentralized growth in the hinterland cities of these regions.

CONCLUSIONS

The problems of rural communities may be usefully viewed within the central place context of low-density labor markets. Community interdependence is the emphasis in this approach and policy strategies and problem analyses must be conducted along the full spectra of city-size classes. Our emphasis is on the availability of employment opportunities and services in a broader regional context, and thus less attention is devoted to the depreciation of physical and human wealth solely within the very smallest rural towns. Though decentralized growth may leave the economic boundaries of these regions less clear, labor markets closely approximate the "daily-activity" context within which residents conduct most of their business and residentiary pursuits, providing a better spatial basis for assessing the development opportunities of the small town resident.

Sectoral development patterns within labor markets suggest an increasing spatial diversity of employment opportunities. Manufacturing employment growth alone should encourage this diversity and increase the possibilities for specialization in the smaller towns both as employment centers and residentiary communities. Centralized population growth patterns appear to have continued throughout the past decade, and this may have an adverse effect on services provided in the smaller peripheral towns. These contrasting trends may in themselves be evidence of an increasing average journey to work expected from the substitution of secondary and tertiary activity for employment in the agricultural sector. This diversity may render it considerably more difficult to predict settlement patterns within these regions in the future.

Congressional proposals emphasize one of four alternative policy strategies for encouraging development within rural communities and may be less compatible with the possible diversification of activity among cities in the long run. The general-decentralization strategy pursued in these programs may also be countered by centralized population trends within these regions. If primacy is a general characteristic of labor markets, investments in spatially-fixed social overhead facilities diffused throughout the many small communities may be both risky and ineffective. Policy emphases more closely attuned to the diversification of economic function among cities by size class seem more compatible with longer run developments within predominantly rural labor markets. Such a policy emphasis should be based on evidence relating specific urban communities to their place within the size distribution of settlements in the labor market system.

GENERAL REFERENCES

Alonso, W. "The Economics of Urban Size," *Papers Reg. Sci. Assoc.*, **26**:67–83, 1971.

Beckmann, M. J. and J. McPherson. "City Size Distributions in a Central Place Hierarchy: An Alternative Approach," *J. Reg. Sci.*, **10**:25–33, 1970.

Fox, K. A. "Metamorphosis in America: A New Synthesis of Rural and Urban Society," in Gore, William T. and Leroy Hodapp (Eds.), *Change in the Small Community,* An Interdisciplinary Survey, pp. 63–104 (New York: Friendship Press, 1967).

Friedman, J. "Poor Regions and Poor Nations: Perspectives on the Problem of Appalachia," *Southern Econ. J.,* **27,** April 1966.

Hansen, N. M. *Rural Poverty and the Urban Crisis: A Strategy for Regional Development* (Bloomington: Indiana University Press, 1970).

Haren, C. C. "Rural Industrial Growth in the 1960's," *Amer. J. Agric. Econ.,* **52**:431–437, 1970.

Prescott, J. R., and W. C. Lewis. "Rural Communities and Regions," *Papers of the Western Agricultural Economics Association,* pp. 213–220, 1972.

Prescott, J. R., and W. C. Lewis. "Labor Markets and Rural Community Development," Chapter S in *Rural Community Development Seminar: Focus on Iowa* (Ames, Iowa: Center for Agriculture and Rural Development, 1972).

The People Left Behind, Report of the President's National Advisory Commission on Rural Poverty (Washington, D.C.: U.S. Government Printing Office), 1967.

3

Labor Markets and Growth Centers

Labor markets are the minimum-sized regional units character-ized by a high degree of functional independence. This region's boundaries contain the rural communities discussed in Chapter 2 and a nodal center to which households in the periphery commute daily. Within this 50–60 mile commuting radius are establishments that provide most of the residentiary goods and services necessary for the region's residents; the latter both earn income and pur-chase daily necessities within the same spatial unit. Regional cen-trality is evidenced by the interconnecting system of urban places surrounding the nodal center often interspersed by agricultural export activity in the smaller labor market regions. The regional node takes on characteristics of centrality itself with a diversity of land uses within the CBD and a significant decline in population density to the city's boundary. The labor market exemplifies the nodal delineation principle with a heterogeneity of activities with-in units and a substantial homogeneity (functional independence) among regions.

Due to this independence, labor markets are also a relatively comprehensive policy unit for a variety of planning purposes. Mul-ticounty labor markets bound the potential number of households using rapid transit systems and highways leading to the nodal cen-ter. The effects of such transit systems on the specialization of land uses with the region suggest that the labor market should also be an appropriate unit for land use planning and zoning. The conse-quences of urban travel (auto pollutants and accidents) are simi-larly concentrated along arterials transcending municipal and county boundaries. Other services not directly tied to transportation may also be logically planned on a labor market basis. Community colleges and urban universities draw their nonresident students from a commuting radius centered on their respective institutions. Public library services are vastly more efficient when supplemented with a relatively rapid system of interlibrary loans, and postal services have already been placed on a regional basis remarkably similar to labor markets. In these numerous applications, multicounty labor markets are important planning regions.

The deliberate concentration of these (and other) activities within the nodal city is a part of the "growth centers" development strategy as discussed briefly in Chapter 2. The efficacy of this strategy depends on employment and population changes occurring within the various sized cities in the labor market and their ensuing effects on commercial services. The transportation linkages both within the region (among cities) and to the larger SMSAs surrounding the labor market will also influence the development potential of the region's nodal center. This development plan will also affect the availability of services and private commercial activities in the smaller, peripheral communities and, hence, the size distribution of central places within the labor market. Expenditure leakages to the nodal center are more likely as central growth within the region is encouraged. These locational shifts of population and commercial activity are the principal development trade-offs involved in the "growth centers" plan.

The purpose of this chapter is to analyze the economic structure of settlements within labor market regions. In the first section, an econometric model (adapted to available census data) is specified and discussed; the principal equations describing population-employment growth and commercial sales are the subjects of the next two sections. The data include observations on 86 multicounty labor market regions for the period 1958–63 collected from four census reports during this period. Some contrasts in labor market and nonlabor market regions from a large sample of Midwestern counties covering the full decade, 1960–1970 are then discussed. The implications of our data for the "growth centers" plan is the subject of a concluding section.

LABOR MARKET STRUCTURE:
AN ECONOMETRIC APPROACH

The labor market sample was systematically selected from Berry's regionalization of 305 Functional Economic Areas (FEAs) from the 1960 journey-to-work data for the United States (Berry and Lewis). Random selection of the 86 regions was deemed inappropriate due to the possible dominance of the largest metropolitan areas within the densely populated regions of the country; three criteria were used in choosing the sample: (1) The central city of the FEA must have a 1960 population of between 25,000 and 100,000 persons, (2) all regions must be devoid of economic or political domination by contiguous urban centers, and (3) the labor market itself should not be unduly concentrated in a few economic or political activities. Labor markets with state capitals, universities, or major tourist centers are excluded from the sample.

The data for the sample were taken from the Censuses of Business, Manufacturers, Population, and Agriculture covering the period 1958–63 and then reaggregated in accordance with the major spatial units within the labor market. Due to the substantial amount of agricultural employment within these regions separate data were collected on productivity characteristics of this sector. In addition to the central city of each FEA, two classifications of the remaining urban areas are used. (1) All data were aggregated for one urban class, termed the periphery. This is necessary due to the absence of employment characteristics for the very smallest cities in each region, and this classification is used in the cross section model described below. (2) A disaggregated urban classification uses commercial sales data available for cities of 5,000 to 10,-000, 2,500 to 5,000, and below 2,500 in population. These data were used in estimating retail, services, and wholesaling equations in a disaggregated model and are summarized later (p. 67).

Table III shows the more dispersed characteristics of the labor market sample compared to similar data for 39 SMSAs. The central cities of labor markets average about 50,000 in population but comprise only 26% of total regional population compared to 51% for central cities of SMSAs. Also, the percent of employment in the central city is uniformly lower for FEAs compared to SMSAs for all four activities shown in Table III. For both the FEA and SMSA, central city percentages of total manufacturing employment are the lowest of all sectoral categories. Several other characteristics from the sample should be noted:

(1) As discussed in Chapter 2, population and employment growth over the period tended to be inversely correlated within city size classes of labor markets. Population growth rates were highest in the nodal centers, while manufacturing employment

TABLE III

Distribution of Total Employment and Population for Labor Market Sample and SMSAs

| | *Nonmetropolitan FEA, 1963* (%) | | *SMSA, 1958* (%)[a] | |
	Central City	*Periphery*	*Central City*	*Periphery*
Population	25.5	74.5	51.3	48.7
Employment:				
Retail	44.1	55.9	66.1	33.9
Selected Services	51.3	48.7	74.2	25.8
Wholesale	53.0	47.0	82.0	18.0
Manufacturing	35.2	64.8	57.2	42.8

[a] Source: Niedercorn, J. H. and J. F. Kain, *An Econometric Model of Metropolitan Development,* The Rand Corporation, 1963 (mimeographed), p. 23.

tended to decentralize to the smaller peripheral communities. As noted in Table I, employment growth rates in the retail, wholesale, and services sectors tend to be inversely correlated with size of city.

(2) Indices were estimated to test for the stability of sectoral activities among the 86 labor market regions. Hoover indices were calculated for both 1958 and 1963, comparing population distributions among regions to other FEA characteristics. (These are defined as, $H = \frac{1}{2} \sum_{i=1}^{m} |a_i - P_i|$ where a_i and P_i represent the proportions of a characteristic and population, respectively, of all m regions accounted for by the ith region.) The land area-population index, for example, rose from 0.32169 (1958) to 0.32287 (1963), indicating a slightly greater disparity in these variables among FEAs. Similar indices comparing retail, selected services, wholesale and manufacturing employment to population showed slight increases over the sample period. With the exception of agriculture, changes in the indices were small (ranging from 1 to 10%), with the smallest increase occurring within the manufacturing sector. The 23% increase in the agricultural sector reflects the differential impact of this sector's decline in the various regions of the United States, but excluding this sector, labor markets appear to be a relatively stable regional unit.

As our concern is with differential population and employment growth between the nodal center and periphery, the model should distinguish the primary determinants of these variables in all major subregions of the FEA. The relative strength of these determinants will then indicate the extent to which the growth center's policy is compatible with development patterns indicated by the model's equations. Additional equations may then show the implications of this spatial distribution of employment and population on the growth of retail, services, and wholesale sales in the various urban communities of the region. This view of development suggests that employment and population in the FEA's subregions influences, but is not influenced by, the levels of commercial activity in these same subregions.

A flow chart of the model is shown in Figure 5. There are three major equation systems and, with the exception of agriculture, each system has separate equations for the two spatial subregions, the central city and periphery: (1) employment in manufacturing, agriculture, and supporting services, (2) population, and (3) sales in the retail, services, and wholesale sectors. The identities define variables as products of other exogenous and endogenous variables in the model. Payrolls, for example, are the product of exogenously determined manufacturing wage rates and employment levels determined within the model. Identity systems 2 and 3 use equilibrium sales in the retail, wholesale, and services sectors to calculate employment levels and the number of establishments in the central city and periphery.

The structure of the model is influenced by the small size of the region considered here, which results in the following problems. (1) The FEAs are connected to contiguous SMSAs by variables termed proximity and gravity in Figure 5. These variables measure the economic impacts on the FEA from being close to larger metropolitan markets. (2) Within the FEA, employment is influenced by rates of compensation determined outside of the region. Manufacturing wages, for example, are usually set by bargaining processes in broader regional or national markets. Interest, dividends, agricultural prices, and major components of transfer and salary income are relatively unaffected by activity within the FEA. Measures of median income and the percentage of families with low incomes are therefore exogenously determined. Also, it is assumed that agricultural output and productivity are influenced by technology, climatic conditions, and prices determined in broad-

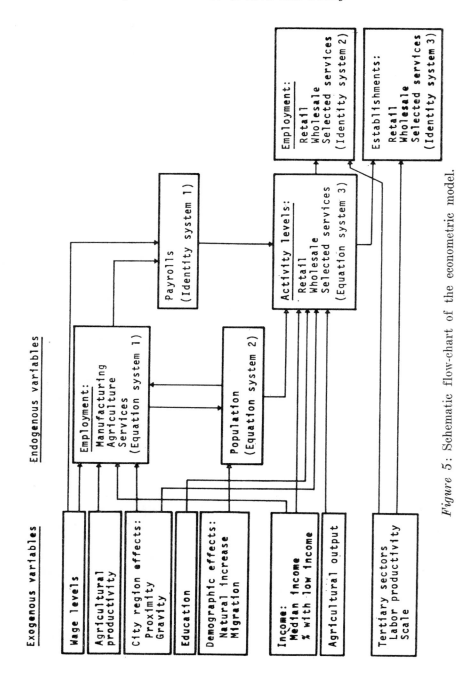

Figure 5: Schematic flow-chart of the econometric model.

er geographic areas. (3) Some data problems suggest a modification of the export model discussed in Chapter 1 in favor of an interdependent system of equations. Predetermined demographic variables measuring percentage changes in central city natural increase and net migration from 1950–60 are included in the population equations, but for the smaller peripheral towns, the data necessary to derive labor supply from population are not available. Also, the supporting employment variable is not the traditional one used in export base studies; this variable includes government, transportation, and utilities employment, which are not solely dependent on the size of export sectors particularly in regions this small. Government employment, for example, includes public services for the nonemployed population, which depends on the age distribution of the population, incomes, and the numerous grant-in-aid programs of the state and federal governments.

The other exogenous variables in Figure 5 are suggested by central place theory. In addition to payroll and population variables, an index of educational attainment is used to measure demands for selected services. Size of establishment and labor productivity in the retail, services, and wholesale sectors are determined by the different level and composition of sales expected in trade centers of alternative sizes. There are 13 structural equations using the variables defined below. Both ordinary and two-stage least squares were used in estimating the parameters of the equations. As the ranked t-coefficients for the variables in each equation generally correspond under both estimating techniques and not all equations are jointly dependent, the coefficients discussed below are the ordinary least squares estimates that are consistent for all equations in the model. The dependent variables, where i indexes the central city as c and the periphery as p, are:

MFG_i	:	manufacturing employment
AG	:	agricultural employment
RT_i	:	retail sales
SV_i	:	selected services sales
SP_i	:	supporting employment
P_i	:	population
WH_i	:	wholesale sales

and the predetermined variables are:

WG_i	:	manufacturing wage; payrolls/employees
PROX	:	highway miles to nearest SMSA

AGSOLD : value of farm products sold
INCMED : median income; central city, 1960
EDHI : percentage of persons 25+ years of age who completed 12+ years of schooling; central city, 1960
NATINC : percentage natural increase in population; central city; 1950–60
INCLOW : percentage of families with incomes under $3,000; central city, 1960
WG/PD : ratio of central city manufacturing wage rate to AGPD
PY_i : total payrolls
GRAV : $([P_c \cdot P_{smsa}]/[PROX]^2)$
AGPD : agricultural productivity
MIGTN : percentage net migration; central city; 1950–60

EMPLOYMENT AND POPULATION

The estimated coefficients below are for equation system 1 in Figure 5. R^2 appears to the right of each equation and t values testing for significant differences from zero are below each variable.

$$MFG_c = -1{,}496 + 0.061\ P_c + 0.139\ GRAV + 0.547\ WG_c$$
$$\phantom{MFG_c = -1{,}496 +} (3.52) \qquad (1.67) \qquad\quad (1.38)$$

(16)

$$R^2 = 0.27$$

$$MFG_p = 5{,}500 + 0.875\ SP_p - 0.378\ AG - 0.618\ AGPD - 0.015\ P$$
$$\phantom{MFG_p = 5{,}500 +} (7.02) \qquad (-2.14) \qquad (-2.52) \qquad\quad (-0.39)$$

(17)

$$R^2 = 0.46$$

$$SP_c = 1{,}944 + 0.132\ P_c + 0.537\ INCMED + 0.003\ P_p$$
$$\phantom{SP_c = 1{,}944 +} (15.19) \qquad (2.08) \qquad\quad (1.42)$$

(18)

$$R^2 = 0.80$$

$$SP_p = 6{,}010 + 0.433\ MFG_p + 0.300\ AG$$
$$\phantom{SP_p = 6{,}010 +} (3.70) \qquad\quad (2.32)$$

(19)

$$R^2 = 0.54$$

$$AG = 18{,}500 - 2.14\ WG_p + 0.198\ SP_p - 0.092\ MFG_c - 99.5\ INCLOW$$
$$\phantom{AG = 18{,}500}\ (-3.19) \qquad (2.35) \qquad (-1.51) \qquad (-1.44)$$

$$- 18.25\ WG/PD$$
$$(-1.80)$$

$$\text{(20)}$$

$$R^2 = 0.21$$

Equation 16 indicates that exogenous variables are the primary determinants of the scale of manufacturing employment in the central city of the labor market. The positive coefficient on GRAV shows that declining distance to (and increasing population in) nearby SMSA markets increases the level of manufacturing employment. Higher wage rates also cause manufacturing employment to rise, probably reflecting the mix effect of higher wage and more strongly unionized industries in the central cities of FEAs. Central city population acts as a labor supply variable though it also may represent the market for products of less specialized firms in these regions. Though more satisfactory labor supply variables could not be constructed, the coefficient on the central city population variable is highly significant.

In contrast to Equation 16, peripheral manufacturing employment is primarily determined by intra-FEA variables. Supporting employment is highly significant statistically suggesting the importance of public and private services to firms located in smaller communities of the region. Peripheral manufacturing employment also tends to be higher in areas characterized by low productivity and declining employment in the agricultural sector. Some evidence also suggests that the effect of declining agricultural employment is more important in peripheral communities than in the central city of the FEA. The agricultural employment coefficient in Equation 17, -0.378, is over four times the size in absolute value than the central city manufacturing employment coefficient in the agricultural employment equation. These coefficients are also of greater statistical significance than the impact of central city population increase on the decline in peripheral manufacturing employment (see Equation 17.) These coefficients suggest that the attraction of expanding job opportunities in the central city is somewhat less important than the growth of peripheral manufacturing employment due to an excess supply of labor in the agricultural sector.

The supporting employment equations indicate differences in the type of public and private services provided by the growth center and peripheral communities and investment differentials required by a changing composition of employment. Population and income are significant explanatory variables in the central city equation, suggesting the importance of transfer programs for the nonemployed population and the influence of income on the demand for higher quality public and private services. In contrast, narrowly defined employment measures are more successful explanatory variables in the peripheral employment equation. The relative sizes of the coefficients on these variables indicate the incremental requirements for supporting employment due to differential growth in manufacturing and agricultural employment. The ratio of these coefficients (0.433/0.300) shows that peripheral supporting employment requirements are about 44% higher for manufacturing than for agriculture.

The most rapid decline in agricultural employment occurs in FEAs characterized by high nonagricultural wage levels, a growing manufacturing sector and relatively low agricultural productivity. As shown in Equation 20, agricultural employment is negatively related to variables measuring the opportunity costs of remaining in the agricultural sector (*i.e.*, the manufacturing wage rate and the ratio of this rate to agricultural productivity). The statistically significant coefficients on the peripheral supporting employment and central city manufacturing employment variables show the importance of local services and alternative employment opportunities in the central city. The income distribution variable measures the effect of employment in this sector due to local purchases of agricultural produce; its negative coefficient probably reflects the importance of locally-sold products in the smaller, more diversified FEAs in the sample.

Given the level of spatial disaggregation, relatively high cross-sectional coefficients of determination are attained. The principal exceptions are Equations 16 and 20 where external demand variables are both more important than in other sectors and very difficult to estimate for regions of this size. These equations do show the strength of intersectoral reallocations of labor particularly in peripheral communities, and the importance of public and private supporting employment growth as agricultural decline is accompanied by a decentralization of manufacturing employment to peripheral communities.

The estimated coefficients for equation system 2 are:

$$P_c = 1,412 + 4.91\ SP_c + 1.42\ MFG_c + 239.8\ NATINC$$
$$\ (13.85) \qquad (4.65) \qquad\ \ (1.54)$$

$$R^2 = 0.83 \tag{21}$$

$$P_p = 26,600 + 4.00\ MFG_p + 4.21\ SP_p + 2.84\ AG - 14.4\ MIGTN$$
$$\ (5.28) \qquad\quad (3.92) \qquad (2.27) \quad (-0.42)$$

$$R^2 = 0.65 \tag{22}$$

The population equations allow for both the employment impacts of the major producing sectors and the influence of local demographic characteristics. Equations 21 and 22 show that employment variables in both the central city and periphery are highly significant statistically. Differences in average employment coefficients between the growth center and peripheral communities are not easily attributable to a single cause, however, since the population variable includes the variant effects of family size, labor force participation, and unemployment rates. The demographic variables are less important as determinants of population levels; the negative sign on the migration coefficient is consistent with intra-FEA migration from peripheral communities to the central city but is relatively unimportant in explaining population levels in the periphery.

RETAIL, WHOLESALE, AND SELECTED SERVICES

The employment and population equations show the major economic variables influencing the spatial distribution of economic activity between the central city and peripheral communities in the FEA. Since shopping trips are dispersed throughout the labor market, we also expect commercial sales to be influenced by these same spatial determinants. The equations analyzed in this section use measures of population and payrolls as the primary variables explaining retail and selected services sales, and they separately estimate the impact of these variables on the spatial distribution of wholesaling activity. These equations generally show the strongest spatial linkages in the model and have implications for the level of sales in each subregion of the FEA due to policies that might promote population and employment growth in the central city.

The coefficients for equation system 3 in Figure 5 are:

$$RT_c = 15,600 + 0.614\ PY_c + 0.659\ P_c + 0.147\ PY_p + 0.029\ P_p$$
$$\qquad\quad (8.51) \qquad\quad (5.31) \qquad (3.04) \qquad\quad (0.720)$$

$$(23)$$

$$R^2 = 0.81$$

$$RT_p = 19,400 + 0.382\ AGSOLD + 0.426\ P_p + 0.392\ PY_p$$
$$\qquad\quad (6.52) \qquad\qquad (4.72) \qquad (2.68)$$

$$(24)$$

$$R^2 = 0.85$$

The retailing equations show the strong influence of peripheral demand variables on central city sales. In the central city equation (23), both central city and peripheral payroll and population have important impacts on retail sales. As expected, the coefficients on the peripheral variables are lower than their central city counterparts and are also of less significance statistically. The ratio of payroll coefficients (0.614/0.147) shows that the per dollar effect of central city payrolls is about five times as important as payroll changes in peripheral communities.

In contrast, only peripheral demand variables are significant in Equation 24, and their coefficients are generally smaller in size, indicating sales leakages to central city retailers. For example, the addition of both payroll coefficients (0.147 and 0.392) equals 0.539 and the leakage to central city establishments is (0.147/0.539) or about 27%. Though disposable income variables are not available, the lower coefficient on gross agricultural sales is consistent with the understatement of rural incomes implied in this variable, and its coefficient is only significant in the peripheral retailing equation. These equations generally show the unidirectional impact of policies accelerating growth in the central city of the FEA. Though the growth center shares in changes in peripheral population and payrolls, the impact of central city growth tends to be spatially self-contained; the spread effects of the growth centers plan appear to be virtually nonexistent in the retail sales sector.

The coefficients for the services sector of equation system 3 are:

$$SV_c = 11,150 + 0.093\ PY_c + 0.039\ PY_p + 0.092\ P_c + 204.2\ EDHI$$
$$\qquad\quad (6.04) \qquad\quad (3.82) \qquad\quad (3.31) \qquad\quad (3.09)$$

$$+\ 8.44\ PROX + 0.0094\ P_p$$
$$\quad (1.52) \qquad\qquad (1.11)$$

$$(25)$$

$$R^2 = 0.74$$

$$SV_p = 992 + 0.084 \ PY_p + 0.416 \ SP_p$$
$$(8.40) \qquad (4.27)$$

$$R^2 = 0.73 \tag{26}$$

Similar spatial purchasing patterns are apparent in the selected services equations despite the addition of variables measuring the competitive impact of larger trade centers, tastes, and the employment effects of services sales in the periphery. The positive coefficient on PROX in Equation 25 indicates that services sales in the growth center are adversely affected by contiguity to larger SMSA markets. The impact on gross sales is about $8,440 per mile and is influential only in the central city equation. The importance of the educational variable is consistent with higher order services available in the larger urban centers of the sample. The highly significant coefficient on the supporting employment variable in Equation 26 suggests the importance of business-related services in peripheral communities.

The coefficients in the services equations are consistent with the generally lower expenditures for services and the spatial purchasing patterns noted in the retailing equations. Both the constant terms and payroll coefficients are lower in the services equation than those for retailing in their respective spatial class. In the central city equation, peripheral payroll and population variables enter significantly, whereas central city demand variables are not important in the peripheral services equation. As above, we estimate the sales leakage from peripheral residents to central city establishments as $(0.039/0.123)$ or about 31%. This is even higher than the corresponding effect in the retail equations and is consistent with the greater availability of more specialized services in the larger central cities.

The final two equations are for the wholesaling sector of the third equation system:

$$WH_c = 64,300 + 1.011 \ RT_c + 0.475 \ RT_p - 2.99 \ GRAV$$
$$(2.64) \qquad (2.42) \qquad (-1.98)$$

$$R^2 = 0.60 \tag{27}$$

$$WH_p = 4,825 + 0.484 \ WH_c + 0.356 \ RT_p - 1.48 \ GRAV$$
$$(3.49) \qquad (2.39) \qquad (-1.82)$$

$$R^2 = 0.56 \tag{28}$$

The wholesaling equations show the strong spatial dependence of this sector on the location of retail trade, some decentralization of wholesaling activity to peripheral communities and the importance of larger metropolitan markets on the level of sales in this sector. Retail purchases by peripheral residents have an even greater impact on central city wholesaling than on this sector in peripheral communities. Larger central city wholesalers are apparently able to stock a wider variety of goods for sale to peripheral residents. The appearance of the central city wholesale variable in Equation 28 is the only example of a central city variable in a peripheral sales equation and confirms the decentralizing trends in the wholesaling sector noted above. Also, the competitive effect of larger metropolitan centers is stronger for central city wholesalers; the coefficient on the gravity variable declines in magnitude and statistical significance from Equation 27 to 28.

Some evidence also suggests that changes in the composition of peripheral employment will influence the spatial distribution of retail and wholesale sales. Changes in agricultural sales in Equation 24 have direct impacts only on peripheral retail sales, while peripheral manufacturing payrolls have a larger coefficient in Equation 24 and an effect on central city retail sales. These results are consistent with the spatial spending patterns expected due to lower incomes earned in the agricultural sector and indicate the somewhat more diffuse impact of employment changes from agriculture to manufacturing in peripheral communities.

To test the strength of these spatial spending patterns, a disaggregated model was estimated using the three-city classification described above. The results, which are summarized below, generally confirm the spatial sales patterns found in the more aggregated model.

1. In all retailing equations population in the same (or smaller) city size class entered as highly significant explanatory variables. The payroll variables were generally of less importance statistically but also followed the same spatial pattern. Though the effect of agricultural sales on retailing activity was spread throughout the three smallest city size classes in the periphery, about two-thirds of its impact is felt in the smallest rural towns of the labor market.

2. The spatial spending patterns in the selected services equations confirmed those shown in Equations 25 and 26 above. Central city establishments serve residents in the smallest rural

towns, which are the only city size class significantly affected by contiguity to larger SMSAs.

3. The wholesaling equations also supported the spatial patterns in the more aggregated model. There is some evidence of a competitive effect between wholesalers in the central city and the next largest city size class. Increases in central city wholesaling reduced wholesaling activity in these smaller communities suggesting an additional negative impact of central city growth on the larger peripheral communities.

The structural model (discussed above) suggests the strength of employment substitution within labor markets and hierarchical patterns of spending among city-size classes. The evidence suggests that significant increases in secondary job opportunities within peripheral communities have resulted from employment declines within the agricultural sector. Also, the strength of spatial spending patterns in the FEA should result in significant reductions in peripheral commercial sales from centralized increases in population; the "growth-centers" plan will strengthen the possible dominance of central cities and adversely influence the commercial health of the smallest towns. These conclusions pertain to structural relationships within these regions; the following section contrasts characteristics between FEA and non-FEA counties.

LABOR MARKET GROWTH: A MIDWESTERN SAMPLE

Over the period 1960–70, national statistics continue to show the strength of centralized population growth between urbanized and nonurbanized areas; population increases of 23.6 and 5.0% were experienced respectively in these regions compared to a national growth rate of 13.3%. The total rural population declined from 54.0 to 53.8 million persons over the same period, though some distributional changes among the smaller towns also occurred. The population of places ranging from 1,000 to 2,500 persons grew by 2.4% while the number of people on farms or living in towns of less than 1,000 population declined. These differential changes may or may not be reflected in counties contiguous to labor market regions, so it is the purpose of this section to examine more recent developments relating central growth in FEAs to characteristics of non-FEA counties.

To test several hypotheses discussed below, data from 543 counties in 6 Midwestern states (Iowa, Kansas, Minnesota, Missouri, Nebraska, and Wisconsin) were collected. Table IV summarizes

TABLE IV

Variable Means and Standard Deviations, Midwestern Sample of Counties, 1960–70[a]

Spatial Class	% Change in Population, 1960–70	Per Capita Income		% Families Below Poverty Line, 1970	% Counties Served...by Inter-state Highways
		1970	1960		
FEA Counties (426)	2.78 (15.90)	$2,568 (388)	$1,418 (286)	12.56 (5.30)	27.7
Non-FEA Counties (117)	-7.40 (11.31)	2,392 (399)	1,320 (296)	16.10 (6.93)	11.9
FEA Counties:					
Central Counties (68)	13.34 (19.20)	2,933 (434)	1,765 (318)	8.60 (3.77)	54.4
Next to Central Counties (191)	3.48 (16.60)	2,549 (345)	1,387 (239)	12.36 (5.10)	28.3
Other FEA Counties (136)	-2.06 (11.50)	2,452 (350)	1,335 (210)	14.26 (5.50)	11.9

[a] The number of counties in each spatial class are shown in parentheses in column 1. The mean of each variable appears in the principal cell for each row; its standard deviation is in parentheses below the mean.

some of the salient characteristics from this sample and shows that measures of economic growth and welfare have been strongest in the central counties of labor market regions. In comparing FEA to non-FEA counties (*i.e.*, counties linked to central cities via commuting and counties not so linked), the average labor market experienced higher rates of population growth (2.8% compared to −7.4%), higher per capita incomes ($2,568 compared to $2,392), and lower percentages of families below the poverty line (12.6% to 16.1%). Also, the average population growth rate and level of per capita income within labor markets declined monotonically from central counties to adjacent and peripheral counties, the average population growth rate being negative for the last category. Consistent with the distribution of average per capita income, the percentage of low income families rose steadily from central counties through this hierarchy. The final column of Table IV indicates the importance of transportation linkages to measures of growth and welfare among counties.

A broad measure of welfare levels reflected in these data might be defined in terms of "the effective range of choice for the average citizen." Such a measure would necessarily include both opportunities for the employment of labor (and complementary productive factors) and the diversity and number of consumer goods and services available within a commuting distance of the residents in the region. The term "effective" implies that income, or some other measure of the ability to take advantage of these opportunities, would have to be incorporated into an operational welfare measure. Also, physical access to these opportunities, as defined by the quality and diversity of transport modes to and from market and/or employment centers, would be an important variable. Such a regional welfare function could be written as:

$$W = W\ (Y,\ R_e,\ R_c,\ A) \qquad (29)$$

where Y is income, R_e and R_c represent the range of choice with respect to employment and consumption respectively, and A is a measure of access. It is expected that all partial derivatives in Equation 29 are positive and the following implicit functions are hypothesized:

1. As will be discussed more completely in Chapter 5, real and money incomes are expected to be positively associated with city size or population (P). Hence, the first term of Equa-

tion 29 is an implicit function of the size of settlement in which productive or consumption activity takes place.

2. R_e and R_c are also related to population through the theory of central places as described in Chapter 1. The range of choice rises as the size of central city increases, providing market scales sufficient to support higher-order goods and alternative occupational choices.

3.   Access is a function of distance to consumption and employment opportunities (D) and the quality of the transportation mode (Q). Access is inversely related to D and positively associated with Q.

From these implicit relationships to the independent variables shown in Equation 29, the hypotheses may be reformulated as:

$$W = W^* (D, P, Q) \qquad (30)$$

where all partial derivatives are positive with the exception of the coefficient on distance (D). Levels of welfare may be indicated by measures of per capita income or population growth as shown in Table IV. Distance is measured between the county in question and the center city of the labor market region. The quality of the transportation mode (Q) is indicated by a dummy variable defined as "1" if the county was served by an interstate highway no later than 1965, and "0" otherwise. An additional variable (FEA) identifies the central county of the labor market as 1, and 0 otherwise.

Table V summarizes regression equations calculated from the Midwestern sample and based on Equation 30. The principal growth and welfare indicators are percentage change in population (1960–70) and levels of per capita income (1970); a third dependant variable (percentage of families below the poverty line, 1970) is utilized as a check on the welfare indicator. The standard errors of the estimates are reported below the estimated coefficients and the rank of the beta coefficient's absolute size is shown on the third line of each cell in the table. Although the coefficients of determination (R^2) are low, the F-ratio equational tests indicate statistical significance at or below the 0.01 probability level. As the data are drawn on a cross section and a multiplicity of influences will affect the dependant variable, the R^2 coefficients are tolerable. All signs of the explanatory variables are correct under the null hypotheses specified above, and only one of the explanatory variables' coefficients is significant at test levels exceeding 0.01.

TABLE V

Regression Equations from Sample of Midwestern Counties, 1960–70

Dependent Variable	Constant	D	P	Q	FEA	R^2	F
(31) Percentage in population, 1960–70	2.801	-0.195**[a] (0.020) (2)[b]	0.031** (0.003) (1)	5.379** (1.385) (3)		0.34	92.65**
(32) Per capita income, 1970	2,506.3	-2.533** (0.643) (3)	0.423** (0.077) (2)	111.33** (38.24) (4)	305.63** (54.51) (1)	0.24	43.20**
(33) Percentage families below poverty line, 1970	12.64	0.055** (0.009) (1)	-0.0067** (0.0012) (2)	-1.147* (0.576) (4)	-2.466** (0.822) (3)	0.21	35.42**

[a] A * or ** indicates that the partial regression coefficient is significantly different from zero at the 0.05 and 0.01 levels, respectively.

[b] Relative rank of the standardized partial regression (beta) coefficient.

Equation 32 in Table V also supports the hypothesis that average levels of economic welfare are highest within central counties of labor markets and decline as distance from that county increases. Central location within the region explains $305.63 of the spatial differential in per capita income. The latter rises at a rate of $0.42 per person in larger counties and declines at a rate of $2.53 per mile for locations in the regional hinterland. Although of substantially less importance than the other three variables in Equation 32, access to interstate highways is a statistically significant determinant of average per capita income. The last equation in Table V confirms the signs and equational significance of Equation 32. As the dependent variable is percentage of families below the poverty line, the coefficients should have the opposite signs to those hypothesized in Equation 32. Though the relative importance of the explanatory variables is changed, the R^2 and F-ratio coefficients are virtually the same as between Equations 33 and 32.

Some additional evidence regarding the relationship between the three dependent variables in Table V and contiguity to central counties is summarized in Table VI. Additional variables measure more precisely the access to the central county of the labor market and are defined as follows:

FEA-1: 1 if the county is in an FEA, 0 otherwise
FEA-2: 1 if the county is adjacent to the FEA central
county, 0 otherwise
FEA-3: 1 if the county is two counties removed from the
FEA central county, 0 otherwise

Arrayed from the most central measure (FEA) to the least central (FEA-3), the correlation coefficients for percentage population growth and per capita income decline uniformly; similarly consistent (but opposite) results are shown for the poverty measure. The presence of a county somewhere in the labor market (FEA-1) is second in importance to the central county of the FEA in explaining the variation in the dependent variables; both FEA and FEA-1 are consistently more significant than for dummy variables indicating noncentral locations within the labor market. These coefficients provide support for the hypothesis that access to populated regional centers tends to be an important determinant of regional growth and welfare.

The statistics from the Midwestern sample indicate that con-

TABLE VI

Correlation Coefficients Between FEA
Locational Variables and Growth/Income Measures[a]

	Percentage △ in Population, 1960–70	Per Capita Income, 1970	Percentage Families below Poverty line, 1970
FEA	0.3099**	0.3840**	−0.3058**
FEA-1	0.2688**	0.1828**	−0.2512**
FEA-2	0.1371**	0.0343	−0.1223**
FEA-3	−0.0983*	−0.1134**	0.0918*

[a] A * and ** indicate that the simple product moment correlation coefficients are significantly different from zero with a probability no greater than 0.05 and 0.01, respectively.

tiguity or access to central counties of FEAs is approximately equal in importance to size of settlement as a determinant of population growth and per capita income. Though the sample was drawn from a region of the United States that includes both smaller and more spatially homogeneous labor markets, it seems likely that the same results would be found in other parts of the nation. The differential growth in FEA central counties versus nonlabor market counties has continued throughout the period 1960–70, and access measures are a significant explanatory variable of this differential. From Table V, it should be noted, however, that regional growth has not significantly narrowed earnings differentials over this decade. The per capita income differential between FEA and non-FEA counties was $98 (1960) and $176 (1970); within labor markets, the central county versus "other county" differential rose from $430 (1960) to $481 (1970). Centralized population growth and enhanced access to the nodal city in the region has not significantly reduced the differential productivity of residents located in the center and on the periphery.

CONCLUSIONS

The labor market is an important regional unit for both analytic and policy purposes. Spatially consistent consumption and production accounts are best approximated by utilizing this areal concept since most factor income and expenditures are disbursed within the region's boundaries. Numerous public services are logical contenders for being administered on a labor market basis, particularly those related to problems associated with the journey-to-work. Due to the multitude of problems attributable to residential decentralization, these regions seem to be most adequately suited as a spatial basis for comprehensive planning; within the smaller FEAs the nodal cities may also be the focus for the "growth centers" development strategy.

For the earlier part of the decade (1960–70), a large sample of low-density rural labor markets showed evidences of population growth in central cities and employment decentralization to peripheral counties. A structural econometric model utilizing these data indicated the strength of manufacturing employment substitution within the declining agricultural sector located in the rural counties of these regions; supporting employment requirements would be expected to increase as secondary job opportunities expand. Among FEAs, agricultural employment decline is strongly associated with the absence of alternative productive opportunities within the labor market.

The incomes generated from employment by spatial sector tend to be expended in a locationally hierarchical manner. Peripheral population and payrolls have substantial effects on sales of retail goods and services within nodal cities but the reverse impacts are absent. The expenditure leakage to central cities is estimated to be about 27 and 31% in the retail and services sectors, respectively. From a disaggregated variant of the econometric model, it is estimated that about two-thirds of the effect of declining agricultural sales is felt within the very smallest towns of the labor market. Wholesaling activity indicated a strong spatial dependence on the location of retailing trade and some decentralization to the smaller communities in peripheral counties. From the viewpoint of commercial activity, the central cities of labor markets have a substantial interest in the economic growth of hinterland cities and towns.

From a sample of Midwestern labor markets covering the full decade (1960–70), strong evidences of centrality are found. Central counties of FEAs grew by 13.3% over this period while non-FEA counties experienced population declines of 7.40%. Per capita incomes uniformly rise from the peripheral to central counties of these labor market regions, and poverty indicators are inversely related to the locational characteristics associated with the income measure. Transportation linkages also have an important influence on the population growth and income measures; about 54% of the

FEA central counties are serviced by interstate highways whereas only 11.9% of non-FEA counties have highways constructed under this program.

Regression equations relating population scale, distance to the nodal center, quality of transit mode to population growth, and per capita income confirm the central locational advantages accruing to firms and households within the region. Correlations between distance to nodal center and the growth/welfare measures decline as successively fewer accessible counties are included in the analysis. The importance of population size and access to central locations within labor markets appears to be relatively equal as explanatory variables in these equations. Central growth of population within FEAs has continued over the complete decade (1960–70), though per capita income differentials between central and peripheral counties do not seem to have narrowed substantially.

The "growth centers" plan would seek to increase measures of growth and welfare within labor markets by centralizing programs of the various governments. From our data, such a plan would be complementary with population growth trends observed over the past decade, but it is substantially less clear that intraregional differentials in per capita incomes would be affected. Nodal population and income growth may increase the range of central goods offered within the region, but it is also likely to cause a further decline in the sales of commercial establishments in the peripheral communities. If noncentralized growth is encouraged, both the central cities and peripheral towns will share in the benefits of development, and it seems more likely that welfare differentials will narrow within labor markets. If, in the long run, secondary employment decentralization continues, peripheral towns should be better able to specialize in particular regional services (not unlike suburban communities in the largest SMSAs) and increase the opportunities for services and employment in noncentral locations. Regional economic growth is not necessarily tantamount to centralization, and it is likely that the "growth centers" development plan would encourage unbalanced economic growth and an even less equitable spatial sharing in its benefits.

GENERAL REFERENCES

Berry, B. J. L., et. al. *Metropolitan Area Definition: A Re-evaluation of Concept and Statistical Practice*, U.S. Department of Commerce Working Paper 28 (Washington, D.C.: Government Printing Office, 1968).

Borchert, J. R., and R. B. Adams. *Trade Centers and Trade Areas in the Upper Midwest* (Minneapolis), Upper Midwest Economic Study, Urban Report No. 3, 1963.

Boudeville, J. R. *Problems of Regional Planning* (Edinburgh: Edinburgh University Press, 1966).

Cameron, G. C. "Growth Areas, Growth Centers and Regional Conversion," *Scottish J. Pol. Econ.* **17**:19–38, February 1970.

Duncan, O. D. *Metropolis and Region* (Baltimore: The Johns Hopkins University Press, 1966).

Fox, K. A. "Metamorphosis is America: A New Synthesis of Rural and Urban Society," in W. T. Gore and L. Hodapp (Eds.) *Change in the Small Community, An Interdisciplinary Survey* (New York, Friendship Press, 1967) pp. 63–104.

Fox, K. A. "The Study of Interactions Between Agriculture and the Non-Farm Economy—Local, Regional, and National," *J. Farm Econ.* **44**: 1–34, 1962.

Fox, K. A., and T. K. Kumar. "Delineating Functional Economic Areas," in *Research and Education for Area Development* (Ames, Iowa: Iowa State University Press, 1966), pp. 13–55.

Fox, K. A., and T. K. Kumar. "The Functional Economic Area: Delineation and Implications for Economic Analysis and Policy," *Papers Reg. Sci. Assoc.* **15**:57–85, 1965.

Hansen, N. M. "A Growth Center Strategy for the United States," *Rev. Reg. Stud.* **1**:161–173, 1970.

Hansen, N. M. "Development Pole Theory in a Regional Context," *Kyklos.* **20**: 709–725, 1967.

Lewis, W. C. and J. R. Prescott. "Urban-Regional Development and Growth Centers: An Econometric Study," *J. Reg. Sci.* **12**, No. 1: 57–70, 1972.

Lewis, W. C. "Growth and Welfare: The Effect of the Spatial Dimension," Utah State University, *mimeo*, 1973.

Robinson, E. A. G. (Ed.), *Backward Areas in Advanced Countries* (New York: St. Martin's Press, 1969).

The Role of Growth Centers in Regional Economic Development, Four Volumes. Report prepared by Department of Economics, Iowa State University, for Office of Regional Economic Development, United States Department of Commerce, 1966, multilithed.

Upper Great Lakes Regional Commission, *Growth Centers and Their Potentials in the Upper Great Lakes Region* (Washington, D.C.: Upper Great Lakes Regional Commission, 1969).

4

Water Resource Development and Interregional Commodity Trade

In contrast to the spatial units discussed in Chapters 2 and 3, the primary focus in the delineation of resource regions is the physiogeographic distribution of a nonhuman characteristic. River basins and watersheds are defined by the spatial area within which a system of water flows are joined in a common course, and the distribution of human activities is of secondary importance. The parts of rivers protected under the Wild Rivers and Scenic Areas Act are selected primarily on the basis of natural beauty as are most of our national forests and parks. Multistate compacts that regulate water withdrawals usually include all government units through which a major river flows. Even the appropriate delineation of an air pollution control district in a large urbanized region should be sensitive to the natural forces of wind velocity and direction.

Public works development, conservation and the regulation of economic externalities are the principal objectives pursued within the regional resource unit. The construction of multipurpose dams, irrigation projects and harbor improvements are among the many water-related activities of the U.S. Corps of Engineers. Reconciling the conservancy and recreational objectives of the public with the private demands for timber is the principal management function of the U.S. Forest Service. The water and air quality legislation of the late 1960's reflects both a national concern for environmental degradation and an attempt to establish regulatory mechanisms that would spatially internalize incentives to control economic externalities.

The long run nature of these objectives presents numerous evaluative problems for the regional economist. Since 1936 the U.S. Corps of Engineers has been required to conduct benefit-cost analyses for flood control, irrigation, hydroelectric power and navigational improvements. Over time the economic basis for evaluating these projects has been broadened to include residentiary, leisure-related activities such as recreation, fishing and wildlife conservation for which few privately determined market prices are available. Evaluating the benefits due to resource conservation is complicated by the importance nonusers often attach to preservation; indeed, with nonrenewable resources the unavailability of the resource to prospective users may constitute virtually all of the social benefit. In any case, prices are not often available for users, and methods of evaluating nonuser benefits are at a very rudimentary state of development. Much of the project's value also may accrue to future generations whose preferences cannot be predicted or assumed to be similar to ours.

The captial-intensive nature of water investments also presents numerous problems in projecting the spatial and temporal distribution of residentiary and productive activity. The benefits due to a flood control project depend on long term changes in the level and type of economic activities conducted in the downstream flood plain. The recreational benefits attainable on a multipurpose dam depend on projected changes in the location of households at some distance from the site itself. The particular resource investment may also influence these patterns of economic growth, so the timing of the construction of dams, levees and river improvements within a water basin may affect the spatial and temporal distribution of the projected activities. Though it is generally thought that differential growth rates among regions in the United States have not been significantly influenced by water resource investments, the spatial distribution of activity within basins and even smaller regional units is undoubtedly affected.

Though numerous problems exist in the regional resources field, this chapter is primarily concerned with the empirical difficulties encountered in estimating interregional commodity trade. For many years the U.S. Corps of Engineers and other federal and state agencies with interests in water resource development have been conducting regional studies. The Missouri Valley and Upper Mississippi basin framework studies, for example, have concentrated on projections of the locational patterns of economic and residentiary activity designed to guide the planning of water investments within these regions. A part of this planning effort is concerned with navigational and port improvements along inland waterways which, in turn, depend on expected commercial traffic carried by inland water transportation modes. The study described in this chapter is representative of normative regional models that attempt to establish cost-minimizing trade flows as standards of transportation system performance. Linear programming is the principal analytical tool, though numerous empirical techniques are combined in the overall model to provide data needed in intermediate stages. The projections period is 1960–80 and the analytical objective is to calculate commodity flows and costs for 19 commodities among the 48 contiguous states. The selected commodities are most frequently carried by inland water carrier and, though the study was originally conducted for the Missouri Valley basin, the long shipment distances necessitated the use of all states as a spatial basis for the model. Due to the substantial amount of data needed to complete the work, we illustrate the principal problems with information for a selected subset of goods and states studied.

For many economists the analysis of spatial flows is the *raison d'etre* of the regional field. The general paucity of good data on the spatial movements of people, capital and commodities necessitates many estimation methods that have become important tools for the regional economist; indeed, even the problem of interpreting existing flows data involves many difficulties that are not widely appreciated. For these reasons much of this chapter concentrates on methodological problems encountered in evaluating the benefits attributable to transportation improvements and the estimation of trade flows. The first section discusses the benefits attributable to harbor and inland waterway improvements and the general structure of the interregional commodity flows model. Some of the specific problems of estimation are then described, with the aggregated flows estimates discussed at the end of the chapter.

DEVELOPMENT BENEFITS AND GENERAL STRUCTURE OF THE INTERREGIONAL FLOWS MODEL

Since the mid-1930's the U.S. Corps of Engineers has been responsible for evaluating the benefits and costs of inland waterways and harbor improvements. Canal construction and channel deepening are examples of projects designed to increase the efficiency of the transportation system. Many types of development benefits may result from such construction efforts, but it has been generally recognized that evaluative criteria in transportation-related public investments have failed to adequately account for the widespread spatial impacts of these improvements. The relation between these development concepts and the objectives of the commodity flows model is the subject of this section.

Development Benefits

An inland waterway or harbor improvement may have several types of localized impacts. The construction of the project itself will generate payments to labor and local suppliers of raw materials and capital goods. These income payments will be spent, in part, on other consumer and producers goods and services available within the community. The investment may also alter the comparative advantage of the harbor in handling specific types of goods at the shipping facility. Channel deepening, for example, may be designed to allow larger ships to use the port and hence alter the composition of commodities passing through the harbor. This, in turn, may change secondary handling facilities at docks, warehouses and transhipment points that subsequently process the in-bound shipment.

Cost reduction is another benefit that may accrue to local firms and households. If it is a general improvement influencing all commodities shipped through the harbor, the delivered price of goods should fall locally. The reduced cost-of-living may be an element in attracting new households to the region and the cheaper price of intermediate goods and shipments may attract firms producing goods for export outside of the region. Land values near the shipping improvement should rise if the project is successful in increasing the level of residentiary and productive activity.

The local benefits generated from the project must be distinguished from those types of economic development effects in the broader region or nation. The general improvement of port facilities and inland waterways will enhance the nation's competitive position in international trade and may significantly influence the location of economic activity within the country. Exporters are able to increase their market areas abroad at the expense of firms in other countries, and reduced prices for imported goods are a benefit to domestic consumers. The coastal ports and cities along inland waterways may differentially benefit from these general improvements in the transportation system.

Though many of these impacts are quite diverse, there are three additional simplified evaluative approaches used by economists in assessing the benefits and costs of public projects:

(1) Consumer's surplus is increased due to the commodity price reduction attributable to the project. The buyer's demand for the commodity increases and the price differential times total output is an approximate estimate of this surplus. The demand curves for the commodities affected by the improvement must be known and since the price effects are not independent of the location of producers and consumers the spatial distribution of firms and households must be estimated. Though a canal improvement may influence the transportation costs of only a small part of the total trip distance, this method ideally necessitates a vast amount of market information both within and outside of the country with the project.

(2) A public project may improve the productivity of a particular input or resource that is not efficiently utilized due to market imperfections or objectives not captured in private competitive markets. Land values may not reflect the most efficient use of this resource if owner's development decisions are mutually dependent. The objectives of public education transcend the student's skill requirements for participation in private labor markets, so the social returns to education are not fully captured by discounted future earnings. Though, as suggested above, land values may be influenced in locations with port or harbor improvements, these affects will be quite diffused throughout the community. Unlike an urban renewal project in the center city of a metropolitan area, the harbor development may affect the locational advantages of virtually all land parcels in the region; calculating the net change in land values attributable to the project is even more difficult. Public objectives in transportation development often include a capability to move goods and passengers during national emergencies, and generally these benefits will not be captured in land value changes at or near the project site.

(3) The method of alternative cost is a third evaluative possibility and has been traditionally used by the Corps of Engineers for inland waterway improvements. The benefits of the project are assumed to exceed its costs, and the analysis determines which of several agencies can most efficiently undertake the development. If a canal is designed to carry a certain commercial tonnage between two cities, then the average cost of providing this service should be less than the most efficient alternative if the project is to be undertaken by the government. Rail movement is the usual alternative consid-

ered since the transit capabilities of these two modes are quite similar. The analysis usually encounters particularly difficult problems in (a) projecting the expected tonnages moving on the canal and (b) evaluating the full costs of the rail alternative.

These evaluative methods cannot capture the diffuse spatial influences that characterize transit-related resource investments. The ultimate origins and destinations for commodity shipments along inland waterways are subject to the changing comparative advantages of production locations and differential growth in major populated centers. Projecting these changes in a comprehensive spatial format involves considerations far beyond the site of the improvement itself, and piecemeal evaluation may entail numerous inconsistencies without estimates of the trade flows among and within the larger regions of the nation. To provide such estimates the Corps of Engineers undertook studies designed to fulfill the following objectives:

(1) Estimate the potential long haul commercial traffic that might be eligible for water-borne carrier among major regions in the United States. The estimates should be based on underlying economic forces influencing the location of production and consumption. The methods should include base year estimates and provision for the projections of these flows.

(2) Calculate the full costs of these commodity flows among the principal producing and consuming centers within the United States and allow for external trade flows that will influence expected traffic within the 48 contiguous states. The data could provide alternative cost guidelines for the rail mode among the various origins and destinations as a guideline for inland waterway improvements.

(3) Maintain the greatest amount of spatial and commodity disaggregation consistent with available data and models capable of projecting economic variables by representing the interdependence of productive activity. This disaggregation is necessary due to the specialized volume and weight characteristics of goods carried by water barge and the unique locations of navigable rivers.

Structural Considerations
for the Interregional Flows Model

Commercial carriers along inland waterways are characterized by high terminal and low line haul costs of shipment. Terminal improvements are therefore a most important consideration in their cost structures; indeed, water carriers pay virtually none of the costs of establishing and maintaining the roadbed. These long haul advantages increase the spatial area within which trade flows must be considered and restrict the commodities necessary to analyze. Flows across basins are at least potentially transportable in part by the water mode and must be added to intrabasin estimates. Bulky, heavy and relatively unprocessed primary goods are most advantageously shipped on inland waterways. While this tends to increase the homogeneity of included goods it also complicates the estimation of intermediate processing locations. The 19 commodities considered here are most frequently shipped by water carrier and include corn, sorghum grain, wheat, soybeans, bituminous coal, crude petroleum, crushed rock, phosphate rock, sulfur, flour, sugar, animal feed, cement, gasoline, fuel oils, alcohols, asphalt, steel pipe and steel mill products.

The degree of spatial and commodity disaggregation attainable is limited by available data and the accuracy of existing projection's models. The information necessary for all components of the model are not available for substate counties or metropolitan regions. The heterogeneity of regional sizes presents some difficulties with state data since the common use of single production centers for each spatial unit may distort commodity flows; Texas, for example, comprises 267,000 square miles, over four times the size of the six New England states. Commodity specialization among alternative modes suggests the necessity for the product disaggregation noted above; however, partial equilibrium techniques tend to provide poor forecasts of commodity demand patterns, particularly for the long run.

Economic interdependence should be allowed for in projecting the production of these goods due to their importance as intermediate inputs in the production process. Input-output models allow for the projected demands of users for a wide variety of goods, though even the largest input-output tables are characterized by a high degree of commodity aggregation. Two goods in this study (corn and sorghum grain) are included with hay, oats and barley in the 1958 sectoral definition for feed grains used by the Office of Business Economics (O.B.E.); these three excluded commodities account for about 40% of total feed grain production. Constant dollar projections of this sector's gross output may be used only if it is assumed that the mix of goods within the sector remains unchanged. Such projections must also be converted to physical volume or weight units (short tons in this study) since transportation costs are defined in these terms.

The physical tonnage estimates for all commodities must be also disaggregated by subarea into production and consumption estimates. The resource-orientation of primary goods usually results in relatively stable spatial patterns of production, and ratios of subarea to total regional production may not change markedly even over long time periods. For goods closer to the final consumer in the production process, locations near populated centers are likely and projected shifts in the spatial distribution of households are needed. The distinction between intermediate and final demand in an input-output model provides a basis for estimating subarea commodity demand. If all of the commodity is purchased directly by final consumers, then ratios of subarea to total regional population may be used as allocators. Alternatively, if the commodity is used primarily as an intermediate input, then the relevant column of the input-output matrix is used to distribute sales to industry and the spatial distribution of each industry is the basis of the locational allocation. Where goods are used by both final consumers and firms a combination of these methods could be used. At this point, initial estimates of the subarea's status as net supplier or demander of each commodity would be available. Out-shipments are expected from net suppliers; each subarea either supplies or demands a particular commodity and cross-hauling is not possible. Several data and conceptual problems should be noted at this point.

(1) Estimation of the underlying economic status of each subarea is a desirable check in existing origin and destination data for the goods included here. The 1% Interstate Commerce Commission (I.C.C.) sample could be utilized, but as with other sources of transit data only the modal trip-ends are distinguished. Intermodal transfers and intermediate lay-overs for warehousing are not usually estimable in official government statistics. The alternative is expensive surveys to trace the commodity movement accurately through a succession of intermediate destinations. Though modal data are useful for other purposes it is a general weakness of transportation censuses that the spatial characteristics of the commodity or passenger trip are usually not emphasized.

(2) Cost-minimizing models are usually incapable of dealing with the cross-hauling problem since each subregion is either a net demander or supplier of the commodity. In the case of inland waterway, however, this problem should not be as serious as with more sophisticated transit modes. When primary goods are fabricated, product differentiation is more likely and spatial demand patterns

become more complicated. Cross-hauling is therefore more prevalent for aggregated commodity classifications containing highly differentiated products, and these goods are more commonly carried by truck or rail. Supply areas for commodities like corn or soybeans also tend to be quite homogeneous and relatively stable over time as noted above. The ability to define more precisely the specialized characteristics of goods is crucial to the solution of the cross-hauling problem, but movements along inland waterway should be least sensitive of all major transit modes to this problem. Though gross tonnages are a better indicator of system use than net tonnages, they should not be significantly different for the goods considered here.

Distances among origins and destinations and cost per ton factors must be estimated under objective (2) above. The 19 commodities can be grouped into agricultural, mining and manufacturing products so some degree of spatial differentiation within subareas is possible. (This should overcome some of the spatial problems connected with using single production centers in each state for calculating distances.) These centers may also be arranged in a hierarchical fashion, so mining and agricultural products flow to manufacturing centers and the latter are the basis for interregional trade in fabricated products. (The manufacturing centers will usually represent the major wholesaling and consuming centers.) Intrastate flows are theoretically possible under the formulation except for the fact that the net demand or supply status is determined by states. Also it should be noted that the distance matrix is not symmetric as in the case in models where single subarea centers are utilized. As the commodities may be transhipped and direct water access to all centers is unlikely, highway distances among centers are used. Published rail distances are insufficiently detailed to show the special agricultural and mining centers that are separately distinguished in each subarea.

Several problems are encountered in estimating transit costs. The absence of very comprehensive data for commodity, distance and direction for truck and inland water modes leaves the published I.C.C. rail information as the most reliable basis for cost estimation. Rail is also the closest competitor with water transit and most closely approximates the alternative costs under objective (2) above. For purposes of long run estimation, fully distributed costs are preferred to rail rates since the latter will be subject to the vagaries of I.C.C. rate decisions. The cost estimates should also be made by commodity type, inter- and intraregional flows, and direction of movement since the I.C.C. data reveal a considerable heterogeneity for these characteristics. Methods of converting railroad rate data to cost estimates are desirable and this problem is discussed more thoroughly in the next section.

Several adjustments to the subarea net supply or demand positions must be made under objective (2). As our interest is primarily in the potential tonnage flows among states along inland modes, movements by intercoastal tanker and barge must be estimated. These adjustments are particularly important for crude petroleum shipments from the Gulf states to the eastern seaboard and grain shipments from the Midwest through the Great Lakes to the East. Had the initial net supply or demand positions not been adjusted, movements of crude petroleum from Louisiana to the New England states would have been considered eligible for barge transit on the inland mode. The size of inland routes typically precludes competition with ocean-going tankers and barge trains, so these projected movements are netted out of the supply and demand tonnages for these states. These adjustments can be made from data on outbound and inbound intercoastal shipments of the 19 commodities for the 31 states with ocean or Great Lakes borders. Since cost data are not available for these shipments, nautical distances among the ports are utilized in these separate allocations. Shipments are subtracted from the net supplying coastal states and receipts are subtracted from the net demanding coastal states.

Export and import adjustments must also be made for all commodities in the study. The distribution of imports and exports by U.S. port will be influenced by the changing spatial patterns of production and consumption in foreign countries, which is outside the scope of the model discussed in this chapter. Projections of commodity imports and exports are also complicated by the influence of governmental programs and international crises; public law 480 shipments and the Arabian oil embargo are examples of phenomena that may cause erratic year to year changes in foreign trade and are also unexplained by our model. Base year ratios of exports and imports to total domestic output may therefore be inaccurate indicators for projections purposes, though their average behavior over longer historical periods may be more stable. Both the intercoastal and foreign trade total tonnages may be projected to grow at rates equal to those observed for commodity production within the United

States. Imports are treated as an increment to supply of the state of entry and exports are an increased demand in the exporting state.

These considerations lead us to the following structural model designed to estimate the interregional commodity flows. A set of balance equations for the kth commodity in the rth subarea are defined as:

$$X_r^k = O_r^k - C_r^k + IR_r^k - IS_r^k + I_r^k - E_r^k \tag{34}$$

where O_r^k = production of kth good in rth subarea (short tons)

C_r^k = consumption of kth good in rth subarea (short tons)

IR_r^k = intercoastal receipts of the kth good in rth subarea (short tons)

IS_r^k = intercoastal shipments of kth good in rth subarea (short tons)

I_r^k = imports of kth good in rth subarea (short tons)

E_r^k = exports of kth good in rth subarea (short tons)

The values of IR_r^k, IS_r^k, I_r^k, and E_r^k are zero in states not bordering the Great Lakes or oceans and may take on zero, negative or positive values in the coastal states with major ports. From these balance equations we define

$$S_i^k = X_r^k \text{ if } X_r^k \geqslant 0 \tag{35}$$

as a net supplying state, and

$$D_j^k = X_r^k \text{ if } X_r^k \leqslant 0$$

as a net demanding state.

The objective of the transportation algorithm is to minimize

$$T = \underset{i}{\Sigma} \underset{j}{\Sigma} c_{ij}^k d_{ij}^k X_{ij}^k \tag{36}$$

where c_{ij}^k = costs per ton mile between i and j for the kth good

d_{ij}^k = distance in miles between i and j for the kth good

X_{ij}^k = estimated commodity shipment between i and j, (short tons)

subject to

$$\underset{j}{\Sigma} X_{ij}^k \leqslant S_i^k \tag{37}$$

$$\sum_i X_{ij}{}^k \geqslant D_j{}^k \tag{38}$$

and

$$\sum_i S_i{}^k = \sum_j D_j{}^k \tag{39}$$

The economic interpretation of these equations is as follows. Competitive firms in the industries producing the goods supply buyers so as to minimize transportation costs. Product supplies in each subarea are drawn down to at least supply domestic consumers and if insufficient, deficits are made up through in-shipments, so gross flows for each commodity are not estimated. (Cross-hauls are estimated in aggregating across goods.) Shipments are no more than the tonnages available in each subarea and receipts fulfill requirements. Total net supplies and demands are equal as are total shipments and receipts by intercoastal barge and tanker. Disparities in domestic production and consumption are adjusted through commodity movements to or from foreign countries. Aggregating across commodities we have the following flows.

$$\sum_k \sum_i X_{ij}{}^k = \text{outbound interregional commodity flows}$$

$$\sum_k \sum_j X_{ij}{}^k = \text{inbound interregional commodity flows, and}$$

$\sum_k \sum_i \sum_j c_{ij}{}^k d_{ij}{}^k X_{ij}{}^k =$ total transportation costs of the potential inland water shipments among regions.

ESTIMATION TECHNIQUES AND PROBLEMS

Numerous estimating problems must be dealt with in preparing the data for the interstate flow allocation. The discussion of these difficulties provides background for recommendations regarding the collection of flows data and the use of alternative regional estimation techniques. In this section we describe the principal steps required to estimate the state balance equations for all 19 commodities in the study; the illustrative calculations are primarily confined to corn and sorghum grain flows within several Midwestern states.

An input-output model provided base and projected year gross outputs as control totals for the 48 states by type of commodity; preliminary calculations are necessary to disaggregate the sectoral estimates and convert them to a physical (tonnage) base. For example, corn and sorghum grain account for 51 and 7% respectively of the feed grain sector (A-6) in the O.B.E. classification. This sector is estimated to increase from $9.6 billion to $18.3 billion over the projections period, and these percentages can be applied directly to the base and projected year sectoral totals. The dollar outputs for commodities are then disaggregated to state of production by percentages of state to total U.S. output; as noted above, the strong resource-orientation of these goods suggests that base year state ratios could also be used for projected year estimates. Sorghum grain, for example, shows a very specialized pattern of regional production with only 23 states producing this commodity. (Texas accounted for 45% of total sorghum grain production in the base year.) Corn production is more diversified among regions but only five states (Indiana, Illinois, Minnesota, Iowa and Nebraska) account for more than 7% of total national production, and Iowa and Illinois alone produce about 32% of this amount.

The state dollar estimates of commodity production must also be changed to a volume or weight basis requiring price and physical conversion factors. In the base year national dollar production estimates and a corresponding physical measure are known. Hence an average price per bushel of corn and sorghum grain may be used to convert state estimates to a physical dimension. Since corn and sorghum grain both weigh 56 pounds per bushel, (56/2000) times total bushels converts the state figures to short tons; the latter is used as a common weight measure for aggregating across commodities. Barrels are also a common volume unit for several commodities in the study, but are less likely to correspond with tonnage estimates across commodities. The barrel/short ton conversion factors range from 0.118 (gasoline) to 0.182 (petroleum asphalt) for the commodities considered here. These factors allow the estimated flows to be expressed in several measures of system use and complete initial steps required to calculate O_r^k in Equation 34.

Distance Matrices for State Production Centers

Flow estimation requires distance and cost factors for the origins and destinations among subregions. Virtually all studies assume symmetry for the d_{ij}^k in Equation 36, and many make the same assumption for the c_{ij}^k. As noted above the states are quite heterogenous in size, so product flows could be misallocated if some degree of spatial disaggregation is not attained. The product heterogeneity represented in the 19 commodities also suggests that geographically selected centers applied uniformly to all goods may substantially misrepresent the true productive locations within states. The mileage calculations distinguish three separate matrices based on the agricultural, mining and manufacturing sectors represented in the commodity list. The selection criteria were as follows:

(1)   The consumption centers were based on 1960 population data for SMSAs and cities and generally corresponded with the manufacturing centers in each state. The manufacturing centers were those cities with the largest number of establishments and/or highest employment in manufacturing according to the 1958 U.S. Census of Manufacturing. Only in the five states of Wyoming, Virginia, North Carolina, South Carolina, and Oklahoma are these two criteria inconsistent, so the consumption and manufacturing centers for all subregions are assumed to coincide.

(2)   The agricultural and mining centers were based on measures of the level of economic activity for each county within the state. The value of crops sold determined the center for agriculture, and employment was used for commodities in the mining sector; the distances for these two sectors were estimated from the largest urban center within each of the counties. These centers show a remarkable diversity. The agricultural and mining centers are the same only in the state of Florida and Massachusetts and along with many small, rural communities are cities the size of Birmingham, Alabama, and Wilmington, Delaware.

Among these criteria there is also a substantial diversity in the selected centers of activity in each subregion. In no state are all three centers in a single city, and the same center for any two of the three sectors occurs in only 13 states; in 8 of these 13 cases the mining and consumption centers correspond. The correspondence is most prevalent in the New England and Southeastern states where errors due to mileage differences would tend to be minor. Although Houston and Los Angeles appear as two centers for the three criteria, the general absence of corresponding centers in the larger states of the middle west and far western regions suggests the distortions that could occur under less disaggregated methods of mileage determination.

Table VII summarizes some of the mileage calculations for selected midwestern states and shows the substantial distance variations encountered under this method. The two rows for each origin show agricultural and mining distances to the common manufacturing

TABLE VII

Distance Matrix of Agricultural, Mining and
Manufacturing Centers for Selected States, Miles[a]

Origin	Destination					
	Minn.	*Iowa*	*Mo.*	*N.D.*	*S.D.*	*Nebr.*
Minnesota	288	540	834	69	325	505
	153	405	699	247	389	511
Iowa	167	130	466	369	158	217
	289	37	322	532	309	159
Missouri	751	541	205	997	814	640
	618	408	72	903	668	488
North Dakota	315	567	861	76	332	512
	645	893	1229	399	620	800
South Dakota	289	210	546	319	63	117
	630	660	996	525	394	574
Nebraska	776	604	919	722	540	465
	738	575	855	781	540	436

[a] The agricultural to manufacturing center distances are in row 1 and the
mining to manufacturing center distances are in row 2 for each state of
origin.

center; the diagonal elements are nonzero since intrastate distances
between the resource and market locations are calculable. The off-
diagonals are nonsymmetric because single centers are not selected
in each state. (This is true only of the agricultural and mining commodities since the consumption and manufacturing centers correspond to each other.)

Both the within- and among-state mileage estimates show a substantial variation. Within South Dakota, for example, a difference
of 331 miles separates highway mileages from the consumption center to the agricultural and mining centers and, with the exception
of Nebraska, roughly similar differences are estimated for the other
states. Agricultural goods produced in Iowa and shipped to Minne-

sota must travel 167 miles, while the reverse flow from Minnesota to
Iowa is three times as far. Shipments from North Dakota to the consumption center in Missouri must travel either 861 or 1229 miles
depending on whether it is an agricultural or mining commodity.
These mileage variations are sufficient to cause significant differences in transit costs per ton and are often within different mileage
blocks used by the I.C.C. in reporting cost and rate data from the 1%
sample. They are also often greater than the highway distances separating the principal population centers among these states and may
therefore cause substantially different flow patterns than distance
estimates based on a single center within each subregion.

Transportation Cost Estimation

The c_{ij}^k in Equation 36 are needed to complete the allocative parameters in the 48-state transportation model. Though symmetry is
also frequently assumed, there is a remarkable diversity in costs per
ton-mile by direction of flow. The I.C.C. rail and cost data are used
here since alternative cost estimates were deemed useful and, in any
case, comprehensive cost information is not generally available for
the truck and inland barge modes. The rail data are disaggregated
by commodity, mileage block and direction of movement, and substantial variations in all these characteristics were noted in these
data. Several objectives were sought in the cost estimation:

(1)   As with the distance estimates spatial disaggregation of the
cost functions is desirable. Separate estimates are made for movements within and among the official, Southern and Western regions
of the United States, so the direction of movement between i and j
is separately distinguished. These cost functions show a substantial
diversity by direction of movement; models, which use undifferentiated distances as cost surrogates, cannot accurately represent the
commercial carrier cost structure for long distance hauls.

(2)   Long-run cost estimates are desired for projections purposes. As noted above, I.C.C. rate decisions may distort rate and
cost structures for particular regions and movement directions. Out-
of-pocket costs may also be subject to variable expenses due to
short-run shifts in traffic volumes. Fully-distributed costs are preferred for this model and must be derived by special estimation
techniques designed to merge the rail and cost data.

The cost data reported by the I.C.C. are unfortunately not directly
applicable to the commodities analyzed in this study. The out-of-

pocket and fully-distributed cost data were reported by miles, tonnage, district and type of car, but not by commodity class. The type-of-car data might be used for goods requiring unique facilities (*e.g.*, refrigerator and tank) since there is probably little variation in usages among regions and commodities, but this seems unlikely for open hoppers, box, flat and gondola cars. For the commodities considered here direct cost estimates could not be made.

The method used in this study begins with estimated rate functions and then adjusts these regressions to a cost basis. The last step is possible due to a known relation between both out-of-pocket (OP) and fully-distributed costs (FD) to revenues that are reported by commodity and regional movement. Several alternative methods of cost calculation are possible with this approach. A rate per ton-mile equation is first estimated as

$$R_{tm}{}^k = a - b \ (d_{ij}{}^k) \tag{40}$$

where $R_{tm}{}^k$ = revenue per ton-mile for the kth commodity

This equation is solved for the mean distance (m^k) for which the ratio of revenue to out-of-pocket costs (R/OP) and revenue to fully-distributed costs (R/FD) are calculated. Thus,

$$R_{tm}{}^k \ (m^k) = a - b \ (m^k) \tag{41}$$

Equation 41 is converted to revenue per ton (R_t) as

$$R_{tm}{}^k \ (m^k) \ x \ m^k = R_t \ (m^k) \tag{42}$$

and

$$(FD/R) \ (R_t(m^k)) = FD \ (m^k) \tag{43}$$

is the estimate of fully distributed costs at m^k distance.

In the next step a constant term (c) is calculated with the aid of (OP/R) as

$$c = FD \ (m^k) \ - (OP/R) \ (R_t{}^k \ (m^k)) \tag{44}$$

and the slope of the fully distributed cost function (d) is estimated as

$$d = (FD(m^k) - c) \ / \ (m^k) \tag{45}$$

Several variants to this estimating method are possible:

(1) As described above, the estimate of the $R_{tm}{}^k \ (m^k)$ can be

determined from the rate regression and the full sequence of calculations can be made. Though this method has the advantage of using all data in the rail rate regression, it tended to seriously over-estimate the costs of long haul. The empirical rate regressions tended to over-estimate $R_{tm}{}^k$ (m^k), $R_t{}^k$ (m^k), $FD(m^k)$ and d. The estimate of the constant term, c, is relatively unaffected because both FD (m^k) and $R_t{}^k$ (m^k) are over-estimated and off-balance each other. Therefore a relatively accurate constant term but an over-estimated slope coefficient results in a progressively more serious over-estimation as the length of haul increases.

(2) Instead of calculating $R_{tm}{}^k$ (m^k) from the rate regression direct estimates are available. These estimates are reported by mileage block, and only interpolation to m^k is necessary. Since the observed $R_{tm}{}^k$ (m^k) tended to be lower than those predicted from the rate regression, the costs were also lower and much more in accordance with independent estimates of fully distributed costs at relatively long hauls.

Table VIII illustrates the cost estimates for corn and sorghum grain calculated from method (2) above for a selected set of midwestern states. These two commodities are chosen for both Tables VII and VIII because their conversion factors from bushels to short tons (0.028) are the same and their transportation cost structure should be quite similar; the tabulated values are $c_{ij}{}^k$ $d_{ij}{}^k$ where distances are the agricultural to consumption center mileages shown in Table VII. There is a slight tendency for estimated corn shipment costs to exceed the cost figures for sorghum grain; in only 6 of the 36 matrix entries does the opposite cost relationship hold. The method of cost estimation tends to predict higher sorghum costs for trip distances less than 310 miles. These disparities are not serious, however, as only 2 cent differences are shown for hauls within Missouri and from South Dakota to Iowa; the percentage discrepancies are also low for both short and long hauls. Method (2) showed equally acceptable results in comparisons to survey cost estimates for corn, soybeans and mixed feed shipments within the midwestern region. The method produced equally good results for other commodities paired by comparable transit characteristics (weight, volume) and was utilized in calculating costs per ton for all goods included in the study.

TABLE VIII

Cost Matrix for Corn and Sorghum Grain
in Selected Midwestern States[a]

Origin	Destination					
	Minn.	*Iowa*	*Mo.*	*N.D.*	*S.D.*	*Nebr.*
Minnesota	431	692	995	204	469	656
	416	636	893	224	448	606
Iowa	305	267	615	515	296	357
	310	278	571	487	302	354
Missouri	910	693	345	1165	976	795
	821	637	343	1036	876	724
North Dakota	459	720	1024	211	467	663
	439	660	917	231	454	612
South Dakota	432	350	698	463	198	254
	417	348	641	443	219	266
Nebraska	936	758	1085	880	692	614
	842	692	967	795	535	571

[a] All cost figures are in cents per ton and are estimated at the distance between the agricultural and consumption centers shown in Table VII. The corn and sorghum grain costs appear in rows 1 and 2, respectively, for each origin state.

Intercoastal Shipments

For several commodities intercoastal shipments are an important component of total trade among the 48 states. Since ocean-going tankers or barges are essentially noncompetitive with inland waterways preliminary adjustments are made to the balance equations for the 31 states with Great Lakes or ocean boundaries. Available data distinguish the Great Lakes and other port states but do not provide information on the inbound origins or outbound destinations. Accordingly, separate distance minimizing allocations among trading states are made where distances are the nautical miles among the eligible subregions. Canadian exports and imports through states along the Great Lakes are treated as foreign trade and are discussed below. Projections of the level of intercoastal flows are based on growth rates of sectoral outputs estimated from the input-output model for the 20 year period; the data discussed below are for the base year.

Table IX illustrates the allocation of Great Lakes corn shipments among the 8 states eligible for shipments or receipts. (The flows are in short tons with distance parameters in parentheses below the interstate shipments.) The model predicts major shipments of corn to New York and Michigan from the major shipping states of Illinois, Minnesota and Wisconsin; Indiana and Ohio ship equal (but relatively minor) quantities of corn to New York. As would be expected in this type of model the most western demanding state (Michigan) imports from Minnesota and Wisconsin while New York shipments originate from the more eastern corn-producing regions. These trading patterns are consistent with the flow of midwestern grain surpluses to larger markets along the eastern seaboard and the major corn milling firms in the Midwest.

Separate data allowed for an allocation of commodity shipments among the remaining coastal states; the latter include flows from and to the Great Lakes ports. For corn, these intercoastal shipments are only one-third the size of trade among the eight Great Lakes states. The major corn shipments originate from Alabama, Louisiana, Ohio and New York. The specialized island economies of Puerto Rico and the Virgin Islands receive most of their supplies by shipments from New Orleans through the Gulf of Mexico. Maine is predicted to receive its corn from Ohio and Illinois while Maryland's inbound corn flows are taken from New York, Virginia and Ohio. All of Florida's intercoastal receipts are attributable to shipments from Alabama, and some Texas and Louisiana shipments are received in Hawaii through the Panama Canal. (The island economies were included for an accurate accounting of coastal flows, but are excluded in estimating the potential shipments among the contiguous states.)

The Great Lakes and intercoastal shipments matrices were estimated for all 19 commodities, completing the calculations of IS_r^k and IR_r^k in Equation 34. It should be noted that these tonnage flows are only first approximations to the ultimate origins and destinations of goods moving among coastal states. The data used in these alloca-

TABLE IX

Allocation of Intercoastal Great Lakes Corn Shipments by State[a]

Origin	Destination								Total Shipments
	N.Y.	*Pa.*	*Minn.*	*Wisc.*	*Ill.*	*Ind.*	*Mich.*	*Ohio*	
New York	(9,999)	(28)	(295)	(276)	(270)	(270)	(222)	(214)	
Pennsylvania	(28)	(9,999)	(323)	(305)	(299)	(299)	(251)	(243)	
Minnesota	(295)	(323)	(9,999)	(74)	(81)	(81)	55,404 (73)	(84)	55,404
Wisconsin	67,220 (296)	(305)	(74)	(9,999)	(8)	(10)	16,390 (54)	(65)	83,610
Illinois	190,570 (270)	(299)	(81)	(8)	(9,999)	(4)	(48)	(59)	190,570
Indiana	10,189 (270)	(299)	(81)	(10)	(4)	(9,999)	(48)	(59)	10,189
Michigan	(222)	(251)	(73)	(54)	(48)	(48)	(9,999)	(11)	
Ohio	10,146 (214)	(243)	(89)	(65)	(59)	(59)	(11)	(9,999)	10,146
Total Receipts	278,125						71,794		349,919

[a] Estimated distances (in units of 10 miles) are in parentheses under the estimated flows. The high diagonal entries preclude shipment from a state to itself. All flows are in short tons for the base year.

tions show port receipts and shipments and not the ultimate source or destination of the product flows. The shipments must therefore be treated on the accounts of the state of entry or exit even though the location of consumption or production may be different. Hence only 31 states have possible nonzero entries for IS_r^k and IR_r^k and for most commodities the number was much smaller.

Exports and Imports

The treatment of foreign trade is somewhat different than the calculations for interstate coastal shipments. Separate data on imports and exports by port state in the base year are used to allocate trade flows to the 31 coastal states. Since it would take nothing less than a full world trade model to detect shifts in the spatial allocation of these flows among the states, base year percentages were assumed to hold in the projection year. Total exports and imports are assumed to maintain a constant percentage relationship to domestic production over the projections period; domestic output projections are provided by the input-output model.

Table X shows the calculation of the aggregate trade ratios for corn. The year to year fluctuations in production, exports and im-

TABLE X

U.S. Exports, Imports and Production of Corn (1956–60)[a]

Year	Production	Exports	Imports
1956	3,075,336	164,789	920
1957	3,045,355	183,628	1,869
1958	3,356,205	214,410	1,138
1959	3,824,598	211,529	1,152
1960	3,908,070	276,552	1,221
	17,208,564	1,050,908	6,300

[a] The reported data are in bushel units.
  Ratio (exports/production) = 0.061065
  Ratio (imports/production) = 0.000366

ports resulted in a substantial instability in the annual ratios. For example, corn production dropped 30 million bushels in 1957 while both exports and imports were increasing. Exports fell by 3 million bushels in 1959 and then increased by 65 million bushels the next year. Other commodities showed an even greater annual instability. Crude petroleum exports (in thousands of barrels) rose from 28,624 (1956) to 50,243 (1957) and then dropped to only 4,346 in 1958. This was due to the Suez crisis and ensuing petroleum shortages in Great Britain and other continental European countries.

Due to the annual instability in the trade ratios, historical averages were utilized for modeling purposes. The trade ratios for corn are calculated at the bottom of Table X; exports constituted about 6% of total production for the period (1956–60) and only minor amounts were imported. For the other commodities, foreign trade can comprise a substantial proportion of total domestic production. High export ratios are found for wheat (0.36), sulfur (0.24), soybeans (0.20) and phosphate rock (0.19). Import ratios tended to be either very high or low for the 19 commodities; the highest ratios were estimated for sugar (0.37), fuel oils (0.19) and crude petroleum (0.13).

Table XI shows the distribution of corn trade flows for 22 of the 31 states in territories that have port facilities. (The nine subregions not shown did not participate in foreign sales or purchases in the base year.) The export and import proportions for each commodity are developed from data distinguishing intercoastal shipments from flows to and from other countries though it is possible that reshipments of coastal flows to other countries occur. (This does not cause a double-counting problem, however, since the increased IR_r^k is offset exactly by the decreased E_r^k.) The aggregation of the data by state and/or the heterogeneity of the commodity may explain the cross-trading flows observed in this table. Six of the 22 trading subregions experienced both imports and exports of corn, so that double entries appear for New York, New Jersey, Florida, California, Washington and the Virgin Islands–Puerto Rico. The latter is a clear exception to the generally low ratios for imported corn. Only Maryland, Virginia and Louisiana accounted for as much as 10% of the total domestic export trade in corn.

The projected tonnages for port of entry or exit are developed from the trade ratios shown in Table XI. Commodity production projected to 1980 provides U.S. control totals for exports and im-

TABLE XI

Foreign Trade in Corn by State of Entry or Exit[a]

State			State		
(1) Maine		0.003117	(12) Texas		0.013970
(2) Massachusetts		0.009148	(13) California	0.031888,	0.001024
(3) New York	0.0000145,	0.006320	(14) Oregon		0.000004
(4) New Jersey	0.000109,	0.005213	(15) Washington	0.000399,	0.000004
(5) Pennsylvania		0.033634	(16) Minnesota		0.084362
(6) Maryland		0.016685	(17) Wisconsin		0.004167
(7) Virginia		0.204442	(18) Illinois		0.097060
(8) Georgia		0.000092	(19) Indiana		0.001102
(9) Florida	0.000073,	0.000308	(20) Michigan		0.007176
(10) Alabama		0.028210	(21) Ohio		0.032921
(11) Louisiana		0.361022	(22) V.I.-P.R.	0.967386,	0.000013

[a] All data are percentages for base year trade. The import and export percentages appear in order for each state or territory.

ports by utilizing the ratios shown in Table X, and the final distribution is then made to the appropriate port of entry or exit. Gross debits and credits are made for states exporting and importing the commodity; for most cases the states either imported or exported the good in question. This procedure was repeated for all 19 commodities, completing the estimation of I_r^k and E_r^k in Equation 34.

Domestic Requirements

The final task is to estimate the C_r^k in Equation 34, completing the subregional balance equations for the 48 states and 19 commodities. Ideally one must know how much of the commodity is utilized by each industry (or government agency) as an intermediate input and where these activities are located. The final demand component of consumption could then be allocated to subregions on the basis of income, population or other demand variables. For five commodities independent state consumption estimates comprising both intermediate and final demand are available and were utilized for the base year allocation; these include coal, cement, gasoline, fuel oils and petroleum asphalt.

For the 14 remaining commodities, separate state estimates are made for both the intermediate and final demand components of gross output. For the feed grains sectoral projection to 1980 of about 018.4 million, $2.5 million represents final demand purchases by consumers and governments. These same percentages are assumed to hold for corn and sorghum grain, and the final demand component was allocated to subregions on the basis of population. (Consumption functions could have been estimated here, but most of these goods have very low income elasticities and the projection of prices for a 20-year period is an additional problem.) For the intermediate demand component, allocators were based for the most part on disaggregated estimates of manufacturing value added.

These sectors are the most significant purchasers of output from the industry producing the commodity in question: food and kindred products (S.I.C. 20) for wheat, soybeans, refined sugar and flour, petroleum and coal products (S.I.C. 29) for gasoline, asphalt, fuel oils, bituminous coal and crude petroleum, primary metal industries (S.I.C. 33) for steel pipe and rolled steel products, chemical and allied products (S.I.C. 28) for sulfur, phosphate rock and alcohols and stone, clay and glass products (S.I.C. 32) for sand and gravel. Cattle numbers by state are used for the intermediate demand component of corn, sorghum grain and prepared animal feeds. The final and intermediate demand components are then added to estimate domestic requirements by state for each of the commodities.

Several alternatives to this procedure (and their problems) should be noted. (1) The final demand components (private consumption, government purchases, etc.) could be separately allocated by state. For most of these sectors population should be a relatively accurate allocator since it tends to be correlated with the size of state and local government budgets and total consumption expenditures. Federal government purchases are the principal problem since the locations of federal installations tend to be spatially heterogeneous, and subcontracting outside of the state of initial expenditure is a common practice. Unfortunately adequately disaggregated statistics for federal government purchases are not available by state. (2) Disaggregated input-output data would be useful for allocating intermediate inputs to the purchasing sector. This information is lost in aggregating sectoral sales and purchases into input-output tables, however, and surveys were not feasible with the resources available for this study. Additional work on disaggregating regional consumption data would be useful.

With the completion of C_r^k all components of Equation 34 may be estimated for each commodity by subregion in the base and projections year. Total supplies for a given state are the sum of production, imports, coastal receipts and Great Lakes receipts; total demands are the sum of exports, coastal shipments, Great Lakes shipments and consumption. (IS_r^k and IR_r^k include both Great Lakes and the other coastal allocations discussed above.) If supplies exceed demands, the state is a net supplier (*i.e.*, has inland shipments of the amount of the excess supply); otherwise the state is a net demander of the commodity. For corn the states of Minnesota, Iowa, Missouri, Nebraska, Illinois, Ohio, Indiana, Michigan, Delaware, North Carolina, South Carolina, Georgia and Kentucky are net suppliers and the remaining states are net demanders. The estimated cost functions are then utilized to allocate inland shipments and receipts among the 48 states in the base and projection year.

THE AGGREGATED COMMODITY FLOWS

The procedures discussed above generate an enormous amount of data for the projections period, and various means of checking the flows were employed. The I.C.C. 1% sample provides origin and destination information though its small size is a severe limitation. Minor corn exports for Georgia, South Carolina and Delaware are predicted by the model, for example, but are not picked up in 1% sample; the remaining flows among states generally correspond. In the early 1960's Iowa total corn exports were growing at a rate of about 800,000 tons per year, a figure consistent with expected out-shipments predicted for 1980. In these ways various cross-checks may be made to assess the accuracy of the model's predictions; because of the vast amount of projected information we confine the discussion here to summaries (by commodity class) for several midwestern and mountain states and the aggregate flows among Census regions.

Table XII shows the gross export and import flows by commodity class for the selected states; the commodity classes are defined at the bottom of this table. The results for agricultural product trade conform to known production patterns for these states. Only Wyoming and Wisconsin are estimated to be net importers of agricultural commodities; Wyoming exports only minor amounts of wheat and Wisconsin specializes in dairy-related products, which are not included in this study. Large proportions of agricultural exports are

TABLE XII

Gross Exports and Imports by Commodity Class, 1980[a]

State	Agricultural Exports (tons)	Agricultural Imports (tons)	Mining Exports (tons)	Mining Imports (tons)	Manufacturing Exports (tons)	Manufacturing Imports (tons)	Total Exports (tons)	Total Imports (tons)
1. Minn.	9,293,405	6,600,405	---	38,866,780	2,692,393	14,015,992	11,985,798	59,482,817
2. Iowa	25,576,106	2,739,475	20,286,725	10,531,028	3,513,824	13,653,330	49,476,655	26,923,833
3. Mo.	5,677,257	---	31,734,154	29,841,418	3,792,233	8,233,412	41,203,644	38,074,830
4. N.D.	10,117,889	2,440,153	25,453,233	11,628	459,684	1,773,573	36,030,806	4,225,354
5. S.D.	3,567,296	1,229,407	22,137,328	3,099,469	---	5,420,692	25,704,624	9,749,568
6. Nebr.	15,473,107	14,075	8,227,532	5,613,877	1,249,126	6,152,230	24,949,765	11,780,182
7. Kan.	25,291,071	3,988,295	21,280,221	1,230,135	25,423,393	2,720,571	71,994,685	7,939,001
8. Mont.	6,803,016	4,374,683	14,720,035	407,494	2,852,588	1,069,388	24,375,639	5,851,565
9. Wyo.	501,685	2,173,787	39,524,737	7,546	11,577,150	643,939	51,603,572	2,825,272
10. Colo.	3,980,383	2,741,344	11,698,672	334,300	3,389,458	3,509,339	19,068,513	6,584,983
11. Ill.	25,715,611	3,240,734	3,721,630	108,571,090	18,758,033	7,800,272	43,195,274	119,613,096
12. Wisc.	---	5,064,836	19,492,340	23,095,119	1,475,227	12,469,321	20,967,567	40,629,303

[a] The commodity groups are (1) agriculture: corn, sorghum grain, wheat, soybeans; (2) mining: bituminous coal and lignite, crude petroleum, sand-gravel-rock, phosphate rock, sulfur and (3) manufacturing: wheat flour, refined sugar, prepared animal feed, cement, finished gasoline, fuel oils, alcohols, petroleum asphalt, iron and steel pipe and finished steel mill products.

accounted for by corn in Minnesota and Iowa; Nebraska and Kansas also export substantial tonnages of sorghum grain. Wheat exports comprise over 90% of agricultural exports from North and South Dakota and 76% of the product tonnage shipped from Kansas. Major soybean exports originate in Minnesota, Iowa, Missouri and Illinois.

The major exports of bituminous coal and lignite come from the states of North Dakota, Wyoming and Illinois. All states with the exception of Minnesota, Iowa, Missouri, Illinois and Wisconsin are net exporters of crude petroleum and are estimated to more than consume their domestic output. Only Wisconsin, Illinois and Minnesota are estimated to be net importers of mining products.

The only net exporters of manufactured products are Kansas, Montana, Wyoming and Illinois. The first three of these states are characterized by low population densities and a relatively specialized manufacturing sector. Kansas, for instance, is estimated to export substantial tonnages of gasoline and fuel oils, a prediction consistent with its position as fourth ranking state in the number of actively producing oil wells in the base year. Flour and cement are also major export products for Kansas. Almost 50% of Montana's exports are concentrated in finished gasoline and fuel oils, and over 90% of manufacturing out-shipments from Wyoming are accounted for by these two commodities.

Patterns of population density also seem consistent with the estimated flows in Table XII. Illinois exports substantial tonnages of prepared animal feeds, gas, fuel oils and lesser amounts of flour and rolled steel mill products. Due to the more diversified manufacturing sector in Illinois (and the relatively concentrated population) much of the domestic production is also consumed within the state. For instance, Wyoming's production of fuel oils is projected at 8.8 million tons and its exports at 7.0 million tons; Illinois, conversely, exports less than Wyoming (5.5 million tons) but is predicted to produce about 29 million tons of fuel oils in 1980. The last two columns of Table XII show that Iowa, Missouri, North Dakota, South Dakota, Nebraska, Kansas, Montana, Wyoming and Colorado have excesses of exports over imports for all 19 commodities; only Minnesota, Illinois and Wisconsin are expected to import more than they export.

Table XIII shows the aggregated trade tonnages for all of the 19 commodities in the study. (Note that the normal Census regions have been redefined at the bottom of this table due to closer trade ties among some states for these commodities.) The dominance of

TABLE XIII

Intra- and Interregional Trade Flows For 1980[a]

Exports to: from:	North Central West	North Atlantic	North Central East	South Atlantic	South Central	West
(1) North Central West	220,324,948	27,704,401	53,163,982	18,897,721	41,638,373	63,827,117
(2) North Atlantic	4,907,703	157,707,689	10,258,112	25,588,685	2,855,139	12,668
(3) North Central East	9,119,028	5,420,569	2,113,567	10,498,024	4,617,042	991,730
(4) South Atlantic	4,203,154	79,747,998	140,819,964	152,362,095	30,048,254	---
(5) South Central	70,718,936	34,322,359	188,181,880	52,095,298	130,642,113	28,240,612
(6) West	24,405,035	---	22,668,740	---	1,761,927	121,302,013

[a] The regions are defined as: (1) North Central West: Minnesota, Iowa, Missouri, North Dakota, South Dakota, Nebraska, Kansas, Montana, Wyoming, Colorado, Illinois, Wisconsin; (2) North Central East: Ohio, Indiana, Michigan; (3) North Atlantic: Maine, New Hampshire, Vermont, Massachusetts, Rhode Island, Connecticut, New York, New Jersey, Pennsylvania; (4) South Atlantic: Delaware, Maryland, Virginia, West Virginia, North Carolina, South Carolina, Georgia, Florida; (5) South Central: Kentucky, Tennessee, Alabama, Mississippi, Arkansas, Louisiana, Oklahoma, Texas and (6) West: Idaho, New Mexico, Arizona, Utah, Nevada, Washington, Oregon, California.

intraregional trade for these larger regions is shown by the usually higher tonnages entered along the diagonals; only the three-state North Central Eastern region shows a substantial departure from this pattern. The principal characteristics of this table may be summarized as follows:

(1) Despite the regionally variant cost characteristics noted above, increasing distances tend to reduce the aggregate flows. The model provides no flow predictions for movements between states in the Western and South Atlantic regions; the West imports minor tonnages from the North Atlantic states but does not export these commodities to the Norh Atlantic region.

(2) Though some of the goods included in the study are manufactured, most of the major flows are from resource-based regions to industrialized states. The North Central East receives substantial shipments from the South Atlantic and South Central states; the North Atlantic region also receives more than it ships from states in the south. The principal trade flows from the North Central West are to the industrialized states in the North Central East and West.

(3) The principal flows from the northern regions tend to display some directional variation and are relatively small compared to the southern states. The major trading partners for the North Central West are directly east and west of this region with some flows through the Missouri and Mississippi basins to the South Central States. The North Atlantic exports to the North Central East but its major shipments go to the South Atlantic states. The industrial states of the North Central East ship minor (and roughly equal) tonnages to the North Central West and to the South Atlantic states.

(4) The major long distance hauls originate in the southern states. The South Atlantic exports substantial tonnages to northern states in the East and Midwest; somewhat smaller tonnages are outbound to the South Central states. The South Central states ship substantial tonnages northward to the North Central West and North Central East and somewhat lesser amounts to the South Atlantic, North Atlantic and Western states. The dominant regions (*i.e.*, those states with greater outbound than inbound shipments with other states) are mostly found in the southern parts of the United States.

The data summarized in Table XIII are aggregated from detailed flows matrices showing the 48 states as origins and destinations. These flows were then assigned to the principal river basin systems with navigable streams for estimating the potential traffic that might be expected to be carried by the inland barge mode. (The estimates are potential in the sense that no allowance is made for the inter-modal split between rail and barge.) These data provide helpful insights into the probable use of newly developed navigable portions of existing waterways, proposed canals, channel deepening and the locational patterns of terminal and transshipment facilities. The cost data could also be utilized to suggest the type of savings expected from improvements along particular navigable routes within the United States.

The data base developed in this study provides a consistent framework for analyzing commodity flows for all the contiguous states so that the spatial interdependence of production and consumptions locations can be allowed for. The objective is an analytical framework extending beyond the consideration of very restricted commodity movements within these subregions; this broadening of the spatial basis for planning is particularly important for commodities subject to the substantial long haul cost advantages afforded by water carrier.

CONCLUSIONS

In this chapter we have discussed some of the most difficult problems of interregional flow estimation facing the regional economist. In most countries the analyst must decide whether to utilize limited commodity flow information or attempt to estimate the underlying economic determinants of consumption, production and trade. Most commodity flow data are collected by mode only, so the true origins and destinations of these shipments may be estimated inaccurately. Sufficiently detailed and comprehensive data for estimating the underlying determinants of trade are infrequently available. In a statistically sophisticated country like the United States information on spatial commodity flows (along with land uses) is at a rudimentary state of development; even less is known about capital movements and human migration.

Studies of the type described in this chapter require the most detailed commodity and spatial disaggregation. The commonly used regional input-output model aggregates commodities within sectors, and inferences about real production are difficult, particularly for interregional models where price variations may be quite substantial. Trade flows emanate and terminate in locations much more diffuse spatially than can be estimated with current data; the distance matrix in the discussion of estimation techniques (p. 92) indicates the degree of spatial specialization found within subregions distinguished in this study. Transportation cost differences by commodity, region and direction of movement are even more variant for hauls of equal length, and numerous estimation difficulties arise in attempting to deal realistically with these differences. Competitive flows between coastal and Great Lakes states and foreign trade further complicate the problem of estimating interstate commodity movements; though port of entry or exit data are available even the immediate origins and destinations are not distinguished. Regional consumption patterns (particularly for the intermediate demands for goods) are infrequently estimated on an adequately comprehensive basis.

As suggested in previous chapters, the development of the interstate highways and technological advances in transportation systems have tended to promote long haul commodity trade and reduce interregional differences in industrial mixes and earnings. These long term developments underscore the need for adequately detailed models and data to guide the planning for these systems on a comprehensive spatial basis. The transportation economist faces numerous problems in dealing with interregional flows models, not the least of which is reconciling the rational cost-minimizing structure of programming with the array of inconsistencies in the rate setting and licensing procedures of the major regulated commercial transportation carriers. In few other problem areas in urban-regional economics are the disparities between theoretical structure and empirical reality so wide.

GENERAL REFERENCES

Cox, P. T., W. Grover, and B. Siskin. "Effects of Water Resource Investments on Economic Growth," *Water Resour. Res.* 7:32–39, 1971.

Davis, H. C. *Economic Evaluation of Water, Part V: Multiregional Input-Output Techniques and Western Water Resources Development*, Water Resources Center Contribution No. 125 (Berkeley: Sanitary Engineering Research Laboratory, University of California, February 1968).

Garrison, C. B. *Effect of Water Resources on Economic Growth in the Tennessee Valley Region* (Knoxville: Department of Economics, University of Tennessee, 1971).

Howe, C. W. "Water and Regional Economic Growth in the United States," *Southern Econ. J.* **29**, 4: 477–499, 1968.

Howe, C. W., and W. K. Easter. *Interbasin Transfers of Water*: *Economic Issues and Impacts* (Baltimore: The Johns Hopkins Press, 1971).

Kneese, A. V. and S. C. Smith (Eds.), *Water Research* (Baltimore: The Johns Hopkins Press, 1966).

Leven, C. L. "A Framework for the Evaluation of Secondary Impacts of Public Investment," *Amer. J. Agric. Econ.*, **52**:723–729, 1970.

Leven, C. L. (Ed.), *Development Benefits of Water Resource Investments* (Springfield, Va.: Clearinghouse for Federal Scientific and Technical Information, 1969).

Leven, C. L., and R. B. Read. *A River, a Region and a Research Problem* (Alexandria, Va.: U.S. Army Engineer Institute for Water Resources, 1971).

Lewis, W. C. "Public Investment Impacts and Regional Economic Growth," *Water Resour. Res.* **9**:851–860, 1973.

Lewis, W. C. et.al. *Regional Growth and Water Resource Investment* (Lexington, Massachusetts: D.C. Heath—Lexington Books, 1973).

Lofting, E. M., and P. H. McGauhey. *Economic Evaluation of Water, Part III*: *An Interindustry Analysis of the California Water Economy*, Water Resources Center Contribution No. 67 (Berkeley: Sanitary Engineering Research Laboratory, University of California, January 1963).

Prescott, J. R. "Potential Water-borne Commerce in the United States," *Report for the U.S. Corps of Engineers*, Kansas City, Missouri, 1968.

Tolley, G. S. (Ed.), *Estimation of First Round and Selected Subsequent Income Effects of Water Resource Investment* (Springfield, Va.: Clearinghouse for Federal Scientific and Technical Information, 1970).

5

Interurban Earnings Differentials Metropolitan Planning and

At the apex of the city size hierarchy are the very largest metropolitan regions; centrality and a rich array of land uses are the most evident characteristics of these regions. The CBD specializes as a high density employment center providing high and low-order services both for regional residents and for export. Interspersed with these employment activities are townhouses and apartment buildings housing the higher income residents of the central city. Less central locations include the older multi and single family residential neighborhoods with smaller retailing centers and public schools. These localized residential communities often include the city's lowest income households and the highest ethnic concentrations within the region. On the fringes of the city residential and employment densities decline to the recently incorporated suburban communities that house the higher income commuters traveling daily to the CBD. Shopping centers provide retail goods and services to suburban residents, and lower land prices and property taxes attract manufacturing firms to industrial parks on the periphery.

The diversity of economic and residentiary activity within the city complicates the planning function of metropolitan governments. The capital-intensive structure of the CBD precludes comprehensive redesign of transportation arterials and encourages the more efficient use of narrow downtown streets. Freeways surrounding the CBD must be adapted to the changing residentiary densities occurring within the city and in the peripheral suburban communities; the construction of new transportation linkages creates a diversity of site value changes for both firms and households. The construction of new schools must be planned with the shifting pattern of residential densities in mind; a number of municipally provided services (police and fire protection, refuse collection, etc.) must also be locationally sensitive to the changing spatial patterns of productive and residentiary activity. These and other planning functions of urban governments may be substantially facilitated by models designed to estimate sectoral levels of economic activity and population over time. The linear simulation model is a particularly flexible tool for analyzing economic growth within the larger metropolitan regions.

Among cities of alternative sizes, economists have also been concerned with the growth implications of money and real earnings differentials. The higher money earnings and amenities of large cities are offset by lower real incomes and the external costs of air pollution and traffic congestion. These trade-offs can be expected to influence firm and household migration among cities along the size spectra and, hence, the size distribution of urban places. Manufacturing employment growth among cities of various sizes is a particularly important sector since it tends to encourage high employment densities and the associated difficulties of air pollution and transit planning; smaller cities may benefit from the higher-than-average earnings paid by most manufacturing firms.

The purpose of this chapter is to describe models designed to facilitate sectoral planning within metropolitan areas and analyze the implications of manufacturing earnings differentials among cities of various sizes. The structure and design of metropolitan simulation models is the subject of the first section. An empirical application for the Des Moines region is then described. A model of interurban earnings differentials is discussed in the next section; the focus of this model is on the implications of earnings differentials for the supply and demand for labor in cities of varying sizes. Some empirical tests are then described, and a concluding section summarizes the discussion of the chapter.

A SIMULATION MODEL OF METROPOLITAN REGIONS

The model described in this section is designed to provide a continuous projections capability for an eight-county metropolitan area centered on Des Moines, Iowa; the emphasis of this section is on the characteristics of the region, their implications for model design and the overall structure of the model itself. This metropolitan area comprises a central county (Polk) and seven contiguous counties that are members of the Central Iowa Regional Planning Commission

(CIRPC). The latter was the first multicounty planning unit established under enabling legislation passed by the Iowa legislature in 1967; these units are responsible for coordinating the planning of public services logically transcending the boundaries of a single county.

As a relatively self-contained economic community, several features of the region influenced the model's structure. First, the inclusion of hinterland communities increases the variance in the region's demographic and employment characteristics. As a nodal region this is apparent with respect to agricultural activity conducted in noncentral counties and the employment profiles of smaller towns suggested by central place theory; the periphery becomes the site of major export activity interspersed with small suburban communities. There is also a tendency for the latter to specialize in particular services accentuating the variation in these characteristics among peripheral counties; towns dominated by universities, government research organizations, state agencies and single plants are examples in the CIRPC region. Six counties, for example, experienced net out-migrant rates varying from —13.2% to —6.2% (1950–60) despite an overall population growth rate of 12.4% for this decade. Boone County in the northwest section of the region had a substantial proportion of retired households resulting in a —0.4% rate of population growth for the period 1950–60, due largely to a particularly low rate of natural increase. These variations in population characteristics suggest the need for a similarly disaggregated age-specific demographic sector within the model.

Second, since this metropolitan region includes an important (but fluctuating) agricultural sector and produces a relatively full range of goods and services for the resident population, the model should allow for the impacts of output changes on investment and alternative sectoral allocations of economic activity. Major shifts in economic activity in the CIRPC region occurred during the 1950–60 decade; agricultural employment fell by 32% and substantial employment increases were experienced in the printing-publishing and finance-real estate sectors. New capital expenditures in manufacturing fell by 35% (1958–63) despite an increase in manufacturing value-added of 22%; service establishments and sales rose by 18 and 45%, respectively, over the same period.

The CIRPC region is characterized by relatively equal accessibility of the peripheral counties to the center (Polk County); Figure 6 shows the eight-county area and the spatial distribution of its

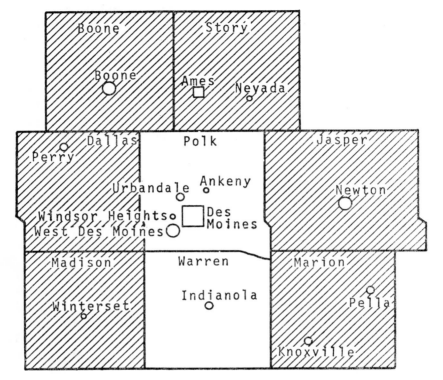

Figure 6: The CIRPC region and major municipalities.

Legend: (population)

☐ 250,000 or more

☐ 25,000-30,000   Shaded counties experienced

○ 10,000-20,000   net out-migration from

○ 5,000- 9,999   1950–1960.

° 2,500- 4,999

principal towns. The even distribution of counties in a regular north-south, east-west configuration of roads, defines Iowa's labor markets as diamond-shaped regions connecting central cities with approximate 50–60 minute auto commuting points along peripheral boundaries. In the CIRPC region this is modified to the extent that major inter-state arterials crossing at Des Moines somewhat reduce commuting times in the direct north-south and east-west directions; the completion of the northern corridor from Des Moines to Ames, for example, reduced the 35 mile trip-time by about 19%. Equal accessibility contours would in this case more closely resemble a four-pointed star. Also due to the substantially independent growth characteristics of Marshall County (directly northeast of Polk County in Figure 6) it has been excluded from the region. Aside from these characteristics, the region is quite spatially homogeneous, possessing a well-developed central urban area experiencing immediately contiguous suburban growth and a fairly regular hierarchy of peripheral communities servicing an agricultural economic base and often specializing in other regional services.

Figure 7 is a flowchart of the simulation model designed for the CIRPC region and indicates the principal interrelationships among the disaggregated subsectors; the latter include separate demographic, employment, output, final demand and capital models. The overall model contains 54 linear equations arranged in a recursive sequence; the computer model is somewhat expanded due to the separate treatment of six age groups in the demographic model and 17 industrial sectors in the output and capital models. Though primary data are always desirable in estimating a model's equations, secondary data sources are sufficient so empirical applications may be extended readily to other metropolitan regions. The coefficients are fixed though the presence of intersectoral regression linkages renders it readily adaptable to stochastic simulation.

From the flowchart the model's principal flows are as follows. The demographic sector accounts for total population, births and deaths by age group. Labor force participation rates determine the available labor force and the employment sector estimates the labor force required to produce industrial outputs from both local and exogenous requirements. An additional migration linkage connects the employment and demographic sectors; migration is in part dependent on unemployment rates that are endogenously determined. Productivity changes are accounted for by output/employee ratios by industrial sector, which also convert outputs to required labor force. Outputs are calculated in an input-output model and three of the final demand sectors (households, state/local and federal governmental purchases) are linked to population changes in the demographic sector. Ratio coefficients connect the capital and output sectors; annual changes in the gross capital stock provide a measure of gross investment in each industrial sector. The latter also provides a linkage between the capital sector and capital accumulation as final

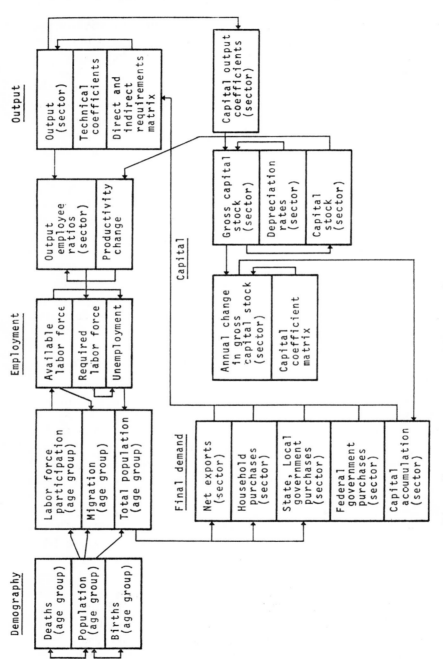

Figure 7: Flowchart of the CIRPC regional simulation model.

demand which influences output and investment. The following sections describe the major sectors in more detail.

Demography

The demographic sector includes a modified cohort-survival model differentiating the following six age groups: 0–13, 14–19, 20–24, 25–44, 45–64 and 65+ years. Birth rates (and their trends over time) are calculated for the four middle age groups and children accrue to group one initially; death rates show substantially less variation and are held constant for all six age groups over the estimation period. The population grows out of the first five groups at a yearly average rate and the sixth group is terminated at death. Migration equations determine either gross or net flows in the five oldest age groups. These migrants are parents and bring with them an average number of children per individual by age group; the oldest age group is assumed not to have children in the 0–13 age cohort. The region's birth rate is applied to the in-migrants as well as those leaving the area due to difficulties in determining origins.

Studies generally suggest that migration is largely determined by measures of employment scale or availability. In this model these variables or close surrogates are used in regression analyses for each age group based on cross section data for 60 State Economic Areas in the midwestern states; two characteristics of these regressions are noted. (1) Unemployment rates did not generally explain much of the variation in migration. Additional internal linkages were provided by allowing available labor force variables to influence migraton in the 20–24 and 65+ age classes. These variables provided a stronger equilibrating relationship and the unemployment rate was bounded to values historically observed within the CIRPC region. (2) The final equations chosen for the model indicated generally improved regression statistics for age-specific population or available labor force variables in the older age classes; the exceptions are in the two cohorts spanning ages 20–44 in which the aggregate available labor force variable was used. (A similar improvement might be made by using age-differentiated unemployment rates, but this was not possible with available data.) These results are at least consistent with the hypothesis that aging itself significantly reduces the age-specific characteristics which influence migration.

With the exception of birth rates most of the demographic characteristics in the CIRPC region have remained stable over time, although variable among sub-regions. The Iowa birth rate fell from 24 to 18 live births per thousand over the period 1959 to 1966; though this is usually attributed to birth control it is interesting that both marriage and illegitimate birth rates have also risen over this period within the state. Though these influences cannot be directly incorporated into this model, exogenous trends in birth rates are allowed for in the experimental runs. (The equational relationships discussed above are provided in an appendix to the Prescott reference.)

Employment

The available labor force is attained by applying labor force participation rates to the population in each age class; outputs are converted to labor requirements through productivity coefficients, and an unemployment rate is determined by confronting labor supplies with demand. Though a capital sector is included in this model, productivity changes occur wholly through changes in output per worker.

Labor force participation rates for the region vary significantly from nationally observed trends. For ages 14–24 the United States (1950–60) figures decline at annual rates of about —0.0045; the comparable Iowa rate is 0.0013. This is probably due to the large net outflows of younger persons continuing their education out-of-state. In the two oldest groups the rate of increase is faster (or in the case of persons 65+ years in age the decline is slower) in the region than for the entire United States, reflecting the lower rates of retirement in the agricultural sector. The occupation-industrial mix of the regional labor force may have substantial effects on the labor participation rate within these regions and should be carefully estimated.

Disparate rates of productivity increase have also caused locational imbalances between the central county and periphery within the CIRPC region. Agricultural productivity increases of about 6.1% annually have been absorbed principally by the slower growth sectors of trade, finance-real estate and services; the latter have experienced annual productivity increases of about 1.6, 1.3 and 1.0% respectively. Though some dispersal of manufacturing jobs is evident in the region, substantial productivity increases and an actual decline in the number of establishments over the period 1958–63 meant relatively lower rates of absorption in these sectors. There is also some evidence that the average scale of manufacturing firm has increased, suggesting that the job creation that has occurred may have been concentrated within the central county. (See Table XIV for the sectoral statistics.)

Output

The output sector is based on a disaggregated 17 sector input-output model in order to reflect the diversity of productive activities in most metropolitan regions; this permits a more flexible analysis of intersectoral allocations of economic activity than is possible with the more frequently used export base regression models. Total outputs are developed from employment and productivity data, and inter-industry allocations are based in part on an aggregation of the U.S. Department of Commerce's 82 sector direct requirements table.

TABLE XIV

Sectoral Output and Productivity, CIRPC Region, 1960

Sector	Area Employment (%)	Output Per Worker ($)	Total Output (%)	Annual Rate of Change in Output/ Worker (%)
(1) Agriculture	9.4	10,505	8.4	6.1
(2) Construction, mining	6.1	17,180	9.0	2.3
(3) Food, kindred	3.3	42,771	12.0	3.1
(4) Textile products	0.4	10,616	0.4	3.1
(5) Printing, publishing	3.4	13,473	3.9	3.1
(6) Chemicals	0.3	49,747	1.7	3.1
(7) Other nondurables	2.3	11,430	2.2	3.1
(8) Furniture, wood	0.5	14,159	0.6	3.1
(9) Primary metals	1.6	13,777	1.8	3.3
(10) Machinery	3.3	21,507	6.0	3.3
(11) Electrical machinery	2.3	10,880	2.1	3.3
(12) Other durables	1.4	14,008	1.6	3.4
(13) Transportation	3.8	13,851	4.5	2.9
(14) Communications	3.1	12,831	3.4	6.5
(15) Trade	19.2	5,817	9.6	1.6
(16) Finance	6.9	30,996	18.3	1.3
(17) Services	23.2	6,592	13.2	1.0

Table XIV shows the sectors selected for the model, their relative importance in the region and the productivity changes noted above. Agriculture accounts for about 8–9% of total regional activity depending on whether output or employment is used as the appropriate measure; trade and services are the largest sectors within the region. Finance, real estate and insurance is also an important activity in the region accounting for about 7% of employment and 18% of regional output. Productivity increases have generally been more rapid in the durable goods manufacturing sectors; overall rates of productivity increase in manufacturing are in the range of 3.1 to 3.4%.

Final Demand

The five final demand sectors allow for the full distribution of regional gross outputs and also appear as payments sectors providing inputs to producing industries. Net exports is the only completely exogenous sector and is estimated by the method of location quotients; the nation, Midwest or state is used for spatial comparisons to the region depending on the market area of the particular sector. Households purchase goods and services from regional residents and are paid wages, salaries, interest and dividends by purchasing industries and other final demand sectors. The two governmental sectors also purchase regionally produced goods and services receiving taxes, fees and fines for government services. In these sectors exogenous trends in per capita purchases are calculated and regional purchases are estimated from population data provided by the demographic sector.

Capital formation refers to inventory accrual (as a purchasing sector) and the approximate cost of plant and equipment utilized in the production of goods and services (as a payments sector). New capital formation values are determined each year in the model by changes in the size of the gross capital stock by industrial sector and an accelerator relation connecting changes in the capital stock to changes in output. This component of final demand therefore differs from the previously discussed sectors in that changes are endogenously determined and there is no direct linkage with the demographic sector.

Capital

A matrix of capital coefficients provides the means of distributing investment purchases for a particular sector to all other sectors.

These coefficients show, for example, that for every dollar invested in agriculture about 35% is spent for purchases for construction and mining, 44% from machinery and the balance from other sectors. Gross investments are constrained to non-negative values but plant depletion may occur after allowances for depreciation. The capital equations relate gross capital stock (by sector) to lagged outputs and apply depreciation rates to the gross stock estimates to calculate the net capital stock by industrial sector.

ILLUSTRATIVE EMPIRICAL APPLICATION: THE IOWA CIRPC REGION

The model's structure is illustrated by an analysis of simulations based on alternative assumptions regarding plausible exogenous changes affecting the region. These alternatives are compared to a base run that incorporates neutral (*i.e.*, observed) rates of change in the exogenous variables and fixed coefficients in the major matrices and regression relationships. The model has been tested under seven alternative conditions over a twenty-year period and monitored at five-year intervals. These runs show in each of the three five-year projection periods characteristics of growth and variance for the major projected variables, which are summarized at the end of this section.

Base Run

The following assumptions were incorporated in the base run. (1) Birth rates were held constant at 1960 levels while death rates were allowed to decline at 1950–60 rates. (The death rate tends to decline at historically steady rates while the birth rate changes during the 1960's are incorporated into an experimental run described below.) (2) State-estimated trends are used for labor force participation, output per worker and purchases by households and governmental sectors. (3) Net export growth is related to estimated population growth rates in the region. (4) The matrices for total requirements, capital-output coefficients and depreciation rates are fixed over the simulation period; regression linkages among sectors remain similarly unchanged.

Figure 8 summarizes the principal demographic changes calculated under base run assumptions. The total population rose at somewhat lower rates than 1950–60 during the first ten years and recovered somewhat during the 1970–80 period. The younger age groups grew

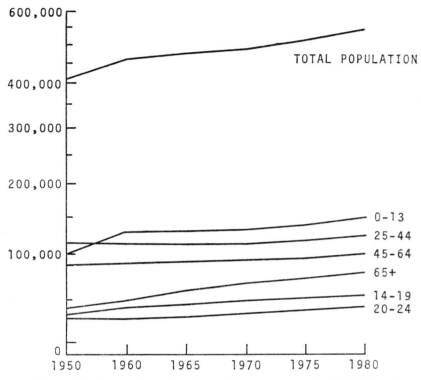

Figure 8: Population (total and by age group), CIRPC region, 1960–80.

at lower (or observed 1950–60) rates due to the lower birth rates used in the base run. Though the population in the 20–24 age group had been declining the model generates sufficient economic growth (primarily through rising levels of net exports, household and governmental purchases) to reverse this trend after 1965. The 45–64 year age group increased only 6.5% over the twenty-year period but the number of retired persons rose substantially; this effect was due to the initial size of the preretirement group and declining death rates. Growth under the base run assumptions was sufficient to generate net in-migration for all age groups.

Some of the principal economic aggregates are depicted in Figures 9 and 10. Though total employment increases by about 32% over the projections period, intersectoral shifts in economic activity continue to occur. Despite a doubling of agricultural output, employment in

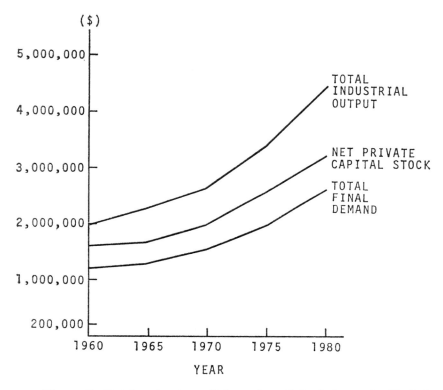

Figure 9: Total output, capital stock and final demand, CIRPC region, 1960–80.

this sector drops by approximately 5,000 workers. All manufacturing sectors show output increases but have relatively small changes in total employment; printing-publishing and nonelectrical machinery employment actually declined. The noncommodity sectors continue to absorb employment shifts occurring in other primary and secondary sectors. Increases in final demands (dominated primarily by household purchases) generate similar trends in total industrial outputs and the net private capital stock. Total capital formation for industrial sectors declined from 1960–70, increasing sharply thereafter. During the first decade the regional economy was not expanding rapidly enough to encourage increasing amounts of gross investment; this was due in part to sharply reduced levels of new capital expenditures over the period 1958–63. These results are the basis for com-

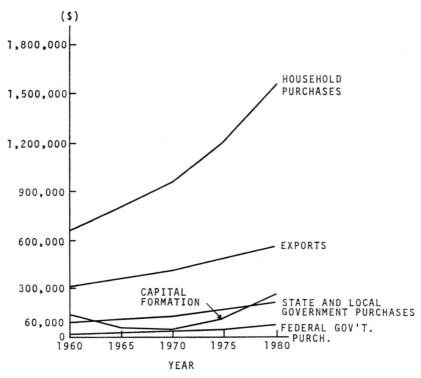

Figure 10: Final demand components, CIRPC region, 1960–80.

paring computer runs incorporating the following alternative assumptions.

National Rates of Labor Force Participation

The strength of national trends in labor force participation (particularly in reduced rates for younger age cohorts) suggests that observed state trends might be reversed. National projections by the U.S. Department of Labor replace regional rates used in the base run. The effect of reduced rates in younger age groups is to reduce the number of persons seeking employment, which tends to hold unemployment rates at levels generally lower than in the base run. The lower unemployment rates ultimately increase in-migration, population and employment to 1980 levels exceeding those in the base run calculations. Since the older age group is less sensitive to changes in unemployment rates, the working age population increases at faster rates.

The somewhat larger population generates output and employment increases (with derived effects on the capital stock) through changes in final demands. Output for each industrial sector is projected at higher levels but the total increase in output is estimated at only about $245,000 greater than the base run level. Though activity levels are all increased, the changes exceed those of the base run only marginally.

Birth Rate Changes

Two runs incorporate birth rate changes. The first utilizes rising birth rates observed over the 1950–60 period in the region and the second uses 1960 and 1965 average rates of decline by age group. In both cases adjustments are made in the average number of children reflecting the increase (decrease) in this variable expected from rising (declining) birth rates. Increasing birth rates result ultimately in increased population, output and employment; the demand effects outweigh labor supply changes reducing unemployment and mildly inducing in-migration. Final demands, investment and capital stock increase, and substantial employment increases in trade and services occur in order to serve the larger population. The opposite reactions are applicable to the case of declining birth rates.

The effects of birth rate changes are among the most important simulated over the projections period. Rising birth rates result in a population approximately 17% higher than in the base run; in the declining birth rate case the population falls by 8.4%. In both cases these effects are naturally felt in the younger age classes, substantially altering the age distribution of the population. Final demand, output and capital formation are the highest of all simulation runs in the rising birth rate case; the effect of falling births is somewhat less extreme but does result in the second lowest level of employment of all the alternatives considered.

Productivity Change

As indicated above intersectoral reallocations of economic activity have implications for variant rates of growth in the metropolitan center and peripheral counties. To test for the effects of these reallocations the annual changes in output per worker are adjusted upward for agriculture (to 7.0%) and downward for the trade, finance and services sectors (to 0.5%). The workers displaced from agriculture are absorbed into the service industries; total employment is about 24% higher compared to the base run in the terminal year of the simulation. In the long run population is approximately the same as that experienced under the rising birth rate computer run but with a noticeably larger concentration in the 25–44 year age group. The latter is partially due to the net positive effect on labor demand reducing unemployment rates and inducing in-migration of workers in their most productive years. Agricultural employment is reduced by about a third; employment increases in the other sectors by 43% (trade), 29% (finance, insurance, real estate) and 26% (services). The increases in employment, output and final demand rank closely to those changes under the increasing birth rate simulation.

Export Change

The CIRPC region has for some time been a center for insurance and other financial institutions; this sector is a major exporter in the model. Estimates indicate that rates of net export increases are in the neighborhood of 3.7%, and to assess the impact of lesser growth rates for this important sector the rate is reduced to 1.3%. The result is a 1980 employment estimate for this sector about 19% below that of the base run and somewhat smaller employment reductions in other sectors. The relatively high unemployment rates tend to retard net in-migration, population growth and final demand. Output, capital formation and total final demands are estimated at levels slightly lower than in the declining birth rate case.

Per Capita Final Demand

A final run adjusted growth rates in the household and governmental sectors to partially test for the effects of policy changes in the region. The following assumptions are made: (1) annual increases in federal purchases from the transportation sector are reduced from 6.19 to 3.10%, (2) annual increases in state and local purchases from the nondurable sector are reduced from 3.60 to 1.78% and (3) annual increases in household purchases from the finance sector are reduced from 6.56 to 3.28%. The results show population and output declining by 5.4 and 15.0%, respectively, relative to base run levels. Lower output results in higher unemployment rates and out-migration. Total output, employment and capital formation are estimated in 1980 to be the lowest of all simulation experiments.

The experiments described above are illustrative of the model's capabilities in providing disaggregated projections for the metropolitan region centered on Des Moines; they are clearly not exhaustive with respect to all possible regional futures and have not included cyclical or highly interdependent variable changes. An analysis of the coefficients of variation of the principal demographic and economic aggregates showed a steady increase over time for most experimental computer runs; exceptions included capital formation due to the accelerator assumption incorporated in this sector and birth rate changes that increased the variation in population estimates for the younger age cohorts among all computer experiments. Though there are qualitative differences in the assumptions underlying each run, an equal number of optimistic and pessimistic simulations were attempted. The annual average changes from 1970–80 indicate a generally improved growth future for the region; growth in output (6.8%), employment (3.2%) and population (1.4%) all exceeded similar indicators for the 1950–60 period.

Linear simulation models provide a particularly useful way of analyzing employment and population changes in metropolitan areas and their resultant impacts on the demand for public services. Water requirements can be estimated directly from the disaggregated interindustry model and total population. The age cohorts within the demographic sector provide data relevant to planning in recreation, parks, education and medical services. The use of secondary county data also extends the number of empirical applications possible with the model described above. Of all the different types of large scale urban models currently available, it seems likely that urban planners and decision-makers will find the disaggregated linear model most useful as a basis for assessing the probable patterns of future urban growth.

A MODEL OF INTERURBAN EARNINGS DIFFERENTIALS

Among urban areas, economists have been concerned with the effects of observed differentials in the return to labor. The positive correlation between city size and money wage rates has undoubtedly been a contributing factor to the redistribution of both the population and employment opportunities among urban places. Population migration may operate to equalize real wage rates, and money wage differentials should result in some decentralization of employment opportunities as firms weigh the production cost advantages of locating in low wage cities against the increased cost of product distribution and input procurement. Neither the migration of households or firms may be fluidly accomplished, however. Spatial immobilities and adverse expectations regarding employment opportunities at the destination city may lower the migratory response of families. Larger cities may be more efficient in the sense that agglomeration economies reduce business service costs to firms or provide sufficiently large labor markets to reduce the costs of adjusting to short run changes in production.

Though many influences have been suggested most of the previous literature on this subject may be usefully dichotomized as to its primary focus on the supply or demand for labor:

(1) Interurban productivity differentials may be reflected in the demographic composition of the resident labor force. Earlier research emphasized the age, racial, labor force and educational characteristics of the city's population in explaining interurban family income differentials. Though variables such as the percentage of nonelderly population and percentage of labor force in manufacturing tend to be positively associated with average income levels, these studies tended to be largely descriptive. Much of the variation remains unexplained, particularly when the data are adjusted for city size differences.

(2) Variations in labor demand may arise from industry/ occupational mix differentials expected in cities of alternative sizes and systematic differences in the scale of firm and factor proportions utilized in various manufacturing industries. Central place concepts suggest the concentration in larger cities of higher paid service and professional employees. Plant size and the proportion of the labor force that is unionized may be expected to influence wage differentials among manufacturing industries. Firms capable of substituting capital for labor may also be expected to locate within the larger metropolitan regions.

Several characteristics of this earlier research should be noted. (1) Existing studies usually treat the firm's demand for labor as independent of the city's proximity to regional markets for its output. As a major export sector, manufacturing firms have spatially distinct markets for products and labor so the delivered price of output will be influenced by factors affecting transportation costs. The effect of locational isolation on the city's mix of industrial activity (and hence on average earnings) may constrain the degree to which interurban earnings differentials may be narrowed. (2) Most studies have **disregarded** the separate factors influencing the demand and supply for labor and their relation to regression coefficients relating earnings to city size and the other explanatory variables that are suggested above. The objective of this section is to interpret such coefficients within the context of the labor supply and demand model and assess their consistency from regression estimates derived from a large sample of manufacturing industries.

The following model shows that, under assumed conditions, the wage differential between two cities is an increasing function of differences in the capital/labor ratio and a declining function of the differences in per unit transportation costs between the cities and a common market center m. The two cities are termed the central city c and a peripheral town p, and the following assumptions are made.

(1) Industry firms in both cities manufacture a homogeneous product under identical production conditions that exhibit constant returns to scale; hence,

$$X_i = F\ (K_i,\ L_i) \tag{44}$$
$$i = c,\ p$$

where X, K and L represent output, capital and labor respectively.

(2) Within each city the labor supply curve is an increasing function of the money wage rate w_i and population P_i where the latter is a shift parameter; so

$$L_{si} = h(w_i) + b_k(P_i) \tag{45}$$

where $dh/dw_i > 0$, $b_k > 0$. Each city constitutes a separate labor market so there is some degree of spatial immobility attributable to the labor force; workers do not migrate to take advantage of modest wage differentials between cities c and p.

(3) The price received per unit of output P_i^o is at least as great in the central city as in the peripheral town. Typically the price received is equal to the market price P^m less the cost of transporting the product to market T_i. As city m may be either a transshipment point or major final market for output, the firm ships most of its output at positive cost. Assuming the central city is closer to the market center, $T_c \leqslant T_p$ which implies that

$$P_c^o\ (= P^m - T_c) > P_p^o\ (= P^m - T_p) \tag{46}$$

(4) The labor demand function in each city L_{Di} is given by the product of the output price received and the marginal product of labor. Due to the linear homogeneity assumption the production function is

$$X_i = L_i \cdot F(K_i/L_i, \ 1) \tag{47}$$
$$i = c, \ p$$

Denoting the capital/labor ratio as r_i and $F(K_i/L_i, 1)$ as $f(r_i)$, the marginal product of labor is given by

$$
\begin{aligned}
dX_i/dL_i &= f(r_i) + L_i \cdot d/dr_i[f(r_i)] \cdot d/dL_i(r_i) \\
&= f(r_i) + L_i \cdot d/dr_i[f(r_i)] \ (-K_i/L_i^2) \\
&= f(r_i) - r_i \cdot d/dr_i[f(r_i)] = q \ (r_i)
\end{aligned}
\tag{48}
$$

From Equations 46 and 48 the labor demand functions for both cities may be written as

$$L_{Di} = P_i^o \cdot g(r_i) + b_1 P_i \tag{49}$$

where $b_1 > 0$, where population is again assumed to be a shift parameter. Note that this specification allows for the effects of services in larger cities that are complementary with the basic productive factors in addition to the impacts of population growth on the firm's sales in local markets. The local price of output is important in considering the spatial distribution of the firm's sales, but does not include the various efficiencies of city size often referred to in the literature on wage differentials.

Equating Equations 45 and 49 the money wage is

$$w_i = h^{-1}[P_i^o \cdot g(r_i) + P_i \ (b_1 - b_k)] \tag{50}$$
$$i = c, \ p$$

As $h'(w_i) > 0$ the inverse function h^{-1} is positively related to the output price received P_i^o, the capital/labor ratio r_i and the effect of local population growth on the demand for output, $(P_i \cdot b_1)$; local population is also a source of labor supply exerting a negative impact on the money wage. For both cities the wage differential is

$$
\begin{aligned}
w_c - w_p = h^{-1}[P_c^o \cdot g(r_c) - P_p^o \cdot g(r_p) - b_k(P_c - P_p) + \\
b_1 \ (P_c - P_p)]
\end{aligned}
\tag{51}
$$

and substituting Equation 46 and defining $P_d = (P_c - P_p)$ we have

$$w_c - w_p = h^{-1}[(P^m - T_c) \cdot g(r_c) - (P^m - T_p) \cdot g(r_p) + (b_1 - b_k) \, P_d] \tag{52}$$

From Equation 52 the signs of the partial changes in the wage differential with respect to the principal variables of interest are:

$$\frac{d\,(w_c - w_p)}{d\,(r_c - r_p)} > 0 \qquad\qquad \frac{d\,(w_c - w_p)}{d\,(T_c - T_p)} < 0$$

$$\frac{d\,(w_c - w_p)}{d\,P_d} \gtrless 0 \qquad \text{as} \quad b_1 \gtrless b_k$$

Several properties of the model should be noted:

(1) For cities of equal size, $P_c = P_p$ and wage differentials arise solely from differences in transport costs and capital/labor ratios. Though central place theory suggests that $T_c = T_p$ in this case, we suspect that wage differentials may be substantial even for cities of equal size.

(2) In the pure export case where firms are entirely resource-oriented, $b_1 = 0$ and hence the population and wage differentials are inversely related. This result may be expected for specialized, resource-oriented firms found in the smaller cities.

(3) If firms serve local markets only, then $T_c = T_p = 0$ and the wage differential is a function of local output prices and capital/labor ratios in the two cities. The local price of output is then a function of demand variables such as income and the prices of other commodities sold locally. In a sample of manufacturing firms this case may be expected for smaller, nonspecialized firms in the very largest metropolitan regions.

(4) When the two cities are within the same commuting radius, then $T_c = T_p$ and the relevant population for both the local demand and supply effects is $(P_c + P_p)$. The labor immobility assumption is violated and the effects of competition within the same labor market should reduce the wage differential to zero. The sampled cities should be sufficiently large to insure that independent labor markets are represented.

(5) Finally, it is suspected that the b_1 and b_k are not constants among cities of different sizes. For a firm of given scale the ratio of

its labor force to population declines with rising city size, and it is likely that the ratio of locally marketed output to population also increases. (The latter is less clear since larger cities provide numerous locational advantages unrelated to size of market alone.) Though the data are for SMSA's, substantially different coefficients on the population variable may be expected for samples of smaller cities.

From the previous studies summarized above our interest is primarily in the combination of forces influencing the equilibrium money wage in each city. Hence our hypothesis may be directly tested by ordinary least squares regression methods; for a given industry the estimated equation is

$$W_i = f(P_i, S_i, K_i/L_i \ D_i) \tag{53}$$

where S_i is a scale variable, D_i is a distance-to-market proxy for transportation costs and, as above, i indexes cities in the sample. To test this hypothesis the following data were collected from a sample of 104 Standard Metropolitan Statistical Areas randomly drawn from those SMSA's defined as of 1960.

(1) Wage rates (W_i): annual production worker wages divided by the number of production workers, 1963.

(2) Population (P_i): population of Standard Metropolitan Statistical Area, 1960.

(3) Employment per establishment (S_i): number of production workers divided by the number of establishments with payroll, 1963.

(4) Capital/labor ratio (K_i/L_i): value added by manufacturing minus payrolls to all employees, divided by production worker man-hours, 1963.

(5) Distance (D_i): highway mileage from the SMSA to major regional market center.

With the exception of variables (4) and (5) above the data warrant little explanation. Measures of the capital/labor ratio in manufacturing industries by SMSA are virtually nonexistent. (The capital stock data reported in the 1958 Census of Manufacturer is given only for states on a two-digit basis and serious questions have been raised regarding its quality.) For our regressions a proxy for the capital/labor ratio is estimated by assuming that the portion of value added not attributable to labor accrues to a broadly defined stock of capital (*i.e.*, all nonlabor inputs). The ratio is estimated by subtracting all wage income from value added and dividing this figure by production worker man-hours; the result is a measure of the nonwage returns per hour of labor input.

Due to the scale of cities included in the sample only six regional market centers are selected; these include the four major coastal cities that represent substantial domestic markets and are important ports for international shipments (New York, Atlanta, Los Angeles and Seattle). Chicago and Dallas–Ft. Worth are market destinations for the smaller SMSAs located in the nation's hinterland. Reasonable geographic representation is favored since the sample is not spatially stratified; size of SMSA alone would tend to overestimate west to east shipment distances due to concentrated populations on the eastern seaboard. The highway distance from each SMSA to the closest of these centers is taken as a proxy variable for measuring contiguity to final (or intermediate) markets.

EMPIRICAL ESTIMATES OF THE INTERURBAN MODEL

To test for the positive relation between average earnings and city size, wage differentials were calculated by industry and the five urban classes shown in Table XV. (The overall sample and industry averages are shown in row 1 and rows 2–20, respectively. The row ranges are shown on the extreme right-hand side and the column ranges for industries are entered at the bottom of the table.) Several characteristics of this table should be noted.

(1) For production workers the earnings advantage of the largest cities is not offset by uniformly lower earnings in the smallest urban size class. Though the all-industry range is substantial ($1147 in row 1) and is calculated from the extreme population classes, there is a negative differential between city classes II and III. The industry data show a tendency for the largest cities to have the highest average earnings, but numerous departures from perfect monotonicity between rising wages and city size class are apparent. The highest average earnings are found in 16 of 20 rows for class V and lowest earnings are distributed as follows: I (5), II (2), III (10), IV (3) and V (0). About 34% of the 65 calculable earnings differentials in Table XV are negative.

(2) Urban size itself does not appear to significantly influence the average interindustry differential or the extreme low and high paying industries that would influence the city's average wage. The lowest and highest interindustry differentials are for city classes I and II; the low differential for the smallest class ($2410 at the bottom of Table XV) is influenced by the restricted range of industries likely

TABLE XV

Differential Annual Wage by Industry and Population Class of City

Industry (Observations)	Population Size Class					Range of Mean Annual Wage by Industry ($) (highest - lowest)
	I less than 100,000	II 100,000-249,999	III 250,000-499,999	IV 500,000-999,999	V over 1,000,000	
(1) All industries	-	715	-217	355	297	1147 (V-I)
(2) Food, kindred (86)	-	312	22	392	602	1328 (V-I)
(3) Textile mill products (30)	-	127	-84	385	281	709 (V-I)
(4) Apparel (44)	*	-	8	-3	558	563 (V-II)
(5) Lumber, wood (46)	*	-	323	791	-72	1114 (IV-II)
(6) Furniture, fixtures (42)	*	-	-67	348	255	603 (V-III)
(7) Paper and allied (40)	*	-	287	70	486	713 (II-III)
(8) Printing, publishing (66)	*	-104	9	444	93	546 (V-I)
(9) Chemicals and allied (43)	*	-	-404	275	263	538 (V-III)
(10) Petroleum refining (19)	*	*	-	-706	904	904 (V-IV)
(11) Rubber products (29)	*	-	-284	309	111	501 (V-III)
(12) Leather products (18)	*	228	-249	-153	778	625 (V-III)
(13) Stone, clay, glass (53)	*	-	74	-90	260	260 (V-IV)
(14) Primary metals (36)	*	-	-15	-51	452	425 (V-III)
(15) Fabricated metals (61)	*	268	-20	263	391	902 (V-III)
(16) Machinery (56)	*	-	-190	97	305	402 (V-III)
(17) Electrical machinery (38)	*	-	-380	690	639	1329 (V-III)
(18) Transport equipment (30)	*	-	-1471	1289	177	1471 (II-III)
(19) Prof. instruments (21)	*	-	166	-696	593	696 (III-IV)
(20) Miscellaneous (37)	*	-	603	211	485	485 (V-I)
Range of wage by city size class ($)	2410 (7-11)	3628 (17-3)	3332 (9-3)	3441 (17-3)	3060 (17-3)	

* Insufficient observations

to locate in SMSAs this small. The difference in the interindustry earnings differential between classes II and V is only $568 and the same industries tend to constitute the extreme high and low figures in each size class. Electrical machinery workers receive the highest average earnings in three of five classes, and, with the exception of the smallest size class, textile mill workers receive the lowest average wage.

(3) The instability in average earnings differentials among size classes and industries suggests that specialized locational factors may be operative. The transportation equipment industry has the largest intercity differentials in Table XV, probably reflecting the specialized locational patterns of auto and aircraft production and the heterogeneity of equipment needs among transit modes. The lowest earnings differentials appear to be characterized by a substantial local market for output (printing-publishing; stone-clay-glass) and a high degree of unionization (rubber products). About 58% of the differentials calculated between classes II and III are negative compared to 30% between II and IV; this is sufficient to produce an "earnings ratchet" just below cities of about a quarter million in population.

For the overall sample (with 794 degrees of freedom) Equation 53 is estimated as:

$$W_i = 4,020^{**} + 0.00938^{**} \ (P_i) + 1.251^{**} \ (S_i) + 119.5^{**} \ (K_i/L_i)$$
$$(45.41) \qquad (3.71) \qquad\qquad (8.41) \qquad\qquad (10.97)$$

$$-0.9756^{**} \ (D_i)$$
$$(-3.84) \qquad\qquad\qquad R^2 = 0.26 \qquad\qquad\qquad (54)$$

where test levels for significantly nonzero parameter estimates are indicated as (**) at the 0.01 level and t statistics are shown in parentheses. Though all coefficients are highly significant, the variables measuring the characteristics of manufacturing firms are of greater importance than P_i and D_i. The signs of the coefficients are in accordance with those hypothesized above; the positive coefficient on P_i is consistent with the somewhat greater influence of local markets for output on labor demand, a result not unexpected for cities of this size.

The stepwise regression results also showed that the influence of S_i and (K_i/L_i) is relatively independent of the principal locational determinants of average earnings. Population size compensates for distance at roughly the ratio of the estimated slope coefficients in Equation 54, controlling on the influence of S_i and (K_i/L_i); this is

(−0.9756/0.0938) or about −10.5 persons per mile and compares favorably with regression estimates containing only P_i and D_i. The latter is (−1.697/0.157) which equals −10.4 and suggests that the importance of scale and capital intensity is relatively unrelated to the net influence of the locational variables.

To test for the stability of Equation 54, separate regressions were calculated by industry; these equations are ranked by significance of the F-ratio test and summarized in Table XVI. As in Equation 54 the signs of the coefficients are generally consistent with those hypothesized above, the only exceptions occurring on the scale and distance variables. The higher earnings attributable to very skilled craftsmen in smaller firms probably account for the negative scale coefficients in the leather, textile and furniture industries. The strong resource and market orientation of the lumber-wood and petroleum refining industries result in positive coefficients on D_i. Two industries have negative population coefficients, suggesting the net supply effect on money wages; the professional instruments industry ranks second only to petroleum refining in the average size of city in which its firms are located. The range in size of coefficient by variable is substantial suggesting the independence of these factors in explaining earnings among industries.

Several tests were performed to determine whether specific characteristics of the industries seem to be correlated with the model's predictive ability. With the following exceptions, these tests confirmed the generality of the model as applied to the individual industry data:

(1) The statistical significance of the equational tests are slightly higher for industries located in the smaller, more isolated SMSAs of the sample. The Spearman rank correlations between the ranks of F-ratio (from highest to lowest in Table XVI and the variable means for P_i and D_i are −0.2342 and +0.2075 respectively. Both the food/kindred and fabricated metals industries tend to be located in the smallest SMSAs of the sample and, as suggested above, petroleum refining firms are found in the largest metropolitan regions.

(2) Rank correlations between the size of coefficient and the ranks of F-ratio also suggest the somewhat enhanced power of the model for industries in the smaller cities and the importance of S_i in determining wages. The ranks of the size of population coefficient and F-ratio have a Spearman coefficient of −0.3550; this result supports the rank correlation for population means as we expect larger positive coefficients on P_i in cities where the net demand effect

TABLE XVI

Regression Estimates for Individual Industry Equations[a]

Industry (S.I.C. Code)	Constant	P_i	S_i	K_i/L_i	D_i	F-ratio
Chemicals and allied (28)	4,274**	0.0467	4.932**	41.06*	-1.262	32.4**
Paper and allied (26)	3,348**	0.0560	6.648**	288.50**	-0.144*	10.8**
Rubber products (30)	3,283**	0.1847**	4.429**	130.50[1]	-0.807	10.7**
Food, kindred (20)	3,513**	0.0955	8.992**	46.67	-1.615	10.3**
Leather products (31)	3,344**	0.1394**	-0.869	44.35	-1.008**	9.2**
Fabricated metals (34)	4,335**	0.1159*	3.485	138.20*	-1.402**	9.0**
Textile mill products (22)	3,404**	-0.0279	-8.114	403.90**	-0.822	8.2**
Stone, clay, glass (32)	4,079**	0.0173	4.047**	193.60**	-0.941	7.1**
Primary metals (33)	5,374**	0.0387	2.349*	67.39	-1.989**	5.2**
Printing, publishing (27)	4,930**	0.1176	2.800[1]	88.34[1]	-1.018	5.2**
Transport equipment (37)	5,239**	0.0021	0.855	195.40*	-2.084[1]	4.5**
Electrical machinery (36)	4,134**	0.2059	0.513	110.00[1]	-1.117	4.3**
Furniture, fixtures (25)	3,471**	0.1519[1]	-0.247	308.50*	-1.171	3.4*
Machinery (35)	4,919**	0.0860	3.483*	92.08	-1.495	3.2*
Lumber, wood (24)	2,751**	0.1853	2.634	383.60**	0.379	3.0*
Prof. instruments (38)	4,636**	-0.0108	0.744	126.70	-2.446[1]	2.5[1]
Apparel (23)	2,708**	0.1405*	0.568	82.44	-0.760	2.2[1]
Petroleum refining (29)	4,550**	0.1164	2.212	88.83[1]	1.097	1.7
Miscellaneous (39)	3,626**	0.1362[1]	2.290	13.60	-0.181	1.2

[a] A [1], * and ** indicate statistically significant coefficients at the 0.10, 0.05 and 0.01 probability levels respectively.

is substantial. The Spearman correlation between the size of scale coefficient and F-ratio is $+0.5005$ indicating the increased predictive ability of the model in industries where the partial impact of firm size on money earnings is highest.

To test for regional and earnings class differences, the data were restratified to estimate the regression equations in Table XVII. (The regression statistics and variable means appear in rows 1 and 2 of this table for each equation.) As in Table XVI most coefficients have the signs hypothesized above, the only exception occurring for the D_i and S_i variables in the southern and low wage equations respectively; all of the population coefficients are consistent with the net demand hypothesis. The values of R^2 are consistent with this statistic in Equation 54 with some enhanced predictive power indicated in the northern industry and low wage equations.

Regional earnings differentials are primarily due to the importance of local markets to southern firms and the greater effect of the S_i and (K_i/L_i) variables in the northern industry equation. The estimated north-south differential is about 16% and is primarily explained by the net demand of southern urban residents for the output of local firms; both the population coefficient and the total effect of the variable (slope coefficient times variable mean) are substantially higher in the southern industry equation despite the fact that southern firms reside in cities about half the size of their northern counterparts. The market orientation is supported by the somewhat higher average distance to marketing center in that region while northern firms are substantially more sensitive to the transportation cost variable.

When the model is estimated by earnings size class, there is an inverse relation between the relative importance of the P_i and D_i variables. Though the average size of SMSA varies little by earnings class, the size and statistical significance of the population coefficient is inversely related to average earnings; the importance of the net demand effect in low wage industries is thus consistent with the significance of P_i in the southern industry equation. Conversely, the impact of market contiguity is more important for medium and high wage industries than for the lowest paying firms in the sample. (The product of the D_i coefficient and average shipment distance for low paying firms is about 14 times this number for medium and high paying industries.) The locational significance of distance is therefore substantially greater for high earnings industries despite the low variance among earnings classes in the distance variable.

TABLE XVII

Regression Statistics and Variable Means for Classified Regressions[a,b]

Equation (degrees of freedom)	Annual Average Wage	Constant	P_i	S_i	K_i/L_i	D_i	R^2
Northern industry[c] (474)	–	4090**	0.0373	3.222**	130.5*	-1.365*	0.31
	$5043	–	1,158,200	164.0	3.91	95.0	
Southern industry[d] (217)	–	3253**	0.5199**	2.188**	119.8**	0.116	0.26
	$4348	–	655,100	142.9	3.88	195.4	
Low wage industry[e] (212)	–	3199**	0.1141**	-0.794	283.1**	-0.102	0.24
	$3803	–	1,170,400	125.5	2.06	135.6	
Medium wage industry[e] (323)	–	4438**	0.1033**	2.171**	56.19**	-1.346**	0.22
	$4914	–	1,079,900	144.0	4.17	135.8	
High wage industry[e] (245)	–	5278	0.0734	2.359**	19.07[1]	-1.367**	0.29
	$5744	–	1,147,400	195.2	5.41	133.5	

[a] The regression statistics and variable means appear in rows 1 and 2 respectively for each equation.

[b] A 1, * and ** indicate statistically significant coefficients at the 0.10, 0.05 and 0.01 probability levels respectively.

[c] Includes New England, Middle Atlantic, East North Central and West North Central regions.

[d] Includes South Atlantic, East South Central and West South Central regions.

[e] Low wage industries are defined as those having a mean wage at least one-half standard deviation ($562) below the overall industry average wage of $4864. High wage industries have annual wages exceeding one-half standard deviation above the overall mean.

The manufacturing variables in the earnings equations show the significance of S_i on average earnings and the consistency of the relation between (K_i/L_i) and relative input costs. The high wage industries have the largest firms in the sample and the impact of scale on earnings is both higher and more significant statistically than in the low wage equation. Conversely, the effect of increasing capital intensity is much more significant in the low wage equation, and the substitution of capital for labor as wages rise is evident from the stratified means of the (K_i/L_i) variable. Assuming that nonlabor input prices are constant between successive classes (low to high wage industries), the ratio of changes in (K_i/L_i) to changes in W_i suggests that the substitution of nonlabor inputs for labor is substantially greater for low wage than for medium wage industries in the sample. Among successive classes $[\triangle (K_i/L_i)/\triangle w_i]$ is estimated as 19.5 (low to medium paying industries) to 1.5 (medium to high paying industries).

The model of earnings differentials discussed in this section suggests the importance of transportation costs and access to markets. The locational characteristics of industries both in the overall sample and the regional stratification support the view that the reduction of transportation costs is probably the most important single factor influencing the narrowing of regional earnings differences. This is consistent with decentralizing locational trends of manufacturing firms noted in previous chapters both within and among the smaller labor markets in the United States.

CONCLUSIONS

The economic complexity of metropolitan growth will probably continue to complicate the planning functions of governments. Disaggregated projections models will be increasingly needed to estimate both the level and spatial location of economic activity and their subsequent effects on the age/income distribution of the urban population and the demands for public services. The simulation model described in this chapter offers a particularly promising approach to the problems of metropolitan planning. It combines economic and demographic models, which allow for a substantial degree of disaggregation with a flexible computational format allowing us to study the effects of alternative urban futures. Several problems with the structure of urban planning models should be noted however.

Metropolitan planning models are typically incapable of dealing with problems of intraannual forecasting. The regular recursive sequence of equations (or even their simultaneous solution) bear little resemblance to the complexity of institutional decision-making within metropolitan regions. The fiscal flows among public institutions both within and external to the city are also excluded from data sources typically used in empirically estimating such models. The conversion of economic-demographic data to social indicators will be a useful extension hopefully increasing the urban modeler's capabilities in predicting short term problems of a sociological nature. Also excluded are institutional bargaining problems (*e.g.*, labor conflicts affecting the provision of public services) which have become more prevalent in the larger urban communities.

The exogenous influences affecting metropolitan growth over the long run also limit the usefulness of projections designed to facilitate planning in the public sector. These influences are not confined to the economic sectoral and population flows accounts (exports, imports and net migration), but may also include major intergovernmental reforms such as the substitution of federal block grants for individual governmental programs or changes in trade policy that influence the comparative production advantages of particular cities. For smaller cities, resource depletion within their immediate regional hinterlands and competition with contiguous towns may also influence long run growth prospects. Inevitably models that focus on the internal complexities of urbanized areas will not be able to deal simultaneously with every conceivable influence external to their immediate jurisdictions. This is particularly unfortunate due to the importance of public facilities planning in the long run within metropolitan communities.

Despite these (and other) limitations, the CIRPC model has provided internally consistent projections of numerous economic and demographic variables relevant to nine public services provided within its metropolitan jurisdiction. Its disaggregative capabilities are useful in pursuing the elusive goal of "comprehensive planning" and the integration of demographic, production and capital accounts provides an element of internal consistency to the projections estimates. Equally important the model's structure is estimable from existing data sources precluding extensive survey work; the basic format for implementing models of its type should be readily adaptable to any metropolitan area.

Among urban areas the continued presence of money earnings differentials will provide incentives for firms and households to relocate in cities along the size spectra. A model is specified that incorporates (1) the implied productive assumptions underlying regression studies of the relation between earnings and city size and (2) the conflicting locational forces of local demand for products and/or labor and the competitive disadvantage of distance from intermediate or final markets for output. The ability of manufacturing firms to decentralize is determined by these locational forces controlling on size and capital intensity characteristics that affect the competitive position of city locations represented in the sample.

Departures from a perfectly positive correlation between city size and average manufacturing earnings are apparent for firms in the sample; though manufacturing wages are highest in the largest SMSAs a substantial variation by city-size class occurs for the lowest paying firms. Also city size does not appear to influence the range of average earnings by industry; the allowable mix of high paying firms is not seriously restricted in the smaller SMSAs in the sample. Regression estimates of the model's parameters confirm the significance of its principal variables. The scale and factor proportion variables are the most significant determinants of annual average earnings, and the net influence of the locational factors is independent of the variables measuring characteristics of firms in the sample. These empirical estimates appear to be relatively insensitive to disaggregation by two-digit S.I.C. code.

Separately estimated regression equations, by region and earnings size class, confirm expected disparities in the explanatory significance of variables in the model. The 16% earnings differential between the North and South is due principally to the local market orientation of the southern region. The higher paying northern industries are able to substitute capital for high priced labor and are considerably more sensitive in their locational decisions to contiguity to their major marketing centers. Also it should be noted that if living costs are positively related to city size, real manufacturing earnings are probably not equal among urban classes in our sample. The "earnings ratchet" in intermediate-sized SMSAs suggests that measurable real earnings differentials may be substantial and could require special explanatory factors. Though the money wage is relevant to firms, the neoclassical mechanism through which real earnings are to be equalized may be subject to some qualifications. Variations in commodity and service demand patterns, psychic and amenity components of real income, and other noneconomic factors among cities of alternative sizes may be additional variables that could be studied usefully.

GENERAL REFERENCES

Bell, F. W. "An Econometric Forecasting Model for a Region," *J. Reg. Sci.* **7**:105–127, 1967.

Burton, R., and J. Dyckman. *A Quarterly Economic Forecasting Model for the State of California* (Berkeley: Center for Planning Development, Research Institute of Urban and Regional Development, University of California, 1967).

Coelho, P. R. P., and M. A. Ghali. "The End of the North-South Wage Differential," *Amer. Econ. Rev.* **61**:932–937, 1971.

Forrester, J. W. *Urban Dynamics* (Cambridge, Mass.: The MIT Press, 1969).

Fuchs, V. R. "Hourly Earnings Differentials by Region and City Size," *Monthly Labor Rev.* pp. 22–26, January 1967.

Hamilton, H. R., S. E. Goldstone, J. W. Milliman, A. L. Pugh III, E. B. Roberts and A. Zellner. *Systems Simulation for Regional Analysis: An Application to River Basin Planning* (Cambridge: MIT Press, 1969).

Hanna, F. A. *State Income Differentials*, 1919–1954 (Durham, North Carolina: Duke University Press, 1959).

Klarman, H. E. "A Statistical Study of Income Differences Among Communities," *Studies in Income and Wealth* (New York: National Bureau of Economic Research, **6**:208–226, 1943).

Lewis, W. C. and J. R. Prescott. "Manufacturing Employment, City Size and Inter-urban Wage Differentials," *Annals of Regional Science*, October 1974.

Mansfield, E. "Some Notes on City Income Levels," *Rev. Econ. Stat.* **38**:474–481, 1956.

Prescott, J. R., and W. Mullendore. "A Simulation Model for Multi-County Planning," *Proceedings of the American Real Estate and Urban Economics Association*, **IV**:183–207, 1969.

Scully, G. W. "Interstate Wage Differentials: A Cross-Section Analysis," *Amer. Econ. Rev.* **59**:753–773, 1969.

6

State-Local Government and
Regional Development Policies

As suggested in Chapter 1, the political jurisdictions of state and local governments may or may not correspond spatially with meaningful economic regionalizations. State boundaries have been historically stable, and the political difficulties often associated with annexation may constrain the spatial jurisdictions of cities to something less than the labor market region they service. Though this may cause difficulties in administering the economic policies of these government units, the latter have evidenced an increasing concern with problems of economic growth. The post-World War II development of the "grants economy" has promoted a closer identification between the federal and sub-federal governments in seeking solutions to problems of low income and inadequate development. State governments have fashioned more sophisticated programs to encourage economic growth within their boundaries, and, on the income side, tax sharing and earnings levies in metropolitan areas represent a political realization of the financial problems faced by local government.

Although of declining relative importance, the property tax has historically constituted an important source of revenue to state and local governments. Economists have been persistently critical of this form of taxation, mainly on the basis of "fiscal unresponsiveness" and administrative inequity. The tax base also may be easily eroded as special groups are accorded exemptions or credits that may have numerous redistributive effects among local governmental jurisdictions within a state. To illustrate some of these effects the first two sections include an analysis of the veteran's property tax exemption used in the state of Iowa. Methods of estimating the impact and

149

incidence of the exemption are discussed, followed by a comparative analysis of policy alternatives used by other states. These sections are designed to show the numerous effects that such exemptions may be expected to have and ways of empirically estimating their magnitudes.

State programs designed to influence industrial relocation have attracted much attention in recent years. These programs are quite varied, ranging from state-established credit institutions to provide low-interest loans for new firms to locally initiated tax forgiveness and/or subsidized leasing programs. A discriminant model, designed to assess the relative importance of traditional arguments advanced in favor of these programs, is discussed. The model distinguishes the existence of a particular program within a state and its extensive use so the specious nature of many state programs may be isolated. Ten independent variables are specified to explain the distribution of programs among the various states, and the empirical results of the analysis are then described.

The objective of this chapter is to focus on the numerous redistributive effects that may be expected when states legislate exemptions influencing locally-levied taxes and the impacts of interstate competition for new firms and plants on national patterns of industrial re-location; several spatial effects are emphasized. State-imposed exemptions differentially influence net tax revenues of local governments since property millages tend to vary among taxing districts. Equitable compensation schemes are discussed and the extent of the net redistribution is estimated. State development programs are expected to influence the locational decisions of firms and households, particularly where such decisions are complementary with locally-based industrial interests. In the absence of a coordinated policy influencing population redistribution at the federal level, the experience of state and local governments provides some evidence as to the extent to which locational patterns of firms may be influenced. Though these spatial effects are not directly attributable to the problems of delineation discussed in Chapter 1, they may exert a significant influence on patterns of substate and subnational economic development.

IMPACTS AND INCIDENCE OF THE VETERAN'S PROPERTY EXEMPTION

Rising property values and taxes tend to increase pressures on state legislatures to accord exemptions and other forms of tax relief to special groups. The elderly, infirm, homeowners and veterans are examples of groups commonly receiving special compensatory relief among the various states. Assessing the effects of these compensatory plans is often a difficult task due to the absence of adequate data and the lack of understanding by legislators of the various impacts that such proposals may have. As a result these plans may be inadequately designed and/or characterized by administrative regulations bearing little resemblance to the original purpose of the exemption.

The veteran's exemption in Iowa differentiates the money claim by the period of military service of the eligible claimant. (Included in the data below are the $500 and $750 claims for W.W. II—Korean War and W.W. I veterans, respectively.) The money value of the exemption is therefore positively related to the claimant's age and undifferentiated by the rank of the veteran during his period of service. The declining real value of the exemption may be offset by its rising tax value where the latter is the product of the local millage and the money claim. The tax value of the exemption therefore varies by the tax district in which the veteran claims his exemption, though it seems unlikely that the spatial distribution of the claimant's property is in any way related to the value of his military service. The data used to empirically estimate the effects discussed below are derived from state data and a special survey of property tax payers for the year 1964.

Under the variable millage form of the exemption, the gross tax loss to the state (millage times claim summed over all eligible veterans) is determined by the total number of exemptions and the spatial distribution of properties; the latter is usually unknown so states do not have good estimates of local governmental tax losses. Existent state data, however, can be utilized to provide approximations to the gross tax loss. From state data for 1964 these are: (1) [(average county millage) (county exemptions)] summed over counties, and (2) [(average urban millage) (urban exemptions) + (average rural millage) (rural exemptions)] summed over counties. The numerical estimates are $10.75 million (method 1) and $11.61 million (method 2). The survey data provide an independent estimate of gross tax loss since they include information on actual millages on exemptions claimed by property tax payers. This figure is $11.69 million or about 10% in excess of the estimate provided by method 1. Because of two possible spatial effects, claimants are able to increase gross tax loss by about 10% over the value of claims taken at average county millages.

Part of the differential may be due to the ability of eligible veterans to claim exemptions at more than one tax rate. Of all property tax payers surveyed, about 20% had at least two properties assessed in different tax districts and only 30% of these veterans failed to take their exemption on the highest millage property. Chi-square tests failed, however, to distinguish between the number of veterans who did and did not claim their exemptions on their highest millage property. The tests distinguished between the millage differential (0–20 mills, + 20 mills) and the tax savings differential (0–$7, + $7) for both groups; their respective chi-square values were 1.11 and 2.94, which are not significant at the 0.01 level. Though increased tax savings are possible by claiming the exemption on the highest millage property, veterans seem to be indifferent to or unaware of these differentials.

Most of the 10% differential is explained by the tendency of claimants to have higher than average property valuations in the higher millage tax districts. About 76% of all exemptions are claimed on residential real property, which carried the second highest millage (101 mills) of all property in the state of Iowa. The survey data also showed that exemption millages are positively associated with family income and that farmers received about 28% less per dollar of exempted valuation than claimants in professional (predominantly urban) occupations. The continued urbanization of the state should differentially benefit nonrural veterans and increase the gross tax loss of urban governments.

Differentials in tax savings also accrue over time within the group of eligible veterans. The data on urban-rural average millages (collected since 1945) allow a comparison of accumulated tax savings by place of residence and size of claimed exemption. Over the twenty year period, 1945–65, the W.W. I urban veteran was estimated to have accumulated $1200 in tax savings compared to $750 for his rural counterpart; the W.W. II differential is calculated at $350 ($800 for urban and $450 for rural veterans). As a percentage of rural tax value the W.W. I and W.W. II differentials are 60 and 78% respectively, substantially higher than the annual urban-rural disparity in benefit payment under the Iowa exemption plan. The variable millage form of this exemption therefore leaves substantial benefit inequities among eligible veterans that are unrelated to the value of military service performed by the claimant.

The incidence of the exemption may be assessed by analyzing the impact of exemption removal on the taxes of nonclaimants and claimants. Knowing the 1964 data (discussed below), estimates of the tax incidence can be made; two assumptions are made in deriving these empirical estimates:

(1) Property taxes collected when the exemption is not in effect equal the sum of taxes collected when it is in effect plus any rebate accorded by the state to local governments as an offset to tax losses. (In Iowa, 5% of gross liquor sales are allocated as a rebate to all local governments in the state.) This may be expressed as,

$$T = T_a' + T_{b_1}' + R \tag{55}$$

where T = the amount of taxes, a = a variable of people having no veterans' exemption, b_1 = a variable denoting the nonexempt property of people having an exemption, prime = a variable denoting the exemption is in effect and nonprimed variables indicate the exemption is not in effect, and R = rebate on real and personal exempted property in the state.

(2) There is no difference in the millages that are applied to the different classes of property. As noted above the average millage on exempt property was estimated to be higher than the average millage on all property, so this assumption is less realistic. The primary interest is, however, in the overall state millage change due to exemption removal and this assumption will not affect the signs of the variables that are changed. This assumption is expressed as

$$M = M_a = M_{b_1} = M_{b_2} \tag{56}$$

where M = millage and b_2 = a variable denoting the exempt property of people who do have an exemption.

The taxes collected when the exemption is and is not in effect may be expressed as

$$T' = (M + \triangle M)\ (V_a + V_{b_1} + V_{b_2}) \tag{57}$$

and

$$T = M\ (V_a + V_{b_1} + V_{b_2}) \tag{58}$$

where V = valuations of real and personal property and $\triangle M$ = the millage differential attributable to the exemption. From these definitions,

$$T/T' = M/(M + \triangle M) = k \qquad (59)$$

and from Equation 55

$$kT' = T_a' + T_{b_1}' + R \qquad (60)$$

and

$$k = (T_a' + T_{b_1}' + R) / (T_a' + T_{b_1}' + T_{b_2}') \qquad (61)$$

The variables in Equation 61 are calculable from available data, which are (in thousands of dollars, 1964);

$$T_a' + T_{b_1}' = 469,375 \qquad T_{b_1}' = 86,556$$

$$T_{b_2}' = 11,691 \qquad T_a' = 469,375 - T_{b_1}' = 382,819$$

$$R = 2,791$$

The estimates of interest are:

$$k = 0.981 \qquad kT_a' = T_a = 375,737$$

$$kT_{b_1}' = T_{b_1} = 84,955 \qquad kT_{b_2}' = T_{b_2} = 11,475$$

$$T_a' - T_a = -7,802 \qquad T_{b_1}' - T_{b_1} = -1,601$$

$$T_{b_1} + T_{b_2} = 96,403$$

The values of T_a, T_{b_1} and T_{b_2} show what total taxes would have been had the military exemption not been in effect. The taxes of those without an exemption would have $7,082,000 less than they were with the exemption. Those who had an exemption would have paid $1,601,000 less on their nonexempt property had there been no exemption, but would have paid $11,475,000 on their exempt property; they would have paid a total of $96,430,000 rather than the $86,556,000 which they actually paid. Hence the veterans who enjoy a benefit of $11,475,000 from the exemption actually pay $1,601,000 of that benefit themselves because of increased millage rates on their nonexempt property. The remainder of the benefit is paid by those without an exemption and the rebate that comes from state liquor sales. Note also that if the rebate R were equal to the tax value of the exemption T_{b_2} then $\triangle M = 0$ and $T = T'$. The fact that the taxes of those without an exemption and the taxes on nonexempt property of those with an exemption are larger when the the exemption is in effect results because the rebate is not as large as the tax loss. Finally, $M + \triangle M = 84.21$ mills for 1964, which implies from the estimate for k that $\triangle M = 1.558$ mills; the increase in millage due to the exemption is slightly less than 2 mills.

Within the class of eligible claimants some would also have lower taxes under exemption removal. An exemption of $500 on property taxed at 96 mills (the estimated 1964 average on exempt property) carries a tax savings of $48, which is equivalent to a 1.558 mill increase on $30,089 of nonexempt property valuations. (A figure of $46,123 results from the $750 exemption.) An exemption claimant with nonexempt valuations exceeding these figures would pay more in taxes than with complete exemption removal and is in effect subsidizing fellow claimants. Even if the eligible claimant has only one-half this amount of nonexempt property, his tax savings are cut in half.

In the absence of precise estimates of local tax losses, states may devise inequitable formulas for compensating local governments. As noted above, Iowa allocates 5% of gross liquor sales as compensation, though there is no direct relation between this amount and the actual losses incurred at the local level. (The rebate as a percentage of estimated tax loss has varied between 31.1 and 17.4% from 1954 to 1965.) Furthermore the Iowa statute distributes this amount on the basis of claimed exemptions evaluated at a maximum of 25 mills. (The law provides for a lower millage for counties below this statutory maximum, but all county millages were substantially in excess of this level in 1964.) Hence, the state rebate is effectively allocated on the basis of the dollar value of exemption claims.

To test for the effect of a more accurately based millage formula, the 1964 county tax losses were estimated by the weighted urban-rural method (formula 2 above) and compared to the state's method of determining the compensation to counties; the results are summarized in Table XVIII. The county strata in this table distinguish counties with SMSAs defined as of 1960 (large) and counties with no city in excess of 5,000 population in 1960 (small). Had the weighted urban-rural millage based formula been used, large counties would have received nearly $130 thousand more in state compensation than they actually received in 1964; six of the seven counties in this stratum would have benefited from the millage based formula. Conversely the rural counties in the small stratum would have received about $120 thousand less in state rebate and 53 counties would have received less in actual compensation. This represents an approximate 12% gain for SMSA counties and a 14% loss for the rural counties. Though it could be argued that the 1964 method at least favors tax districts with relatively low valuations, the redistribution of revenues toward rural counties is probably an unintended consequence of the law and should (if desired) be the subject of separate legislation with this particular objective in mind.

The redistributive effects of the Iowa veteran's property tax exemption indicate the extent to which administrative convenience may obscure the legislative intention underlying a particular subsidy. The spatial disparities in the exemption's value have no discernible relation to the social benefit of the veteran's service. The formula for determining the compensation for tax losses to local governments combines an arbitrary earmarking rule with an allocative formula that neither recognizes the millage effect on tax loss nor uses available state data to improve on the existing formula. Though there are many advantages to earmarking not often perceived by economists, the net effect of the veteran's exemption substantially negates the purpose of the statute. In the next section, alternative state plans dealing with veteran's property tax subsidies are analyzed as an alternative to the exemption.

POLICY ALTERNATIVES AND THEIR EFFECTS

States often adopt different approaches to subsidizing selected groups providing a relatively rich array of alternatives to a specific

TABLE XVIII

Distribution of the 1964 Iowa Rebate
to Local Tax Districts

County Stratum	Large	Medium	Small	Total
Stratum rebate ($):				
1964 method	1,021,243	928,010	841,924	2,791,177
Weighted method	1,149,945	918,238	722,994	2,791,177
Counties in stratum	7	32	60	99
Counties benefiting from weighted method	6	13	7	26

state plan. Estimating the effects of these alternatives on Iowa veterans provides a useful comparative framework within which policy recommendations can be formulated. In advance of discussing these alternatives, at least two adjustments might be made within the context of the present exemption plan:

(1) The veteran's exemption may be viewed as a partial compensation for the personal costs of military service or a contribution for the benefit that society derives from that service. (In both cases an allocative problem among subnational governments exists since the conflicts are national in scope; we will disregard this difficulty in our discussion.) If personal costs are evaluated at the best civilian opportunity, rank and/or age may not be a good basis for prorating tax relief since civilian compensation for these skills is not necessarily related to these criteria. The millage component of tax value may be related to opportunity costs, however, if the higher valued skills are practiced in high millage tax districts. As a payment for benefits derived, rank or age may constitute acceptable criterion if the employing agency (the military) accurately evaluates the productivities of its employees. The subsequent location of the veteran's properties is unlikely to be related to the value of his military service.

In the absence of a prorating criteria to compensate for the capricious effects of property locations, the veteran's exemption might be evaluated uniformly at a millage rate reflecting state average tax values or tied to overall property tax millage levies. This would be tantamount to a credit plan (discussed in more detail below), leaving the recipient's compensation independent of the spatial distribution of his property. The rebate to local governments might then be prorated on the difference between the local levy and the uniform millage.

(2) A second problem is concerned with the appropriate definition of the eligible tax base. Exemptions taken on productive property may encourage inefficient allocations of economic activity by maintaining marginal firms who might otherwise be better employed in producing other goods and services. (Commercial and industrial property, both real and personal, are eligible for the exemption under Iowa law.) Confining the exemption claim to residential real property would at least subsidize a necessity from the recipient's viewpoint, and avoid these direct effects on the allocation of productive activity. About 80% of nonagricultural exemptions are claimed on residential real property and it is likely that most of the 18% of ex-

emptions taken on agricultural real property could be specifically applied to an owned home.

Alternatives to the variable millage plan include (1) the imposition of means tests, (2) restrictions on the veteran's lifetime tax savings and (3) credit plans. The effects of these plans on Iowa veterans are suggested below.

Means Tests

A number of states have imposed income or asset limitations on the eligibility for an exemption. For example, family income limits of $7,500 and $3,000 have been instituted in the states of Michigan and North Dakota; wealth restrictions have been applied in New Hampshire (value of residence less than $10,000) and Arizona (value of all property less than $5,000). Means tests may leave the exemption structure intact though applicable to a smaller group of eligible claimants. The impact on tax value disparities in the exemption depend on (1) the effect on eligibility from the choice of wealth measure and (2) the distribution of eligible properties among tax districts.

Table XIX shows the effects of various income and net asset limitations when applied to Iowa veterans; both criteria would sub-

TABLE XIX

Effects of Income and Net Asset Tests
on the Iowa Veteran's Exemption, 1964[a]

	Veteran's Exemption (Dollars)	Tax Value (Dollars)	Claimants (Number)
Income limits:			
less than $3,000	18,250	1,701	31
less than $5,000	46,515	4,290	81
less than $7,000	69,147	6,459	128
no limit	122,299	11,692	236
Net assets:			
less than $5,000	10,286	901	25
less than $10,000	33,882	3,249	70
less than $15,000	54,578	5,261	111
no limit	122,299	11,692	236

[a] All units in the body of this table are in thousands.

stantially reduce the coverage of the exemption plan. Income limits of $7,000 and $3,000 would have reduced the value of claimed exemptions by about 42 and 85% respectively; the number of claimants would fall from 236,000 to 128,000 or 31,000. The tax value (or loss) due to the exemption would have been reduced to $6,459,000 or $1,701,000 with a corresponding increase in net taxes levied, assuming that millage rates remain unchanged. The impact of net asset limitations of $15,000 and $5,000 would result in even larger reductions in the dollar value of claimed exemptions and tax values; only 111,000 and 25,000 claimants would remain in the program under these limitations.

The rather substantial effects on the program attributable to income and net asset limitations used in other states suggest that the higher income and net asset classes contain substantial proportions of total claimants. For these families the loss of the exemption is unlikely to significantly influence their real standard of living, whereas for the most severe income and net asset restrictions shown in Table XIX the remaining claimants may suffer considerable losses under complete exemption removal. The administrative savings attained by such restrictions may outweigh the loss of benefits to wealthier veterans and some of the more objectionable redistributive effects analyzed earlier may be avoided. Where income limitations confine the eligible claimants to the poorer rural tax districts, for example, millage disparities may be substantially alleviated. It should also be noted, however, that the specific form of restriction may differentially affect occupational groups, particularly in rural states; farmers may be eligible under fairly restrictive income limitations but ineligible under net asset means tests of a far less confinng nature.

Maximum Lifetime Tax Savings

Wyoming is the only state that has placed a maximum on the aggregate lifetime tax savings of claimants; after a veteran has accumulated $800 in tax savings he is no longer eligible for the exemption. Each veteran therefore receives an equal aggregate tax savings and the exemption is terminated in a shorter time period than if eligibility extends over the life time of the claimant. The millage on exempted property has no effect on aggregate tax savings except to allow urban claimants to reach the maximum more quickly. The present value of the aggregate payment is thus greater for veterans in high millage tax districts though the actual money payment is equal for all claimants.

The major effect of this plan is to (1) cause some disparities in the time period of eligibility among veterans and (2) reduce the stock of claimants. To evaluate these effects average urban-rural state millages were used to calculate accumulated tax savings for W.W. I, W.W. II and Korean War veterans. (The millage data were available only from 1945, so W.W. I claims prior to this time could not be evaluated.) From 1954–1964, the accumulated tax savings of urban and rural W.W. I veterans were $1,200 and $750, respectively, so even if the $800 restriction applied to this group on exemptions claimed after 1945, few W.W. I veterans would have been eligible in 1965. All Korean War and rural W.W. II veterans would have remained in the program as of 1965; urban W.W. II veterans would have exceeded the $800 limitation by this year. Estimates were also made of the time differential for urban and rural claimants within the program who are eligible due to participation in a given national conflict. On the basis of millage rates extrapolated at historical rates of increase, the $800 restriction would have left rural W.W. II and Korean War veterans eligible for exemptions for a period of nine and seven years longer than their respective urban counterparts. All Iowa veterans currently eligible for exemptions would be excluded from participation in the program by 1978.

The maximum tax savings restriction tends to exclude the oldest veterans eligible for exemptions. These are often the lowest income families and though their accumulated lifetime tax benefits are substantial, the restriction is probably more severely felt within this group. Administrative cost savings may or may not be attained since more detailed records would have to be kept on a smaller number of exemption claimants. The relative costs for rural governments would undoubtedly be greater since the average rural veteran would be in the program longer than veterans residing in higher millage tax districts. Additional costs would be necessary to insure that terminated claimants did not reapply for an exemption in other tax districts in the state. The principal advantage of the restriction is to eliminate the worst disparities in lifetime savings based mainly on location of eligible properties.

Credit Plans

Finally, an unrestricted credit plan could be adopted. New Jersey, for instance, has allowed a deduction of $50 annually from the property tax bill of eligible veterans. This would equalize the annual money benefit to urban and rural claimants and provide an exact basis for compensating local tax districts. Each veteran claiming an exemption receives an equal amount of tax savings each year.

The survey data allow a comparison of sets of credits that would (1) closely maintain the relative amounts of compensation among groups under the Iowa exemption and (2) approximate the estimated 1964 tax loss in Iowa. If credits of $40 and $60 were substituted for the $500 and $750 exemption and the small number of pre-W.W. I claims are replaced by a $240 credit, the total state credit would be $10.6 million; these credits are equivalent in tax savings to $500, $750 and $3,000 (the pre-W.W. I exemption) taxed at 80 mills. The corresponding exemptions taxed at 100 mills would result in credits of $50, $75 and $300, with a total cost to the state of $13.2 million. These plans would benefit veterans claiming exemptions at less than 80 and 100 mills, respectively.

These alternative state plans suggest the numerous ways in which the most pernicious effects of exemptions may be avoided. Though individual claimants may be insensitive to differentials in money benefits, the aggregate effects may be substantial particularly as they influence the distribution of net tax losses among urban and rural tax districts. Though substantial differences in money benefits and local tax losses per dollar claim persist under the exemption plan, a system of credits would (1) equalize dollar benefits among claimants and (2) provide an exact basis for compensating tax districts. Though determining the appropriate compensation for veterans seems an impossible task under any plan, the credit form of payment minimizes the underlying redistributive effects of the exemption type of plan.

State planners and economists should probably reexamine the impacts of selected group exemptions particularly where pressures on the property tax as a revenue source are substantial. The ease with which such exemptions are often accorded by state legislatures and their frequently unintended consequences render state tax policy a most useful field for economists interested in problems of public finance; most state policies influencing local tax structures (homestead credits, agricultural land tax exemptions, etc.) have similar redistributive effects among local governments. At the very least, the prevalence of highly questionable earmarking procedures and fixed allocative formulas should be investigated more thoroughly. Though it is possible for such budgetary rules to be acceptably efficient, the heavy reliance placed on fixed rules automatically transferring revenues to specific expenditure programs probably often results in allocations of funds ill-attuned to the purposes of state programs.

STATE LOCATIONAL INCENTIVES: A DISCRIMINANT MODEL

Among states the competition for new industrial plants and firms has resulted in numerous legislative statutes providing various forms of subsidies. The impact of these state and local financial incentives is often analyzed by correlating indices of economic growth (*e.g.*, manufacturing value-added, employment) with some measure of the extent to which these programs are utilized. Such studies are usually unable to control on the numerous factors influencing economic development within and among states or provide sufficient insight as to the relative importance of socio-economic characteristics of states which may determine both the authorization and extent-of-use of these programs. This suggests a reversal of the causal linkage usually assumed in such studies, namely that the continued authorization and extent-of-use are primarily determined by the past socio-economic performance of the state. If this is true, then states lacking the desirable configuration of characteristics should concentrate their development policies in other areas. Also by contrasting authorized and extensively used programs we may analyze the differences between commonly suggested beneficial effects of these programs and those factors that *de facto* influence their success.

The development plans included here involve a public subsidy of the following forms. (1) Tax exemptions on income, sales, specific excises and property are often accorded at the state or local level. Local exemptions are primarily applicable to property taxes and are often confined to the school district levy. (2) Industrial bond financing includes the flotation of issues by a local government for the construction of commercial and industrial facilities. The latter are then leased to new firms entering the local government's jurisdiction often with an additional property tax exemption. These bonds may be general obligations of the government or revenue issues backed by the rental income attained from the leased facilities. (3) State industrial finance authorities have made direct loans to industry (often as a partner with the Area Development Administration) and guarantee private loans to industrial firms. As of 1963, about 416 state direct loans had been made, totaling about $56 million. (4) Statewide development credit corporations make loans to small manufacturing firms. Much of the aggregate amount of these loans

(75% in 1963) have been made to instate firms, the balance going to new enterprises and out-of-state firms relocating or building new plants in the state. Both (3) and (4) above are state-authorized and -operated institutions often charging interest rates below those offered by banks or other financial intermediaries.

If the status of these programs (as of 1963) was randomly distributed among states, then presumably the net benefits they generate are zero or difficult to assess. (Their status includes authorized or nonauthorized programs and active or nonactive if the particular program is also authorized.) Alternatively there could be influences unrelated to net benefits and a questionable independence of the distribution of programs among states. An element of randomness would be introduced, for instance, if older statutes exempted technologically obsolete industries. Regional "bandwagon" effects may be operative and program complementarities may obscure the independence suggested above.

The evidence seems to support the view that due to the real costs (and supposed benefits) that are entailed in these programs their status as of particular dates is not specious. The three states of Florida, New Jersey and Virginia have repealed state authorized tax exemptions. Where exemptions are restricted to particular industries the latter have included pulp and paper, textiles, beet sugar and oil refining; these industries could hardly be termed obsolete. Also we know of no single instance where an existent exemption applies to a subsequently repealed tax. The hypotheses below are therefore formulated in terms of past influences (independent variables) measured over the period (1954–63); these variables are hpyothesized to explain the existence of development legislation as of 1963 regardless of when the state actually adopted the program.

There is some evidence of a regional effect though it is impossible to determine whether it is due solely to the effect noted above or to common characteristics of a broader multistate region. In any case, when the data for the four programs are grouped by the nine census regions, two effects may be distinguished. (1) There is a marked decline in the number of states with any kind of development legislation in the western regions. Only Washington, Montana and Wyoming have any type of plan in the 11-state Mountain and Pacific regions. This could be due to the somewhat unique resource endowments of many of these states; California's growth experience has probably not necessitated these types of programs. (2) Eastern states tend to prefer state-wide credit corporations while tax exemptions and industrial bond financing are more popular in the central northern and southern regions. This suggests that the relative strength of private credit institutions and/or local governments may be an important factor in determining the state's preference as to type of development plan.

The tetrachoric correlations among types of programs indicate the independence of these development plans among states. As expected these correlations are high where the variables are for authorized and active plans for a given type of program (*e.g.*, the highest correlation is 0.8230 for state-wide development credit corporations). However, among types of programs (for either authorized or active plans) the correlations range only from 0.3963 to –0.0100. The highest coefficient (0.3963) is for state tax exemption and industrial bond financing programs, both on an authorized basis. There is even a slight inverse correlation between states having active local industrial bond financing programs and those with state-wide industrial finance authorities and credit corporations (either authorized or active).

The discussion above suggests that the dichotomy between each currently authorized and nonauthorized (or if authorized, nonactive and active) program may be explained by socio-economic conditions in a state experienced prior to 1963. The following ten variables are utilized to explain the distribution of programs among states:

(1) *Welfare-market.* Levels or growth in per capita income reflect the welfare of the state's citizenry and its potential as a market for locally produced, income-elastic goods and services. (X_1 – percentage change in per capita income, 1954–63.)

(2) *Welfare.* The prevalence of low incomes within a state may influence legislators to enact these development plans. Alternatively, poverty states may not adopt these programs in deference to various types of categorical assistance and state welfare plans deemed to be more directly beneficial to its poorest citizens. (X_2 – percentage of families with less than $3,000 money income, 1959.)

(3) *Industrialization.* The absence of an extensive industrial base restricts the provision of business services and processed inputs to new firms and expands the range of potential in-migrant firms through the reduced competition for local markets and productive factor inputs. (X_3 – manufacturing value-added per capita, 1962.)

(4) *Industrial growth.* Even if a strong industrial complex exists, new firms may prefer industrial locations where the longer run prospects for growth are good. (X_4 – percentage change in manufacturing capital expenditure, 1954–62.)

(5) *Resource base.* States with resource-oriented economic bases may find that a wide array of inducements are necessary to promote a diversified industrial economy particularly if the primary industry has been historically declining. (X_5 – agricultural and mining employment as a percentage of total employment, 1960.)

(6) *Market location.* A high population density and presence of concentrated urban markets reduces the need for legislation designed to attract market-oriented firms. (X_6 – population density, 1960.)

(7) *Political.* Diversified economic interests may be reflected in the political inability to enact development legislation, and strongly unified interests may stifle or amend such legislation particularly where competition is feared. Political scientists have developed indices to measure the degree of political unity and diversity within states. Degree of state cohesiveness is an addend of four factors measuring the deviation of the state from national norms and policies; the lowest positive score indicates maximum unity. State traditions of centralism and localism is a similar index, with the lowest and highest indices given for localistic and centralistic states, respectively. (X_7 – degree of state cohesiveness and localism in political traditions.)

(8) *Wealth-demand.* The relative wealth of a state will be reflected in the quality of its public and private services and will indicate its ability to underwrite the costs of development programs and provide residential amenities for the labor force of in-migrant firms. (X_8 – per capita direct general expenditures of state and local governments, 1962.)

(9) *Labor market.* Labor availability may be an important consideration especially in states with relatively low density rural populations. Unemployment may indicate the availability of low wage labor or inadequate skills. Manufacturing employment growth will indicate the availability of an array of skills for new firms competing in local labor markets. (X_9 – percentage change in manufacturing employment, 1954–62.)

(10) *Debt.* Levels of public indebtedness reflect the desirability of encouraging in-migrant firms to support local and state services through expansion of the tax base. (X_{10} – per capita state and local debt outstanding, 1963.)

These ten variables (or close proxies) are hypothesized to explain the distribution of the four programs by state as of 1963. The discriminant model assigns 1 or 0 values to a particular state, depending on whether it has authorized the program or not, and if authorized whether the program is extensively used or not. Several additional points are important in interpreting the results of the discriminant functions. (1) The relative importance of the independent variables is evaluated in two ways. The contribution to the overall score is $(k_i \overline{X}_i)$, the product of the discriminant coefficient and the overall mean of the ith variable. As the latter does not account for the dispersion around the two means of the i variables, we have also evaluated $k_i (\overline{X}_i - S_{x_i})$, where S_{x_i} is the overall sample standard deviation of the ith variable, and the signs are determined so that $|k_i (\overline{X}_i - S_{x_i})| < |k_i \overline{X}_i|$ In Table XVI (p. 000) the rank scores are $|k_i \overline{X}_i|$ and $|k_i (\overline{X}_i - S_{x_i})|$ respectively. (2) The signs of the k_i coefficients depend on the way in which the vector of mean differences is calculated. In our analysis the average scores for states that have authorized plans are numerically smaller than the states that do not. If our hypothesis cannot be rejected, the negative product of the $k_i \overline{X}_i$ indicates a higher probability that the state has authorized legislation. The next section evaluates the empirical results of applying the discriminant model to the data discussed above.

EMPIRICAL RESULTS OF THE DISCRIMINANT MODEL

The empirical estimates for the model are summarized in Table XX; there are several characteristics typical of all nine equations. (1) With the exception of numbers 2 and 7 all equations are statistically significant at or exceeding the 0.100 level. Both exceptions are for authorized programs involving state programs or taxes. (2) Whether evaluated at the overall means or one standard deviation below their means, the rank scores generally correspond. The rank differences are distributed as follows: (zero differences, 52 coefficients), (1 difference, 22 coefficients), (2 differences, 6 coefficients) and (3 differences, 6 coefficients). (3) The signs of the coefficients are generally quite mixed among equations. This is to be expected because the independent variables may influence states in several ways. For example, rapid growth in personal income (X_1) may either render these programs unnecessary or induce further development efforts through the recognition of their benefits and the availability of resources for its pursuit. There are no consistently expected signs for the independent variables shown in Table XX.

The results for tax exemptions (TE, Equations 1–3 in Table XX) show several consistent relationships. The welfare and wealth-demand variables consistently ranked high as important discriminatory vari-

TABLE XX

Discriminant Coefficients and Rank Scores[a]

Equation/Variable	X_1	X_2	X_3	X_4	X_5	X_6	X_7	X_8	X_9	X_{10}	R^2 (test level)
(1) TE (any kind, authorized)	0.00173 (2, 2)	-0.00509 (1, 1)	-0.03243 (5, 5)	0.00006 (10,10)	0.00053 (9, 9)	-0.00012 (6, 6)	0.00833 (4, 4)	-0.00023 (3, 3)	0.00049 (8, 8)	-0.00003 (7, 7)	0.559 (0.100)
(2) TE (state taxes, authorized)	-0.00071 (7, 5)	0.00644 (1, 2)	-0.07661 (3, 4)	-0.00001 (10,10)	-0.00350 (5, 7)	0.00002 (9, 9)	-0.01875 (4, 3)	0.00039 (2, 1)	0.00249 (8, 8)	0.00002 (6, 6)	0.341 (0.500)
(3) TE (local taxes, active)	0.00065 (5, 3)	-0.00991 (2, 2)	-0.02825 (7, 6)	-0.00000 (9, 9)	0.00268 (4, 7)	-0.00021 (6, 5)	-0.00072 (1, 1)	0.00002 (3, 4)	-0.00144 (8, 8)		0.586 (0.025)
(4) IBF (authorized)	-0.00158 (2, 2)	-0.00439 (1, 1)	0.00051 (10,10)	0.00026 (6, 6)	-0.00038 (7, 7)	-0.00078 (5, 5)	0.02239 (3, 4)	-0.00023 (4, 3)	-0.00003 (9, 9)	0.00146 (8, 8)	0.481 (0.100)
(5) IBF (active)	-0.00427 (1, 1)	0.00550 (2, 3)	-0.06945 (5, 5)	0.00010 (7, 8)	-0.00395 (6, 6)	-0.00204 (3, 2)		-0.00043 (4, 4)	-0.00026 (8, 7)	0.00141 (9, 9)	0.638 (0.025)
(6) SIFA (authorized)	-0.00191 (1, 1)	0.00096 (4, 4)	0.02678 (2, 2)	0.00001 (9, 9)	-0.00067 (8, 8)	-0.00006 (7, 7)	0.00157 (6, 6)	0.00000 (10,10)	0.00111 (5, 5)	-0.00011 (3, 3)	0.518 (0.100)
(7) SIFA (active)	-0.00060 (2, 1)	-0.00071 (6, 5)	0.01435 (3, 3)	-0.00008 (8, 8)	0.00160 (4, 7)	0.00001 (9, 9)		-0.00001 (5, 4)	0.00107 (7, 6)	-0.00009 (1, 2)	0.369 (0.250)
(8) SDCC (authorized)	0.00085 (3, 3)	-0.00464 (2, 2)	-0.00980 (7, 4)	-0.00011 (9, 8)	0.00239 (4, 5)	-0.00102 (6, 9)	0.04294 (1, 1)	-0.00000 (10,10)	0.00059 (8, 6)	-0.01283 (5, 7)	0.748 (0.025)
(9) SDCC (active)	-0.00037 (5, 3)	-0.00298 (1, 1)	0.03428 (2, 2)	-0.00027 (6, 7)	0.00179 (3, 6)	-0.00011 (7, 8)		-0.00001 (4, 4)	0.00086 (8, 5)	-0.00618 (9, 9)	0.759 (0.010)

[a] Variable substitutions by (equation, variable) are: State traditions of centralism — Localism, (2, 7), (4, 7), (8, 7); Bank assets per capita, 1963, (3, 8), (6–9, 8); Average unemployment rate, 1957–63, (3, 9); Per cent urban, 1960, (4–5, 6); Tax revenue per capita, 1963, (4–5, 8); Debt per local government unit, 1962, (4–5, 10), (8–9,10); Value added per manufacturing establishment, 1962, (6–9, 3); Counties per SMSA, 1960, (8, 6).

ables though the coefficients are mixed in sign. The distribution of incomes and levels of public expenditures are consistently important factors influencing state tax exemption plans. The least important coefficients are on the industrial growth and labor market variables though again the signs are mixed.

Several variables in the tax exemption equations show substantial disparities in rank scores in at least one of the three equations. The welfare-market variable is important for authorized state and local exemptions; the political variable is similarly influential in the equation for actively used local tax exemptions. The sign on the latter indicates that states with active local tax exemption programs are likely to have strong traditions of intrastate cooperation. Of lesser importance are the resource base and market location variables, which have tied ranks of nine in one equation; neither of these variables is very important in discriminating the state classifications.

Equations 4 and 5 are for authorized and active local industrial bond financing (IBF) programs. Both the welfare and welfare-market variables consistently rank highest as important discriminatory variables. The market location variable is somewhat more important than the resource base variable, especially for actively utilized programs; industrial growth is also more influential than in the tax exemption equations. The least important explanatory factors are the labor-market and debt variables.

The difference between authorized and extensively-used programs arises principally from the changed rank order of the industrialization and market location variables. An industrial base and concentrated markets are much more important in determining "active-use" than authorization of the program; the signs on several variables also corroborate this relation. The low-income states are more likely to have industrial bond financing programs but less likely to use them. The industrial states are less likely to have authorized plans, but of the states with programs the more industrialized are likely to have actively used plans.

Equations 6–9 summarize the results for industrial finance authorities (SIFA) and state-wide development credit corporations (SDCC). The differences in the importance of these variables for these two types of credit institutions are substantial. (1) For SIFA, the most important variables are welfare-market, debt and industrialization with consistent signs for all three coefficients for both authorized and active equations. The industrial growth and market location variables are relatively weak discriminators. (2) For SDCC, the welfare variable is most significant. States with a higher proportion of its citizenry with incomes less than \$3,000 are likely to have both authorized and active programs. Industrial growth, labor markets and debt are the least important discriminatory variables though all have consistent signs in the two equations.

Disparities in the importance of variables between authorized and active equations are evident for both SIFA and SDCC. The availability of local private credit institutions (X_8 – bank assets per capita) is more important in the active than authorized equations for both SIFA and SDCC. For both plans the sign change is consistent and suggests that though the lack of credit institutions influences authorization, their availability is important in determining extent-of-use. The industrialization variable (X_3 – value added per manufacturing establishment) for SDCC also shows a considerable difference between authorized and actively used programs. The sign change indicates that states with relatively large scale enterprises are more likely to authorize legislation, but less likely to be active users. The political variable is also more important in the SDCC equation for authorized plans.

Table XXI summarizes the outlier and mean score statistics for all nine equations listed in Table XX. (The term *adoptor* indicates states with authorized and extensively used plans; the outlier definition is given in footnote *a* to Table XXI.) There are 12 outliers for adoptors and 9 for nonadoptors. The states of Illinois, Massachusetts, Washington and West Virginia are outliers in two equations. Of these states only Illinois is misclassified in two major types of development plans. The development problems associated with West Virginia and Massachusetts are well-known and probably account for their misclassification; special factors may explain the misclassification of Washington.

The tax exemption equations (1–3) misclassify five nonadoptors and only two adoptors, though the standard deviations are lower for nonadoptors than adoptors in all three equations. The local industrial bond financing equations (4, 5) misclassify six adoptors and no nonadoptors; the standard deviations for adoptors exceed those for nonadoptors in both equations. The results for both types of credit plans (Equations 6–9) are mixed in relative magnitude of the standard deviations for both adoptors and nonadoptors.

The empirical results of the discriminant analysis may be summarized as follows:

(1) Regional factors appear to slightly influence both the authori-

TABLE XXI

Outlier and Mean Score Statistics for Discriminant Equations

Equation Number	(1)	(2)	(3)	(4)	(5)	(6)	(7)	(8)	(9)
(1) Number and name of states "incorrectly" classified[a]									
Adoptors	1 (SC)	0	1 (Vt)	4 (Ill, Ind, Colo, Wash)	2 (La, Wash)	1 (W Va)	2 (W Va, Ky)	1 (Idaho)	0
Nonadoptors	1 (Tex)	3 (NJ, Ill, Nev)	1 (Ark)	0	0	1 (Mass)	1 (Mass)	0	2 (Tenn, Ala)
(2) Adoptors[b]									
Mean score	-0.09582	0.10136	-0.52628	-0.21070	-0.21387	-0.06145	-0.06143	-0.00589	-0.07999
Std. deviation	0.03618	0.03670	0.05362	0.03496	0.04025	0.02963	0.03221	0.03455	0.04105
Number	16	7	7	23	13	17	13	28	19
(3) Nonadoptors									
Mean score	-0.04339	0.15820	-0.42666	-0.17053	-0.14650	-0.01580	-0.02437	0.05801	-0.01503
Std. deviation	0.03252	0.03491	0.04538	0.02219	0.03754	0.03246	0.02690	0.04083	0.03517
Number	32	41	41	25	35	31	35	20	29

a The outlier states are those with standardized scores less than or exceeding the mean standardized score of their appropriate group.

b Mean scores for both adoptors and nonadoptors are obtained by substituting the variable means for both classes into the discriminant function. The standard deviations measure the dispersions around the mean scores for both adoptors and nonadoptors.

zation and type of development plan used by states. State-wide credit corporations are more prevalent in eastern states, and tax exemptions and industrial bond financing programs are preferred in the central (northern and southern) regions. Very few states in the western regions utilize any type of development plan.

(2) Correlations among types of programs for a given state are very low. This suggests a lack of complementarity among programs and/or the presence of very specialized factors in explaining the type deemed most suitable for a particular state.

(3) Measures of personal income growth or the distribution of income are consistently important explanatory variables. States appear to be more sensitive to broader welfare measures than to specific conditions within the manufacturing sector. Growth in manufacturing value added and industrial labor are variables with the consistently lowest discriminatory power.

(4) The locational attraction of either a strong resource base or market potential is relatively unimportant in discriminating between states with or without financial incentive plans. The ranks of these variables are consistently low and do not differ significantly from each other.

(5) Some evidence suggests that the traditional arguments for these programs have a relatively minor influence on their authorization and use. Neither the inconsistent sign or low discriminatory power of the public indebtedness variable lend credence to the "tax base expansion" argument often used in support of these programs.

(6) Finally it seems doubtful that those factors that motivate legislatures to adopt development plans are the same variables influencing the success of these programs. The variables showing enhanced importance in the actively used equations are usually economic. For example, the industrial base and market location variables are more important in the active use of local industrial bond financing programs than in their authorization. Similarly the existence of private credit institutions is of much greater importance in determining the success of both types of state-sponsored credit plans. These results are at least consistent with the view that the development efforts of states are not sufficiently sensitive to their specific comparative economic advantages.

CONCLUSIONS

The two studies discussed in this chapter have suggested the types of spatial effects that state policies may have both within and among their jurisdictions. State-enacted exemptions from the payment of property taxes cause inequities in benefits to recipients and local government jurisdictions based solely on locational characteristics associated with the variant desires of communities for local public services. Though these inequities may not influence the residential choices of exemption claimants, the disparity in benefit payment is unrelated to the objectives of the exemption, and the differential net effect on rural and urban governments is undoubtedly an unintended consequence of this policy.

Among states, the attempt to attract new firms or plants does not appear to have had a substantial impact on the spatial distribution of industrial activity. Those factors influencing the authorization of locational incentives are often different from characteristics of states that *de facto* affect their success. Indicators of economic growth in the industrial sector are not very effective in discriminating between states that do and do not have legislation designed to attract new firms or plants; traditional arguments related to tax base expansion also appear to be ineffectual in the authorization of these programs. The evidence suggests that politics (not economics) is the more important consideration in determining the distribution of incentive programs among the various states; the absence of a notable economic impact from these programs may be due in part to their prevalence.

As policy units, the historical stability of state boundaries and legal statutes may exacerbate these effects over time. To the extent that the variance in millage rates increases with urbanization, the inequities associated with local exemptions also increase. The inability of state legislatures to continually review and assess every statute in light of changing economic conditions increases the likelihood of new and unintended effects. The development of regional economies transcending state boundaries may result in a commonality of interests not easily recognized due to the strength of local interests and loyalties. Multistate compacts may be much more effective than interstate competition, for example, in promoting industrial and commercial development. Thus, economic change both within and among states may influence the ability of these units to fashion effective economic policies for their citizenry.

These (and other) studies lead us to conclude that the role of state governments will be continually diminished by the substitution of special districts more attuned to the realities of spatial economic change. The creation of multicounty districts to deal with problems of transportation and other public services will probably continue as the economic boundaries of urbanized regions expand. Problems of a broader regional nature will similarly require the cooperation of numerous state governments, induced, perhaps, by the availability of resources from the federal government to pursue particular objectives. The discussion in this chapter has not directly touched on problems of the appropriate functional distribution of responsibilities between the state and local government or the question of scale economies in the provision of public services. Given the problems inherent in the stability of these policy units, these considerations may be substantially less important than the interest shown by the state and federal governments in promoting substate and multistate units capable of dealing effectively with the problems of regional development.

GENERAL REFERENCES

Bloom, C. C. *State and Local Tax Differentials and the Location of Manufacturing,* Bureau of Business Research, University of Iowa, Iowa City, Iowa, March 1956.

Bridges, B. "State and Local Inducements for Industry," *Natl. Tax J.* **18**:1–14 and 175–192, 1965.

Brown, G. W. "Discriminant Functions," *Annals Math. Stat.,* **18**: 514–520, 1947.

Campbell, A. K. "Taxes and Industrial Location in the New York Metropolitan Region," *Natl. Tax J.* **11**, 1958.

Due, J. F. "Studies of the State-Local Tax Influence on Location of Industry," *Natl. Tax J.* **14**:165–183, June 1961.

Eisenbeis, R. A., and B. Avery. *Discriminant Analysis and Classification Procedures* (Lexington, Mass.: D. C. Heath—Lexington Books, 1972).

Lewis, W. C. "Tax Incentives and Industrial Location," *Rev. Urban Econ.* **1**:29–51, 1968.

McCracken, P. W., (Ed.), *Taxes and Economic Growth in Michigan* (Kalamazoo, Mich.: The Upjohn Institute for Employment Research, 1960).

Morgan, W. E. *The Effects of State and Local Tax and Financial Inducements on Industrial Location,* unpublished doctoral dissertation, The University of Colorado, Boulder, Colorado, 1964.

Prescott, J. R., and W. C. Lewis. "State and Municipal Locational Incentives: A Discriminant Analysis," *Natl. Tax J.* **22**:399–407, 1969.

Prescott, J. R., and G. Gruver. ''The Veterans Property Tax Exemption: Incidence and Policy Alternatives,'' *Land Econ.* November, 1971, (pp. 410–413).

Spears, M. ''Veterans' Property Tax Exemptions,'' *Natl. Tax J.* **11**:129–137, 1958.

Tintner, G. *Econometrics* (New York: John Wiley & Sons, 1952) Ch. 6.

7

Federal Policy: Experimental Cities and New Towns

A coordinated policy toward urban resettlement can best be pursued at the federal level since many of our current urban problems are attributable to interstate migration patterns. Though only one element in an overall policy strategy, new community development has attracted widespread attention due mainly to (1) projections of high density corridor development and (2) rapid rates of decentralization in existing metropolitan regions. The vision of linear urban concentrations that destroy the identities of two or more existing metropolitan communities has suggested the need for entirely new urban developments. Other than the post-W.W. II redevelopment in European cities and Brasilia, few precedents are available in guiding the planning of cities this large. Continuing suburbanization in existing cities decentralizes population from metropolitan cores and raises issues regarding the desirability of unplanned peripheral growth and the possibility of residential redevelopment in centralized locations.

Entirely new metropolitan communities may complement (or hinder) the balance of intercity economic relationships within their spatial spheres of influence. As discussed in Chapter 1, central place theory provides a basis for analyzing the effects of intervention and issues related to optimal location for these cities. The planning objectives established for the new metropolitan community also will affect its viability as an independent unit and the growth characteristics of nearby communities. The Minnesota Experimental City is a particularly interesting example since a variety of urban objectives have been specified for it; most significantly, its structural flexibility (both social and physical) allows for the experimental testing of various urban technologies less easily adapted within existing metropolitan regions.

Small community development has emphasized residential relocation and a changing pattern of private and public services provided to households. The much-discussed new town movement has generally encouraged decentralized growth, while other efforts have attempted to revitalize older residential areas within the metropolitan core. Both development efforts face the problem of a threshold scale sufficient to sustain growth, though the specific nature of the scale problem is quite different in these two cases. Centralized redevelopment encounters substantial competition from a variety of nonresidential land uses while the decentralized new town must attain a scale sufficient to satisfy the higher-order service demands of its residents. As residentiary services and life styles are of primary importance, various social objectives are common to both efforts.

Regardless of the scale of development, the planning of new urban communities assumes some notion of optimal population size. The specification of such planning targets, however, encompasses a host of urban attributes not easily collapsed to a single dimension. The relation of public service costs and city size has been a traditional focus in the urban public finance literature; analogies to the average and total product curves of the theory of the firm have also been constructed. Though central place theory and the observed variation in city sizes run counter to the idea of single optimal size, the growth characteristics of urban systems provide some criteria for specifying planning targets at all levels within the size spectra.

In this chapter we discuss some issues of intervention at both spatial scales. The first two sections include some of the planning considerations associated with the Minnesota Experimental City, while the third contrasts small community residential development in central and decentralized locations. The problem of specifying "optimal" planning targets within the context of city systems is then discussed.

DEVELOPMENT OBJECTIVES FOR
METROPOLITAN REGIONS

The proposed "experimental city" in Minnesota is probably the most comprehensive urban development that has ever been planned in the United States. The planning period is short and the population target large, but even excluding these problems its unique objectives further constrain the actual processes of development. Environmental considerations are of primary importance, as a wide variety of urban technologies are to be tested within its boundaries. These include social and physical innovations that are seldom found in established metropolitan communities due to the diffusion of land ownership and the inherent inflexibility of capital-intensive public and private technologies. The interactions between these unique objectives and the numerous problems associated with physical implementation are the focus of our discussion.

As noted above, rapidity and scale are the principal difficulties in the city's physical development. Initial objectives suggested a 10–15 year planning horizon for a population of 250,000. These objectives imply average annual growth rates of 6–10%, over twice the average metropolitan growth rate during the 1950's. Public investments of about $10–15 billion will be required for the city's residents and must be phased logically with the growth of the private sector. The site will probably be undeveloped, so a substantial effort in parcel consolidation and preparation must be made.

The rapidity with which the city is to be developed poses several problems. (1) The public and private capital stock will initially have a very limited age distribution. Presumably new technologies will be implemented over the planning period and this could eventually result in erratic cycles of maintenance and replacement. Extending the development period and phasing the construction of major systems would tend to alleviate this problem. The developers might purposely select investments of varying economic lives or already-depreciated assets, though the basis on which such selective judgments would be made is unclear. To simply replicate conditions in existing cities seems inconsistent with the experimental objective, though it may minimize problems encountered after the city is well-established. (2) There is also the problem of compatibility with regard to the uniform adoption of the latest technologies. New innovational design must be sensitive to the mixture of old and new technologies in most cities, and development bottlenecks may occur if such complementarity is not attained.

The totally comprehensive nature of the planning effort presents problems of coordination and control. In the absence of a settled pattern of land uses, investment risks in the private sector will be substantial. The planning authority may have to provide guarantees of at least the broader contours of spatially-allowable activities and the provision of essential public services. Overly extensive controls, conversely, may cause substantial inefficiencies in the private sector that discourage firms from locating in the city. Land use plans may have to be supplemented with controls on land values, rents and wages particularly if a decentralized location is chosen. The post-W.W. II redevelopment of European cities suggests the need for such controls; these problems are of an altogether different nature than those encountered by "new town" developers.

The planners will also have to clearly define the appropriate environment for experimentation. The city's innovational experiences should be relevant to the future development of other cities and this suggests a broadly similar social and physical structure. But the presence of substantial innovational activity itself precludes such a structure; in any case, the city will be quite atypical in its earliest years. Experimental activity also suggests a flexible structure and controlled environment. Rigidities such as highly capital intensive physical structures and bureaucratic public organizations must be avoided if the social costs of innovational changes are to be minimized. The ability to effectively control the social and physical environment suggests an extraordinary range of powers vested in the planning authority.

The types of socio-physical innovations tested within the city are also dependent on the external environment and the choice of site. Locations close to Minneapolis-St. Paul will substantially restrict the success of projects designed to provide higher-order, competitive public and private services. Alternatively, hinterland sites will result in high transportation and location costs to private firms and may hinder the city's economic growth. The extent and size of contiguous towns will also influence residential locations, shopping patterns and home-to-work trips, which may, in turn, preclude certain types of experiments with transportation systems. The demand and employment complementarities of the city with these communities will determine the magnitude of its "spread and backwash" effects, which will also influence the success of innovational activity in the city.

The range of basic economic activities within the city will affect both the service sector and the interdependence of all urban sectors with the regional periphery. In the northern counties of Minnesota a forest, minerals or recreational base might develop and the city would be subject to cyclical and seasonal fluctuations in output, employment and local migrational patterns. A more southern location favors heavy manufacturing, agri-business services and a more diversified range of basic economic activities, which may alleviate the cyclical sensitivity of the service sector to fluctuations in external demand. Other public sectors may be less sensitive to problems arising from alternative locations within the state. A public university or highway commission would contribute a relatively high income, cyclically stable component to an otherwise unstable range of basic economic activities. The presence of these activities would also increase the range of services demanded by the high income and younger residents of the city. Though states have rarely pursued an economically-consistent policy with regard to the location of public activities, such a policy could be used to supplement the otherwise less desirable economic characteristics of sites within the state.

The political structure of the city may also be substantially different from existing communities due to the nature of the physical development and innovational activities within the city. The state legislature may not favor the institutional structures necessary if the planning process itself is to be innovative since safeguards for local communities may restrict the type and scope of the development. It is likely that during the initial period a planning authority will be created to carry out the physical development and its organizational structure and powers will substantially influence the types of problems inherited by the metropolitan government. The latter should be organized to encourage innovative activity within its departments and a substantial portion of its efforts will be devoted to program evaluation. The ability of the city government to develop success criteria and to control or change the planning process itself may be the most crucial characteristic in the ultimate success of the city's experimental efforts.

Though experimentation is the primary objective of the city numerous secondary goals have been suggested.

(1) The city will provide job opportunities for the region's under- and unemployed. The size and type of the in-migrant flows will primarily depend on the location and economic base of the city itself. A state-oriented employment policy would provide preferences for instate residents and/or active encouragement of industries using local skills in excess supply, though the strict adherence to such a policy could jeopardize the city's long-run growth prospects.

(2) The city could act as a regional training center preparing potential out-migrants with job skills essential in the larger urban communities. In contrast to (1) above, this objective accepts out-migration from the region and seeks to minimize the adjustment costs on the individual; a "spillover benefit" is provided to the

destination city. Though there is some evidence that even smaller cities *de facto* provide this function, the absorption of these costs suggests a policy of uncommon magnanimity. A wider range of employment and training opportunities in both the public and private sectors would be necessary under this objective. Programs could range from formal schooling with the tuition costs absorbed by the city or subscribing company to on-the-job training seeking a partial recovery of program costs. Firms with their own training programs would be given high priority for locations in the city under this objective.

(3) Employment policies might seek a "maximization of the human input" by encouraging job opportunities with a closer labor-product identity. This is consistent with the view that the city should not be (at least totally) a capital intensive, technologically advanced community. A more balanced mix of human and machine-vending technologies could be sought by encouraging artisan's fairs and farmer's markets; public halls and museums could be more effectively utilized in encouraging local talents.

(4) Some programs might seek a redistribution of nonmonetary income and a social externalization of the efforts of private organizations. The latter includes the leisure time of families and the adoption of community programs by business enterprises. Participation in these programs might be voluntary or actively encouraged by a system of tax credits. A vast untapped reservoir of talents and experience available in the modern leisure-economy could be more effectively utilized.

(5) Social goals could include a more spatially homogeneous socioeconomic order and a closer identification of the resident with his immediate community. The use of neighborhood modules seeking balanced income and racial mixes has been proposed to lessen disparities in financial resources among school districts; its application on a sufficiently broad scale has not yet been attempted. Cooperative retail outlets and local organizations equipped to provide construction, repair and management of public facilities would enhance the individual's personal and public interest in locally provided services.

The interdependence of the city's physical characteristics and its socio-economic objectives is a central element in its ultimate success or failure. Unlike existing communities, the city's planners have the unique opportunity of fixing totally the type and spatial distribution of its stock of public and private facilities within a very short period of time. The benefits and costs of marginal changes will be difficult to evaluate and respond to in an environment of rapid and total development; social relationships will be similarly unsettled and lacking in historical continuity. It seems likely that under such conditions the original objectives and purposes of the city may be easily obscured unless very careful attention is paid to the appropriate strategies for implementation that are compatible with goals of the city.

PLANNING STRATEGIES FOR GROWTH

The planners of the city view the early commitment of large firms as a crucial determinant to subsequent economic development. Flexibility with respect to site selection would be maintained if the private costs of processing and distribution were relatively independent of market or resource-oriented sites. The larger firms should also be relatively independent of the need for very specialized private or public services; agglomeration economies in a city of 250,000 are probably insufficient to provide a permanent base for very specialized services. In the earliest development period, it will also be desirable to minimize the use of regional transportation facilities, and firms with high weight or volume shipping requirements should probably be discouraged. Similarly, firms with labor forces that are both highly mobile and have specialized demands for residential amenities may have difficulties in these earlier years. Efforts should be taken to insure the permanency of the commitment; the decision to locate in the city must be based on profitability of production, not on short-term promotional considerations.

An alternative (or concomitant) strategy is to focus existing private or public investments within the region. As noted above, this could include the relocation of federal, state and county offices providing regional services in addition to site priorities for new governmental installations; a substantial component of the economic base could be developed around these governmental activities. Private recreational investments might be concentrated in a "Tahoe-complex," considerably increasing the range of recreational services provided in the central lake region of Minnesota. In the subsequent attraction of new economic activities to the region the comparative advantages of these activities would hopefully be enhanced.

The city could be developed as a regional or national "showcase community." The development process itself will attract world-wide attention and the presence of innovative physical features (*e.g.,* community domes) would be a permanent attraction for visitors. A substantial flow of tourist income would result and the city would require special residentiary and transportation services to accommodate nonresidents. It is also likely that private firms might base promotional activities in the city that are of particular interest to tourists. Though such an emphasis would again be atypical of existing communities, the planning authority does have strong leverage over income levels by its policy toward physical innovations.

The site selection process for the city presents both political and economic problems for the planners. Incorporated cities and towns may not favor nearby locations and attaining a concensus in the state legislature may be very difficult; alternative sites may be politically restricted to relatively uneconomic and sparsely populated areas. Parcel consolidation on privately-owned unincorporated lands will present substantial difficulties due to the concentration of land necessary for a development of this size. A federally-owned site on Indian or military reservations would somewhat alleviate this problem, but these areas are usually less suited for intensive development. Site alternatives might be restricted to a location roughly centered among the cities of Minneapolis, Winnipeg, Duluth-Superior and Fargo-Moorhead on the expectation that the city would become a nodal center for transportation among these urbanized areas. In these ways the numerous regional site alternatives may be restricted.

The short development horizon suggests the need for a careful selection of priorities in the planning process; the temporal ordering of basic construction activities will have a particularly important impact on the locational decisions of private firms. It has been estimated that about 25% of the target labor force (80,000 persons) will be needed for basic construction to include, in the earliest years, land clearance, underground services, streets and dwellings for residents. The latter might be mobile homes to be used as shells for permanent housing later on in the development period. In later years the construction work force will be occupied with public structures of lower initial priority such as sports areas and the municipal auditorium.

The phasing of publicly provided services will depend on the specific nature of the activity. Regulatory services such as police and fire protection must be provided throughout the development period. From the viewpoint of attracting permanent residents for the city, excellent primary and secondary educational facilities will be an important on-going public service. Sewer, water and gas services may have to be expanded slowly due to the uncertainties about the spatial distribution of the population. Transportation services will be similarly affected by the locational patterns of firms and households and, in addition, they must be logically coordinated with the existing regional transportation network.

Basic economic activities should be given priorities in site development and materials. A fully operational target of 3–4 years might be established for committed firms; the provision of certain low-order public services, amenities and transportation facilities will be necessary for their efficient operation. Some planning flexibility is desirable for it may develop that very specialized services are necessary in the early life of the city. A services complex might be constructed providing office and meeting facilities, hotel and recreational space. Planning and governmental personnel might also be housed in this complex, and if the structural shell is not overly specialized it might be converted to other uses as these services are developed elsewhere in the city. Higher order and larger scale business and household services could be provided in later years when the permanency of the city is assured.

Figure 11 summarizes the development sequences discussed above. In general nonessential activities should be minimized and services not directly contributing to the city's development should be given low priority. A university for example, would require numerous supporting services for faculty and students and should not be constructed in the earliest years. Similarly, hospital and medical facilities should not be expanded beyond a scale necessary to deliver the most essential services to the resident population. The planning authority will have to spatially allow for the ultimate development of these facilities, and this might be done through land acquired for subsequent conversion to public uses. Finally, as shown in Figure 11, spatially determining activities may have to be developed slowly in the earliest years. Only the most efficient services should be provided to minimize capital losses in future years due to spatially unpredictable patterns of development.

The degree to which structures may be rapidly "filtered" into alternative uses will, in part, depend on the land use powers of the planning authority. If the latter possesses strong land use controls, the risks of uncertain spatial distributions of economic activity will be less and specialized investments will be made. This is contrary to the notion of flexibility and should perhaps be discouraged. Less specialized shells allow for more alternative uses and would reduce

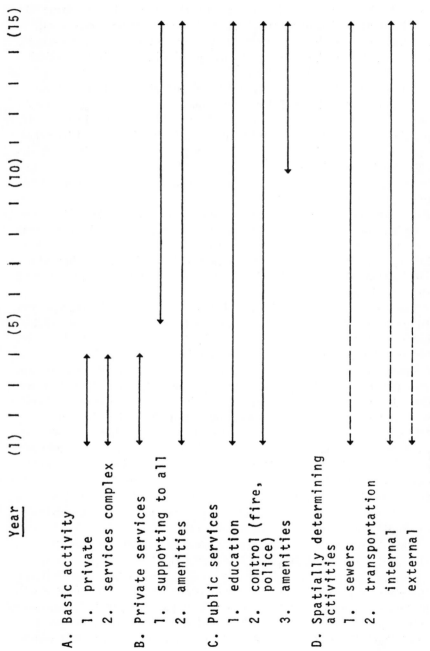

Figure 11: Activity sequence for metropolitan development.

investment costs in temporary structures. Construction technologies that allow for horizontal expansion would avoid problems of uncertain density requirements in different parts of the city.

The utilization of mobile structures will also increase the flexibility with which land may be used during the development period. Numerous public and private services could be regularly provided in mobile units, deferring the investment decision in spatially fixed facilities until higher priority land uses had been established. Any frequently purchased and easily transported commodity or service could be restricted to distribution in these mobile units; library services, food and paper products are examples. These mobile units might be rented at low cost to concessionaries and subsequently converted to public uses.

The rapidity of development will complicate the spatial basis for planning by obscuring the most efficient land uses. The planning authority could reserve sites for possible future public uses and/or resale to private interests when contiguous land uses were established. This would maintain flexibility during the years of uncertainty and allow for low cost expansion of needed public services in areas where rising land valuations rendered such expansion infeasible. A less intensive, dispersed development strategy such as spiraling would avoid premature commitments to inefficient land uses in addition to evening out disparities in the age distribution of the capital stock.

The planning authority must also consider the use of existing facilities and the planned dispersal of major sectors. Rental housing for construction workers might be provided in contiguous cities and towns; some public services (*e.g.*, primary and secondary education) could also be decentralized. The planning authority would have to compensate the cooperating local governments for public services and plan for supplemental transportation services. Many of the spatial planning problems could be alleviated if certain sectors were developed away from the city itself. Centers for the university and government services complex could be planned in outlying locations up to 20 or 30 miles from the city. These service centers could be constructed later in the development period and would relieve pressures on public land uses within the center city.

Manpower planning also involves timing considerations during the development period. Priorities might be established for single males or married couples without young children where the wife can provide a needed public or private service. Efforts should be taken to minimize the variation in the age distribution of the population, thus restricting the range of public services (*e.g.,* medical care and education) needed in the earlier years. Individuals with a fairly wide range of skills and low preferences for specialized amenities would contribute to the stability of the resident labor force.

The development of the city will be influenced by the types of criteria of success that are applied to investment projects in the public sector. These criteria presuppose the existence of normative targets of performance to control the "irreversibility" of less desirable characteristics of urban growth. Automatic planning guidelines or more formal benefit-cost analyses could be institutionalized in the public sector. A beginning could be made by allowing a range within which discretionary judgments are allowed; the early incorporation of these guidelines into the planning process could be a most strategic step in promoting consistent public decision-making in the development and operation of the city.

The numerous practical difficulties of development are additionally complicated by the experimental objectives. Though several physical innovations have been proposed, their capital-intensive nature may preclude further experimentation after the city is established. The alternative to these substantial investments is a flexible environment of rapid experimentation, but some stability must be provided if the city is to be livable and the innovational tests are to be accurately evaluated. There are also a variety of social innovations that have been proposed for the city.

The most radical physical innovation is partial or complete enclosure. Environmental benefits (snow and air pollution exclusion, regulated temperature and sunlight, etc.) are possible by excluding or regulating activities within the enclosed air space. The proposed scale of dome ranges from 1–2 miles in diameter down to the neighborhood level. Air pollution control requires the exclusion of major pollutors and regulation of energy uses inside the domed area; electricity is the most desirable form of energy. Openings in the dome's shell can be used to recirculate the air while sunlight and heat levels can be controlled by the transparency of the dome's windows. Nuisances such as the noise of jet aircraft would also be excluded.

Several sources of efficiency are claimed for the dome. Snowfall removal could be attained by embedding heat wires in the skin of the dome, thus regulating the rate of run-off. Both rain and snow water could be directed into canals around the base of the dome and then into large reservoirs. These water reservoirs could then be drawn down during water deficit periods. Seasonal activities such as construction and recreation could be conducted throughout the year. In addition, the dome would more effectively conserve the heat energy dissipated by open cities.

A vast tunnel complex underneath the city has also been proposed and is designed to provide for the movement of goods, solid wastes and people. The tunnels would provide direct access to underground utilities reducing the repair costs of power and sewer systems. Auto pollutants could presumably be trapped and filtered and the seasonal public service and congestion costs of surface transportation modes would be reduced. Additional cost savings are possible if the tunnel shell can be used as a foundation for ground level structures.

In addition to the substantial costs of these investments there are problems of timing and relevance to environmental conditions in other cities. The external effects on land uses and values from partially doming an existent city would cause political problems possibly even more serious than those associated with rapid transit systems. Implementation may only be feasible in a new city at an early stage of its development and therefore irrelevant for problems in other communities. Similarly, a tunnel complex constructed in advance of a well-established residential sector may create many inefficiencies in the transportation system.

Restrictive practices in urban communities also affect the physical and social environment and have been frequently attacked by planners and public administrators. Physical restrictions include ineffective enforcement and design of maintenance and building codes and the improvement disincentive effects of the property tax. Social and institutional restrictions primarily affect labor market efficiency and residential locational choices; these include restrictions on production techniques, membership in labor unions and trade associations and socially discriminatory practices in housing and education. In such a new city, the planning authority should be in a good position to eliminate these problems particularly if they are institutionalized in the development plan during the earliest years. Some would be avoided due to declining social acceptability; it is presumed, for example, that an open-occupancy statute will be operative. Also the inadequacies of the property tax and the increasing reliance of cities on nonproperty sources of tax revenue will lessen some of the disincentive effects noted above.

Public services planning is an important area for experimentation due to its impact on the quality of the city's residents as producers and citizens. More emphasis might be placed on technological adaptations in the service sectors, particularly at the administrative level, and experimentation with spatially extended planning jurisdictions. Organizational arrangements for a more comprehensive coordination of programs for the precollege population could be attempted in addition to programs for the more active involvement of retired families in community affairs.

In summary, a strong commitment to experimentation will provide the city with the capability of effectively controlling and changing its environment. At the same time long term investments that may be deemed necessary to solve environmental problems will impede the future flexibility of the city's institutions. The planning authority will have to carefully consider these longer term trade-offs; in addition, it must also recognize that the qualitative problems that arise during the development period will be of a different nature than those recognizable in existing metropolitan areas.

With few exceptions the problems associated with the planning of the Minnesota Experimental City will be common to whatever future efforts the federal government may take to develop large metropolitan regions in entirely new locations. The frequently-heard projected need for 10–20 new cities each of a quarter million population by the year 2000 has been tempered by declining rates of natural increase in recent years; nevertheless, it reflects the discouragment of many planners with the unbalanced accommodation of new urban residents in existing cities and the continuing decline of the metropolitan core. If these cities are ever developed they may not have to cope with the complications posed by "physical and social experimentation," but they must avoid the most glaring inflexibilities associated with existing metropolitan regions.

The two major characteristics in planning large cities are the totality of the development and the absence of previously established institutions. The planners of the Minnesota Experimental City will learn much about the problems of physical development on such a scale, but the degree of social experimentation will probably be determined early in the city's life. After the development phase is over, it is doubtful that an environment of "total experimentation" will (or should) be maintained. The success of the city will be difficult to determine but considerable weight will probably be placed on the fate of its physical innovations rather than on the more obscure problems of social welfare and productivity. It is also likely that, once begun, it will not be allowed to flounder further complicating the evaluation of its relative successes and failures. It therefore seems likely that the city's development will provide more insight into problems of (1) resettlement rather than renovation and (2) planning for substantial changes in social institutions, rather than restructuring those in existing urban communities.

SMALL COMMUNITIES AND NEW TOWNS

At the other extreme in the urban size spectra are efforts to encourage residential redevelopment either within metropolitan centers or somewhat beyond the fringes of existing suburban communities. Residential redevelopment downtown must solve the problem of contiguous neighborhood decay and high rates of housing abandonment. Policy approaches must be highly selective spatially since average residential densities within many metropolitan cores are declining and the long run prospects for the housing sector are not encouraging. Most developmental efforts downtown are therefore designed to attract very selective income and occupational groups. At the urban fringes a somewhat opposing set of development problems must be solved. The residential sector tends to be of lower density, and a broader ''income-mix'' of families may be encouraged. Employment opportunities are developed within the new town and the problem of accessibility to high-order central city amenities must be faced. Though of substantially smaller scale than the proposed city discussed earlier, these two development efforts provide sharp contrasts in objectives and planning problems.

Within core areas it has frequently been argued that contiguity of housing units precludes redevelopment expenditures that are ''socially optimal.'' Decision-makers are mutually dependent on their own development decisions so inaction may be privately optimal, although socially inadequate. Residential blight occurs and redevelopment is possible only if these mutually dependent incentives are internalized within a developmental unit with broader planning powers. The urban renewal authority is an example of such a unit with very substantial land use controls, though smaller neighborhood improvement organizations are designed to overcome similar problems. Other difficulties such as high crime rates, inadequate educational services and the absence of employment opportunities may or may not be causally related to this problem but undoubtedly contribute to it. Physical deterioration occurs though the combined forces of family ties and low income may preclude high rates of residential relocation particularly if the phenomenon is common elsewhere in the city.

Reconversion to nonresidential uses is impeded by several problems. Residentiary services such as retail stores face declining local incomes and population in addition to competition from larger scale super-markets that may be located nearby. Zoning ordinances may preclude large-scale productive activities such as manufacturing and ware-housing; for many other reasons these firms are tending to relocate away from core areas anyway. Land ownership in the blighted neigh-borhood also faces the prospect of subsequent reconversion to public use due to the construction of transportation arterials or the expan-sion of existing institutions (universities, governmental offices, etc.). These factors suggest the numerous interdependencies and dynamic considerations not readily analyzed in the traditional theory of land rents summarized in Chapter 1.

Dwelling unit abandonment is frequently the result of these eco-nomic forces and a most serious indication of the condition of urban land markets. The expected future tax claims on the property exceed the prospective resale or reconverted returns and a dynamic process leading to owner abandonment proceeds. First, maintenance expendi-tures decline and rental delinquencies increase. In early stages evic-tions may occur but later on rental adjustments are usually made as vacancy rates rise. Then tenant abandonment may occur, resulting in zero rental revenues. As vacancies rise and neighborhood deteriora-tion continues, deposit charges are dropped and end-of-month move-ments increase. Rental collection expenses exceed revenues from the tenants and itinerant families are free to occupy the unit. Finally as the landlord perceives no alternative uses for the property, tax pay-ments and utility charges go unpaid and title is abandoned. The unit is totally unmanaged and becomes a shelter for drug addicts, gangs, dying animals, etc.

Though the abandonment process appears to be quite spatially selective, many of the older cities have recognized the problem and attempted to deal with it. Atlanta, Baltimore, Chicago, Detroit, New York City, Philadelphia and St. Louis are cities with programs at various stages of development. In Philadelphia about 350 housing units are abandoned per month in diverse areas such as West Ken-sington, Mantua-Heddington and the north and south central districts surrounding the central city. The census tracts with the heaviest abandonment rates in Philadelphia ring the downtown area at a distance of approximately 2–3 miles; residential redevelopment in center city has taken the form of high-density apartment or town house construction for higher income families. Several approaches have been taken to the abandonment problem.

(1) Early attempts in Philadelphia have been directed toward the classification of neighborhoods by the degree of deterioration with a corresponding differentiation in policy approaches. Various social indicators reflecting racial composition, condition of the housing stock and their changes over time are calculated for the most blighted neighborhoods and compared to similar indicators for stable census tracts. The latter serve as approximate targets for redevelopment in the blighted communities.

Tracts that appear to be on the verge of experiencing high rates of housing abandonment may be designated for a substantial upgrading of municipal services; relatively stable residential densities accompanied by declining incomes are the principal classifying indicators. Special efforts in trash collection, street cleaning, police and fire protection, health services and education would be the major policy instruments in preventing further deterioration.

Rapidly declining residential property values characterize tracts at a more advanced stage of deterioration. These neighborhoods also qualify for the service priorities noted above in addition to more stringent controls over residential development. The economic goal is to maintain commercial and residential investment at a level necessary for self-sustaining growth and a desirable living environment. Some proposals include a community housing corporation overseen by political and real estate representatives who would review grants, loans and mortgages requested by landlords and homeowners to ensure that property transactions are compatible with the overall development goals of the community. This corporation might also provide low-cost guarantees for residential investments to lower the risks inherent in neighborhoods undergoing rapid rates of abandonment.

A final category distinguishes census tract sections for which clearance seems to be the only remedy in the long run. Areas with abandoned properties constituting upwards of 40% of the housing stock have few prospects for redevelopment with existing structures and reconversion is much more likely if these buildings are razed. Resources are needed to finance relocation payments to tenants and resident landlords, acquisition costs and the expenses of demolition and clearing the land. Properties may be taken under eminent domain, and redevelopment occurs under planning processes similar to those in the traditional urban renewal program. Though this stage is similar to other urban redevelopment programs, the less drastic categories discussed above provide for some prescriptive measures that have not usually characterized existing programs for metropolitan areas sponsored by the federal government.

(2) A somewhat less centrally planned approach is to offer abandoned dwelling units at low-cost long-term leases with property tax forgiveness up to the period when the resident attains title to the unit. Normally incurred housing expenses are devoted to redevelopment for a period of about five years and the successful "urban homesteader" may resell or continue to reside in the unit after the leasing period is terminated. The city eventually attains tax revenues from the parcel, though resale for nonresidential uses is precluded. Some initial successes with urban homesteading appear to have been achieved in Wilmington, Delaware.

Successful residential developments in central cities have usually been oriented toward higher income families in very selective stages of the life cycle. Georgetown, Society Hill and the less spectacular condominium developments recently constructed in many cities offer excellent access to work or centrally located amenities at relatively high housing costs. Suburbanites who are disenchanted with rising property taxes and commuting expenses may readily be attracted back to the central city, particularly if the children are in college or have established families of their own. Younger, childless business executives may also find the attractions of the central city preferable to lower density living in less accessible locations.

The potential demand for higher income downtown residences may therefore be significantly influenced by existing tax and service disparities between the central city and suburban locations. The latter offer precollege educational services usually superior to public schools in the central city, and, where private schools are not available, high-income residents may choose noncentral residences to educate their children. Through later stages occupational earnings differentials may act as a filter separating back-migrants to the central city from longer term suburban residents. Professionals and business executives will be more likely to relocate centrally than school teachers and other public employees. Relocation patterns may be even more sharply differentiated as retirement approaches. The highest income families can afford expensive central city apartments whereas the less wealthy may move to a retirement community beyond the suburban fringe. The lower income retired family may stay in the paid-off home or relocate locally in a modest apartment.

For many of the older metropolitan communities these forces have resulted in fairly disparate patterns of population change among neighborhoods. Census tracts in core locations show substantial variations in population change as the higher density residential development may be quite close to a tract undergoing urban renewal or conversion due to freeway construction. Several miles from the central business district more stable rates of population decline occur, and their prevalence accounts for the net decline in central city populations that have been observed in many larger cities over the past several decades. Beyond this ring of declining tracts the population stabilizes and decadal rates of change show less variation. Finally, in the suburban community ring positive (but more variant) rates of population change appear.

Federal policies have tended to influence residential rings within metropolitan regions showing highly variant population changes and also seem to have been directed toward residential decentralization and employment centralization. The home mortgage guarantee programs of F.H.A. are often cited as an important contributing factor to suburban growth and downtown residential decline since single family home ownership has been emphasized. Freeway construction has had its most visible impact on neighborhoods within metropolitan cores and has generally been designed for the auto home-to-work trip connecting decentralized residences with jobs located downtown. The urban renewal program has also encouraged commercial and industrial activity back to centralized locations and, more recently, the numerous poverty programs have attempted to reemploy low-income families in central work locations.

Though uncoordinated, the overall thrust of federal policies in metropolitan regions has been to increase home-to-work transportation expenses and promote costly urban sprawl; within core areas high cost and risky locational redevelopments have been encouraged. Though increasingly sensitive to the cohesiveness of communities within the broader urban area, neighborhoods have been disrupted and residents diffused throughout the region. Rather than beginning with the goal of neighborhood development, traditional policies have been primarily designed for suburban nonresidents and centrally located commercial interests. Though the interests of all these groups are interdependent, it is not unlikely that unless more emphasis is placed on the central resident, core areas of the future will be reserved solely for higher order amenities and work place locations.

The term "new towns" has been applied to highly diverse set of community developments often characterized by the opposite problems to those discussed above. Company towns, communes, religious communities, large suburban tracts and "project cities" associated with state or federal resource developments have been included by various writers as new towns; the semiautonomous, privately financed communities of Reston and Columbia are a somewhat closer representation to the traditional new town concept used in England. Several common characteristics of these efforts can be contrasted to the problems found in established cities.

(1) Development is usually comprehensive and at some distance from established urban areas. Parcels of rural land must be consolidated, usually by a large private or public corporation and the rates at which new in-migrants are attracted largely determines the financial success of the development.

(2) The low density character of the new town necessitates large investments in social overhead facilities. The transportation grid, water supply and sewerage systems are initially constructed and amortized in the costs to residents. Depending on the age distribution of the local population, educational and recreational facilities may also be needed.

(3) Unlike the redevelopment of urban neighborhoods, substantial efforts are usually made to attract an employment base since few nonagricultural work opportunities are available locally. Craftsmen, artists and writers are engaged in relatively footloose occupations and may be readily attracted to low density residential towns. As in many cases the attraction of the new town is its semirural nature; heavy industrial and commercial activities are usually excluded, and industries closely related to the agricultural base (furniture, food processing, textile products, etc.) are established.

(4) The development of new community relationships, not the preservation of traditional ones, is a major problem for the new town. Though many new communities have relied on a single motivating objective, the plurality of interests found in the resident population often results in unsatisfied demands for a wide variety of services. If the primary objective (employment, religious homogeneity, etc.) is not attained, then the town's longer term future is threatened. Also, unlike the neighborhoods of the larger, eastern metropolitan regions ethnic homogeneity has not been an important cohesive factor, though some writers have argued that much of the

impetus to white outmigration from central cities to new communities is due to the changing racial composition of urban cores.

(5) The new community usually must make a concerted effort to satisfy both a particular need of its residents and an external demand for its services. A residentiary service that is unavailable elsewhere must be efficiently provided and, where local productive activity is a crucial determinant of income, the community must be willing to effectively compete in its external environment. In the absence of public or private subsidies, few towns can survive unless there is competitive will and cooperative cohesion quite atypical of neighborhoods within larger cities. The Amana towns in Iowa are an example of this competitive determination combined with a primarily religious objective; they have prospered where numerous religiously-based resettlement efforts have failed. Often this social cohesion has been attained only at the expense of individual freedom, and subtle authoritarian pressures may be exerted. In many cases the inability of the new town to survive is directly related to the lack of diversity in productive activities or amenities.

A federal policy toward new town development should probably not attempt to accommodate all the types of resettlements noted above. Aid to religiously based towns is legally suspect and the private sector's residential developments should be subsidized only if a very clear public policy objective is to be satisfied. The various objectives underlying the establishment of communes do not appear to warrant public support, and since the "project city" type of development is usually short-lived the continued subsidization of these communities seems wasteful. Currently only a limited number of planning grants have been accorded to new towns with primarily residential characteristics, and many object to the limited perspective of the new town movement implied in "subsidizing the suburb."

The benefits attributable to decentralization are one basis on which public policy guidelines could be established. A clear definition of the irreversible development patterns in central cities that result in substantial social costs (or preclude further growth) would suggest the types of decentralized satellite communities that might be encouraged. Weekend-based recreational complexes or productive activities that are excluded from centralized locations would be several possibilities. In the context of broader regional development new towns may provide a means of overcoming particularly severe impediments to locational change and redevelopment. Under this guideline the grantor requires a detailed study of development patterns in all cities within the region and a clear justification for the basic objective pursued by the new town.

The new community may also add significantly to the national cultural heritage. Towns that effectively market the products of less advantaged minorities and in other ways encourage the survival of their cultures might qualify for subsidization on this basis. Artisan communities with a promising artistic tradition or an ''established school'' of residents is another type of town providing benefits for the general populace. Communities that service the tourist population near established historical or natural landmarks might similarly be encouraged. Such efforts could promote national or international tourism and provide substantial benefits by preserving local traditions that have played an important historical role in the nation's development.

Social and technological experimentation is another objective that might result in development benefits that are useful to the broader national community. As discussed above, architectural designs that represent a broader income and racial mix of the resident population have attracted much interest in recent years. Experimentation with low-density transportation innovations and less easily adapted methods of instruction in primary and secondary schools are additional examples. Indeed, the general testing of public service delivery systems that encourage the substitution of capital for labor might provide numerous insights into the problems of service cost reduction.

The development of small communities and new towns necessarily involves a less comprehensive planning effort than the larger urban complex described earlier (pp. 176–181). Because of the specialized nature of the problem that may justify redevelopment it is less easy to draw general principles and objectives on which a national policy might be based. The enormous resource waste that accompanies high rates of housing abandonment requires ameliorative measures to ease the transition for affected residents. Conversely, the justification of new towns need not rest on problems of market failure in the larger cities and may offer highly imaginative and innovative experimental insights. Despite such diverse justifications for public intervention, planning criteria have tended to emphasize population size and density in attempting to develop guidelines for urban redevelopment; it is to these criteria that we now turn.

OPTIMAL CITY SIZE

The discussion above has emphasized problems of urban redevelopment at the extremes in the size spectrum. The very largest metropolitan regions are characterized by increasingly severe problems of congestion and environmental pollution; the net external costs associated with these regions can be reduced by encouraging decentralized growth patterns. Small towns, neighborhoods in larger cities and specialized communities lack the scale sufficient to provide high order services or the resources needed to solve particularly severe economic problems. Hence a solution to the problems of large metropolitan areas (*i.e.*, small community development) may present difficulties unless an intermediate size represents an optimal scale of city.

Many writers suggest that cities in the approximate population range of 100,000 to 400,000 are both able to avoid the problems of environmental degradation and provide a reasonable range of high order public and private services. (The planning target of 250,000 persons for the Minnesota Experimental City reflects these considerations.) Though these criteria are not comprehensive, their detailed specifications might provide useful guidelines for the urban redevelopment policies of the federal government. Residentiary services and interdependencies are usually emphasized and the more important economic considerations underlying the formation of city systems are often neglected. Even the term "optimal city size" is suspect since historically stable size distributions have been empirically observed. Several interpretations of optimality have been discussed.

(1) A single city may be interpreted as a productive unit similar to a firm in an industry, but with population as the principal independent variable influencing costs and output; the latter includes the dollar production of all private and public goods and services within the urban economy. If the stock of public and private facilities constitute the fixed plant, then a U-shaped average total cost curve might be hypothesized, and the minimum per capita costs at a particular population level would be one definition of optimal size. Other defined optima depend on the relation between population size and average per capita output. If total output has a maxima, then the city is a sales maximizer at that population scale. The size at which marginal costs and marginal revenues are equated would normally provide another scale at which per capita net product is maximized. Given a linear average per capita output function and a U-shaped cost curve there may be a range in which net product is positive on a per capita basis.

Most of the optimizing criteria would normally fall within this range. Small cities are not large enough to efficiently utilize the plant of optimal scale, and negative net product results in out-migration and population decline. The very largest cities attract populations that overcrowd the fixed factor, and congestion raises the per capita costs of producing output. Though it is unclear that even the largest cities have reached this point, the negativity of net per capita output should similarly result in out-migration and population decline. The cost and product curves may shift over time, so cities that grew in population at one point in time may subsequently decline and vice versa.

One problem with this interpretation of optimal size is that over time the range of viable population sizes has enormously increased. Many of the smaller rural communities have decreased in size, but stabilized at lower levels as they have adapted to specialized functions less dependent on the agricultural sector. (The Midwestern rural retirement community discussed in Chapter 2 provides an example.) Some very small towns and hamlets continue to exist at sizes that are probably little in excess of minimal scales typically found a century ago. At the upper end of the size range, the scale frontier steadily continues to be pushed back. Despite the decline of some metropolitan cores, the urbanized regions continue to grow into the suburban fringe and the maximum size has yet to be determined. This raises the possibility that positive net product per capita is virtually constant for a wide range of scales, and the notion of an optimal size is of little use in this case.

Another difficulty with the single city-firm analogy is that it obscures the variations in product-mix suggested by central place theory and evident in empirical observation. Within size classes of cities producing a similar mix of outputs there may indeed be a variation in net per capita outputs that could be usefully analyzed. These variations may be due to inefficiently provided public services, lagging adaptation of newer techniques in the private sector and other causes. The city may have just reached a population threshold justifying several new but initially high cost public and private services, which renders a comparison with costs at the previous product mix difficult. If anything, cities are multiproduct firms with a highly positive correlation between size and number of products, and the range of problems (joint supply, input complementarities, etc.) are only assumed away under single product and cost curves.

(2) Other studies have attempted to empirically estimate per capita

cost functions for a variety of public services. Population is again the scale measure, but it may refer to either city size or the number of persons within a service district. Though some variations are found among these studies, it is typically concluded that horizontally integrated services (police, fire) tend to be provided at constant cost whereas some vertically integrated services (water supply, sewerage systems) may be subject to declining cost to scale.

Under this criterion the optimal-sized city depends on the cost characteristics of each public service district. Some city sizes may be too small to efficiently conduct a particular service at its optimal scale. If the minimum cost service district is less than the city's population then, aside from the indivisibility problem, that service can presumably be provided at relatively low cost. Since public services do not show strongly hierarchical patterns among cities of different sizes as in the private sector, comparisons along the size spectra can be made. Several problems are also apparent with utilizing the public service criterion as a planning guideline.

Cost minimization is not net benefit maximization. Though school districts, for example, may be subject to a range of declining per capita cost it seems doubtful that the optimal cost scale is sufficient to internalize the benefits of the service. Since students typically out-migrate from the district after high school it has been argued that school boards underinvest in educational facilities as their constituents receive little benefit from the service. Though primary/secondary education is a service eliciting the most citizen interest and may therefore be the least likely area to which this argument should be applied, the general principle remains. "Spill-out" benefits accrue to the citizenry outside the district and cost minimization is not the only consideration.

Another consideration in interdistrict equity in financing the particular public service. Cities with public service districts of minimum cost scales may also have substantial variations in property taxes per family. Depending on the spatial distribution of wealth, rearranging district boundaries to reduce these variations while maintaining the size that minimizes costs may or may not be possible. This problem is increasingly important in the core areas of metropolitan regions as the out-migration of commercial and industrial wealth sharpens resource disparities between the nodal center and peripheral communities. Nonminimal costs might have to be incurred to even out the access of residents to high quality public services.

Though of increasing importance, public service costs are not the only consideration for the establishment of new towns or the redevelopment of smaller communities. As suggested in the discussion on small communities and new towns (p. 189), numerous private market phenomena and socially important objectives may constitute legitimate grounds for publicly planned development. It has also been suggested in Chapter 1 that means of more flexibly reconstituting metropolitan and public service boundaries might do much in easing the various types of problems underlying the "urban fiscal crisis." The latter is probably not an inherent problem of urban scale and density alone.

(3) Central place theory emphasizes the interdependence of cities of different sizes within a cohesive regional system of settlements. Unlike the absolute population size criteria discussed above, this concept provides a better means of analyzing systematic disparities in a regional system of cities along the entire size spectrum. Cities may also provide specialized functions for the broader regional community (transhipment node, political capital, etc.) and these particular roles are not distinguishable under the population scale criterion above.

Within the hierarchical city system, cost curves for private services are L-shaped with no unique minima for a particular size of settlement. The specific service is found within the lowest order city constituting the size threshold and in all cities exceeding that size A fine continuum of thresholds among services provides a well-differentiated hierarchy, and the opposite would occur in systems where the minimum-sized scales were clustered at distinct points along the population scale. If technologies are uniformly adaptable within the city system, then the height of the cost function is of little importance, but technical change may lower or raise the threshold sizes of services over time therefore changing the service-mix of activities among cities within the region. Changes in the demand for particular services will also affect their availability in similar cities near the threshold. The presence of a good or service offered only in one city or a selective set of urban size classes would contradict the cost conditions implied in central place theories.

Within the size distribution no particular urban scale may claim to be optimal or nonoptimal. Regions with very dominant centers and less well-developed peripheral towns may coexist with city systems where the opposite conditions are found. Though various causal factors may be operative in both cases, this concept allows for a finer differentiation of the particular problem that may characterize the regional system. In the former case, low peripheral incomes, barriers to the decentralization of services and an inadequate intraregional transportation system may favor centralized growth and another set of problems may be found where regional centers are undeveloped. Though an entirely new community may not be necessary in this example, the notion of a single-sized optimal city is of little use in appreciating the many possible reasons for disparities within the size distributions of these two cases.

Functional specialization is another phenomenon that seems relevant to planned development, but less easily adapted under the absolute scale criteria for optimality. Individual cities of alternative sizes often play specialized roles such as tourist centers, retirement communities, and commercial transportation nodes, and the planning for new towns must be sensitive to these concentrations of service activities within the region. The interdependence of communities within the region is perhaps best exemplified in the various functional categorizations distinguished by economic geographers; wholesaling, stock and commodity exchanges, cultural centers, etc. are additional functions that may dominate the economies of particular cities. Though central place theories do not offer adequate explanations of these patterns of specialization, the diversity of city sizes that are emphasized are more compatible with the functional phenomena.

Spatial relationships are also emphasized within the context of central place systems and not usually considered under the absolute size criterion; systems of cities within very low-density agricultural regions may play similar roles to those found in the more urbanized areas, though the minimum and maximum city sizes are quite different. In such comparisons, it is difficult to conceive of an absolute optimum-sized city compatible within both regions. The distances that separate cities of a particular size may also vary considerably among low and high-density regions, so the competitive pressures to specialize may also vary.

This discussion suggests the range of unsettled issues and problems in specifying planning criteria for urban redevelopment. Many of the objectives and justifications for intervention are a mixture of economic and noneconomic factors, so single-dimensioned criteria are probably insufficient. Table XXII shows recent population growth trends that will undoubtedly influence the success or failure of whatever policy guidelines might be developed. In both decades, population growth in urbanized areas (*i.e.*, essentially cities in excess of 50,000 persons) was about double that of the nation whereas the

TABLE XXII

Population by Size of Place for the United States:
1950, 1960 and 1970

	1950ᵃ	1960ᵃ	1970ᵃ	(% change) 1950–60	1960–70
United States	150,967	179,323	203,212	19.0	13.3
Urban	96,468	125,269	149,325	29.9	19.2
Inside urbanized areas	69,249	95,848	118,446	38.4	23.6
Outside urbanized areas	27,598	29,420	30,878	6.6	5.0
Places of:					
25,000 or more	7,406	6,935	6,932	-6.4	-0.0
10,000–25,000	8,248	9,238	9,687	12.0	4.9
5,000–10,000	6,300	6,918	7,739	9.8	11.9
2,500–5,000	5,643	6,330	6,521	12.2	3.0
Rural	54,230	54,054	53,887	-0.0	-0.0
Places of:					
1,000–2,500	6,473	6,497	6,656	0.4	2.4
Under 1,000	4,031	3,894	3,852	-3.4	-0.1
Other rural	43,725	43,664	43,379	-0.0	-0.0

ᵃ In thousands

Source: U.S. Bureau of the Census, *U.S. Census of Population: 1960 and 1970*, Volume 1.

growth rate in urban places under 50,000 was less than 40% of the national growth rate. Between 1960 and 1970, population in the average city outside of urbanized areas increased by only 5% (an average rate less than that expected from net natural increase) resulting in a sizeable net out-migration. Though some diversity in growth experience is found along the city size continuum, the predominant trend is towards centralized growth within the very largest metropolitan regions.

CONCLUSIONS

In this chapter we have discussed some problems of direct intervention at the lower and upper extremes in the urban size spectra and the specification of planning criteria for urban redevelopment. The developers of the Minnesota Experimental City would be faced with an enormous number of objectives, alternative strategies and problems of physical implementation; truly comprehensive planning would be necessary. The development of a new town usually involves a more limited objective that is primarily residential in nature, though an equally diverse array of goals seems to have historically motivated various attempts to establish these communities. The specification of adequately detailed planning criteria for the size and location of new settlements is vastly complicated by the wide variety of these goals.

The "irreversibility" of growth processes in large cities and the need to accommodate an increasing population in new urban developments are common arguments in support of these efforts. In the larger metropolitan regions many planners suspect that reducing observed disparities in public services between the central city neighborhoods and suburban communities is no longer possible and that programs should be designed solely to ease the severest consequences of locational transition to a primarily nonresidential core. Though Table XXII reflects declining birth and population growth rates in recent years, it also shows the steady increase in the share of total population that prefers urbanized regions. From 1960–70 the population in urbanized areas grew by about 25 million persons, enough to accommodate about 100 cities the size of the metropolitan community planned in Minnesota. The percentage of total population that is urbanized increased by 7% from 1950 to 1970.

These autonomous development efforts should be incorporated within a framework of a national policy toward urban growth and resettlement. The various locational influences exerted by present programs are frequently inconsistent, inadequately recognized and uncoordinated both within and among urbanized regions of the nation; they are certainly not spatially neutral in their impacts. The traditional programs of state and local governments are ill-attuned to exerting significant leverage on locational growth patterns and could not be well-coordinated on a national basis. The development of substantially more sophisticated resettlement criteria would be a substantial aid in formulating such a policy and should be extended to include the various socio-economic objectives discussed above, in which a clear national interest is involved. Experimentation with these objectives in the actual development of prototype communities, if only on an initially limited scale, could be an important step in structuring planning processes that might ameliorate some of the worst consequences of urban growth.

GENERAL REFERENCES

Alonso, W. "The Economics of Urban Size," *Papers Reg. Sci. Assoc.* **26**:67–83, 1971.

Cameron, G. C. *Regional Economic Development: The Federal Role* (Baltimore: The Johns Hopkins Press, 1970).

Cameron, G. C. "The Regional Problem in the United States—Some Reflections on a Viable Federal Strategy," *Regional Studies,* Vol. 2, 1968.

Chinitz, B. "Appropriate Goals for Regional Policy," *Urban Studies* **3**:1–7, 1966.

Committee for Economic Development. *Distressed Areas in a Growing Economy* (New York: Committee for Economic Development, 1961).

Friedmann, J. *Regional Development Policy: A Case Study of Venezuela* (Cambridge, Mass.: MIT Press, 1966).

Friedmann, J., and W. Alonso. *Regional Development and Planning Part IV,* "National Policy for Regional Development," (Cambridge, Mass.: MIT Press, 1964).

Hansen, N. M. *French Regional Planning* (Bloomington: Indiana University Press, 1968).

Hirsch, W. Z. "The Supply of Urban Services," in *Issues in Urban Economics,* (Harvey Perloff and Lowdon Wingo, Eds.) (Baltimore: The Johns Hopkins Press, 1968).

Leven, C. L. "Establishing Goals for Regional Economic Development," *J. Amer. Institut. Planners* **30**:99–105, 1964.

Lewis, W. C. "Public Investment Impacts and Regional Economic Growth, *Water Resour. Res.* **9**:851–860, 1970.

Pittsburgh Regional Planning Association, Economic Study of the Pittsburgh Region, Vol. III, *Region With a Future* (Pittsburgh: University of Pittsburgh Press, 1963).

Prescott, J. R. "The Planning for an Experimental City," *Land Econ.* **46**:68–75, 1970.

Wilson, T. *Policies for Regional Development,* University of Glasgow Social and Economic Studies, Occasional Paper No. 3 (Edinburgh: Oliver and Boyd, 1964).

Winnick, L. "Place Prosperity vs. People Prosperity: Welfare Consideration in the Geographic Distribution of Economic Activity," in *Essays in Urban Land Economics* (Los Angeles: University of California, 1966).

8

Summary and Conclusions

In this book we have considered numerous methodological and policy issues along the size continuum of subnational regions. From State Center, Iowa, with a population of 1,200 to the 7 million inhabitants of greater Chicago there is an astonishing diversity of economic and demographic characteristics. An underdeveloped public and private service sector and a declining agricultural population encourage out-migration from the State Centers of the rural hinterland; congestion, pollution and the inefficiencies of high density employment erode the economic base of the metropolitan core. The diversity apparent in these extremes is primarily the result of economic interdependence and spatial specialization, a secondary theme that has characterized the work in this volume. The task of this chapter is to summarize our discussion and synthesize some issues among the spatial units considered in the previous chapters.

SUMMARY

Three models of urban-regional structure form the basis for most empirical work on subnational economics. (1) The spatial distribution of urban land uses is determined by the ability of productive units to simultaneously outbid competitors for land parcels and pay transportation costs to market their products. An analogous choice between commuting and housing costs for households determines the spatial distribution of residences around central work place locations. (2) Economic base models emphasize the role of exports in determining regional levels of aggregate economic activity and population. The locational incidence of employment growth is not distinguished in the traditional base model, and the influences of increasing household income and sectoral shifts in the mix of economic activities within the region are not emphasized. Though economic base concepts are most applicable to the smallest regional units, the recursive sequence from exports to local activity is usually a part of all regional models (input-output, multiequation econometric, etc.) applied to various spatial scales. (3) Central place theories emphasize the interdependence of rural and urban communities and the size distribution of urban places within a region. The increasing size of minimum market threshold determines the array of economic goods and services provided at various levels in this distribution. Interdependence among regional units results in rank-order criteria that may be used to test the stability of urban systems.

Principles of spatial economic delineation usually have been based on concepts of homogeneity and nodality, instead of the models noted above. The distribution of a characteristic within and among regions is the basis for regional selection and usually no consideration is given to the functional relationships described in economic models. Rural communities are dependent nodal units embedded in a fairly homogeneous agricultural plain; labor markets include a full hierarchy of communities centered on a daily commuting radius. (The latter is, indeed, a spatial economic characteristic but not a direct consequence of regional theory.) Geographic attributes define river basins, and the most central of places are the heterogeneous, quasi-independent metropolitan regions. The federal, state and local governmental units have evolved as policy regions with somewhat obscurely defined boundaries of functional specialization and do not conform to the more general delineating principles discussed in Chapter 1. As suggested there, currently used regionalization concepts are very general and should be better integrated with theories of regional economic structure and growth.

The extreme dependency of rural communities suggests that their problems must be considered within a fairly broad spatial framework. Fluctuations in agricultural income and competition with larger trade centers within the region combine to constrain the availability of locally-provided goods and services and threaten its financial institutions. Regional specialization may provide some degree of independence from these economic forces, though it is usually a second-best substitute for a healthy economic base. Indicators of labor force and sectoral productivity are not markedly adverse to the development prospects of the smallest towns, but scale differentials among city-size classes are apparent; the decentralization of shopping centers from labor market central cities will cause a further decline in small town retail establishments. Community consolidation seems unlikely, but is an apparent prescription from rank-size studies that generally reflect the underachieving status of the smallest towns. Proposals that encourage a general decentralization of policy resources to the smaller communities of labor markets seem ill-attuned to the probably more viable long run patterns of economic specialization. Certainly the development of spatially-fixed, capital intensive service facilities in towns experiencing long run population decline is not likely to be successful.

Labor markets are the minimum-sized regions characterized by both a well-developed urban hierarchy and a substantial degree of economic independence. The "growth-centers" development strategy would focus programs in the central cities of these regions with the expectation that their development benefits would be diffused throughout the hinterland. The econometric model described in Chapter 3 does not generally support the presumption that centralized population and income growth will have positive "spill-over" effects in the smaller communities. The spatially hierarchical patterns of spending are remarkably strong within these regions and centralized growth would probably be detrimental to the retail and service sectors of noncentral cities. Some encouraging patterns of employment decentralization were also noted from statistics underlying the model, a trend that might possibly be discouraged by centralizing the residentiary growth of the region. From 1960–70, population growth continued to be centralized within labor markets, a trend that was also noted for the period 1958–63. Intraregional differentials in per capita incomes and their distribution also favored central counties, and some evidence suggests that the development of transportation facilities linking central counties to other regions may have played a significant role in encouraging these growth patterns. The evidence from both samples discussed in this chapter suggests that though centralized population growth characterizes these regions, the benefits of this growth are probably not widely diffused throughout noncentral counties.

The development of inland waterway and harbor facilities among and within river basins presents numerous difficulties to the regional economist. Traditional evaluative procedures for waterway investments emphasize localized patterns of trade and ignore the broader interdependence of long haul commodity flows among regions in the United States. Chapter 4 describes some of the most important problems encountered in estimating interstate commodity flows that are potentially eligible to be carried on inland waterways. Most of these problems stem from the inadequacies of existing interregional flows data and the tendency to collect statistics on a modal basis. Programming techniques are combined within input-output projections and regression analyses to estimate base and projected year flows for 19 commodities over the period 1960–80. The spatial and commodity disaggregation necessary in this study revealed a substantial heterogeneity of regional characteristics that may influence the correct estimation of subnational commodity trade. The estimation problems associated with transportation costs, interregional distances, coastal trade, foreign exports and imports clearly suggest the necessity of collecting more accurate origin-destination data for studies of regional trade.

Metropolitan regions are the most spatially and sectorally heterogeneous units considered in this book. At the top of the central place hierarchy, a wide variety of private and public services are offered within metropolitan boundaries, and the spatially compact nature of the largest cities presents numerous planning problems. Projections models that can sufficiently reflect this diversity of activity are useful tools in this planning process. A model described in Chapter 5 combines dynamic cohort-survival and input-output techniques to simulate a variety of economic activities for the eight-county region centered on Des Moines, Iowa. Alternative assumptions regarding the projection of exogenous activities provide the basis for assessing the model's structural sensitivity and numerous uses of the model's outputs are discussed. A second major part of this chapter analyzes a model of interurban earnings differentials that incorporates the derived demand and supply of labor within metropolitan regions. The effect of access to major markets is also included in this model and regression analyses suggest the importance of transportation costs in explaining interurban earnings differentials. Though substantial disparities in the correlation between city size and average earnings are noted, the reduction of transportation costs appears to be the single most important factor in narrowing these differentials; this result seems consistent with spatially decentralizing trends in the manufacturing sector over the past 15 years.

Two studies illustrate the diverse spatial impacts that may characterize economic policies pursued by state and local governments. The exemption form of property tax relief in Iowa differentially benefits veterans in urban and rural tax districts and results in compensatory payments that are inequitably redistributed to local governments. The variations in the tax value of the exemption among veteran's families have no *a priori* relation to the benefits received from their military service by the state's citizenry or society generally. The effect of alternative benefit plans (means tests, maximum lifetime exemptions and credits) are assessed on the Iowa data, and it is concluded that, at the very least, a system of tax credits should replace the present exemption legislation. The study revealed the prevalence of fixed earmarking rules used by state governments, and the inadequate appreciation of how the specific form of instrument (*i.e.*, the exemption) may subvert basic objectives of the legislation. Among states the competition for new industrial plants and firms has intensified in recent years. Programs ranging from local property tax exemptions to statewide credit corporations have sought to increase the industrial base of states and metropolitan areas. Though there is some regional variation in the type of plan used, the general impact of these programs on economic development is not substantial The most intensively used programs are usually found in states with high rates of economic growth, and the commonly used arguments in favor of these plans are not justified. Both studies discussed in this chapter suggest the insensitivity of state legislatures to the actual economic impacts that their various programs may have.

At the federal level, population redistribution may be influenced by programs encouraging the development of new metropolitan regions and smaller communities. The discussion in Chapter 7 suggests the wide range of unresolved issues in developing criteria for the scale and location of new urban settlements. If undertaken, the Minnesota Experimental City will have a substantial impact on the economies of nearby communities, and the internal structure of the city will be directly influenced by the planning authority. The city's objectives are unique and some compromise between experimentality and the relevance to other cities of its innovations will have to be reached. The redevelopment of neighborhoods in the largest metropolitan regions and the establishment of new towns present a similar array of issues. The abandonment of residential assets in the larger cities imposes severe hardships on families in core neighborhoods, and a well-defined set of criteria relating national objectives to the various types of decentralized new town developments is needed. Existing criteria for the optimal scale of planned development are inadequately sensitive to the varying characteristics and objectives of urban settlements of alternative size; well-defined and implementable criteria for the optimal location of new communities are yet to be developed. Though birth rate declines beginning in the early 1960's have alleviated some of the concerns regarding population growth, a policy framework for resettlement may yet be needed and should be based on more comprehensive studies of central place systems.

METHODOLOGICAL AND POLICY ISSUES

Data availability is one of the primary methodological problems facing the urban-regional economist. As discussed in Chapter 4, the absence of good origin-destination commodity flow information often necessitates very indirect estimation methods, and even existing interregional data are ambiguous with respect to the true sources and destinations of these flows; similar comments are applicable to population and capital movements. Perhaps even more surprising is the absence of statistics on land uses and ownership, which is the fundamental information needed to analyze environmental and transportation problems.

Several difficulties are a result of these data limitations. (1) Allocative methods are often needed to make spatial inferences from locationally static information. Minimum requirements and location quotients are examples of methods used to determine interregional exports and imports which require very specific assumptions regarding spatial demand and productivity characteristics. (Location quotients were used to determine export final demands in the CIRPC model described in Chapter 5.) (2) Methods of consistent spatial disaggregation are useful since better data are always available on larger regional units. Particularly difficult problems rise in estimating the components of models for substate non-SMSA regions.

Data problems have also tended to limit the number of empirical applications of the models discussed in Chapter 1. The export base model has traditionally been utilized for urban planning purposes and is probably the most extensively used concept in regional economics; however, many of those studies are highly simplified representations of complex economies. More sectorally disaggregated state input-output models were developed during the 1960's, but most of these efforts relied heavily on national coefficients and spatial interrelationships within states were usually excluded. Indeed, almost all the urban and regional input-output models are structural replications of the larger national tables. The bid-rent model has not been empirically applied to urban areas, though some larger scale simulation models have incorporated residential land values and rents. City size distributions have been studied, but the structural relationships among hierarchical levels have not been estimated comprehensively; there is no empirical analog to the central place system discussed in Chapter 1 for a nation or large region. More extended data bases would undoubtedly encourage a broader range of empirical applications.

Theoretical work will probably continue to emphasize spatial and sectoral refinement. Locationally hierarchical relationships as are found in some urban areas have not been adapted within input-output models. An ultimate objective of the larger regional simulation efforts might be to consistently disaggregate regional totals to the firm and household level. Though some progress has been made in this regard, current models are still not capable of dealing with spatial externalities between contiguous land parcels. Estimating the size distribution of firms by industry is another important problem in land use modeling that has yet to be resolved in a theoretically satisfying manner. The identification of specific attributes of firms and households is also impossible within the framework of most currently available urban-regional models; for many planning applications regional dollar or employment totals are not particularly useful.

The gap between the model builder and user is a final methodological problem that should be noted. The modeler is rarely able to deliver the exact type of information required by using agencies due to data limitations or theoretical specification difficulties. The user, conversely, is typically incapable of interpreting proxy estimates, and the vast number of interrelationships that are often present in complex models. It seems likely that the continued growth of large scale planning agencies will tend to bridge this interpretive gap as specialization occurs within these organizations. Currently, however, the sophisticated structural relationships within these models are not utilized well in the planning process.

A major policy issue in subnational development will continue to be the coordination of the various federal agencies that are primarily responsible for programs at each regional level. The U.S. Department of Agriculture, Economic Development Administration, Corps of Engineers and Housing and Urban Development are the principal agencies concerned with the regional entities discussed in Chapters 2 through 5. As yet there appears to be little governmental recognition of the interdependencies of these efforts and no policy status encompassing development at all subnational levels.

The spatial inflexibility of subnational governments is perhaps the most common theme in discussions of urban policy problems. The absence of a close spatial correspondence between the socio-economic community and the governmental unit is particularly apparent in the largest urbanized regions. The problems of suburban competition in providing public services and internalizing the costs of metropolitan services to nonmetro residents are examples of issues with important spatial dimensions. Intercounty cooperation in transportation planning is another problem found in both the high and lower-density urbanized regions. Aside from special districts, few important changes in the spatial jurisdictions of subnational governments have occurred in the last century, and it is unreasonable to expect them to service well a community that transcends their political boundaries. Though some efforts have been made by the federal government to encourage cooperative planning among traditional governmental units, better means of overcoming these spatial problems are needed.

Spatial comprehensiveness is a theme of previous chapters that also has implications for policy formulation. Delineating criteria are particularly important here and, as suggested above, should be broadened to incorporate theories of regional development not just the spatial distribution of social and physical attributes. Rural communities are embedded in a system of urban places and their development problems should be analyzed within a regional context. Labor markets contain a hierarchy of places with economic interrelationships and linkages to larger urbanized areas that must be considered in assessing the impacts of the growth centers policy. Planning for the development of inland waterways must be based on a national network of interregional trading relationships. The spatial interdependencies that link urbanized areas and the more rural regions must be better understood if the impacts of development programs are to be accurately assessed.

A final policy issue is the specification of criteria for governmental intervention particularly in relation to spatial interdependence. Evidence of market failure (production and consumption externalities, noncompetitive factor and product markets, etc.) are the usual criteria used by economists. (It should be noted that though benefit-cost criteria are usually developed within a comparative statics framework, many urban phenomena are problems of optimal transition; the profession has substantially less to say about such matters.) The discussion in Chapter 7 suggested the complexity of effects expected from governmental intervention within a central place system. Few guidelines or definitional criteria exist for identifying the under- or overdeveloped status of a particular regional unit, and almost nothing seems to be known about how selective intervention would influence the entire city system. Until convincing work is accomplished on this problem, a policy framework for new metropolitan and small town development will probably flounder on the many (and sometimes contradictory) objectives and benefits claimed for these communities.

Our discussion has not led us to a single integrative principle on which an overall policy stance toward urban-regional development might be based. The various methodological and policy issues described in these chapters seem too diverse for such an undertaking. Perhaps a conscious recognition of this diversity within the existing framework of governmental units is the best that can be presently hoped for by social scientists interested in the spatial aspects of socio-economic development. But it may also be mistaken to think only of the traditional phenomena such as urban-rural migration and metropolitan congestion as the basis for policy formulation. As noted above, the noncongruity of the governmental unit and its socio-economic constituency is a remarkably persistent theme underlying the discussion of urban-regional problems and should perhaps be the key element in policy formulation.

INDEX